McGraw-Hill's

500
Microeconomics
Questions

Also in McGraw-Hill's 500 Questions Series

McGraw-Hill's 500 American Government Questions: Ace Your College Exams
McGraw-Hill's 500 College Algebra and Trigonometry Questions: Ace Your College Exams
McGraw-Hill's 500 College Biology Questions: Ace Your College Exams
McGraw-Hill's 500 College Calculus Questions: Ace Your College Exams
McGraw-Hill's 500 College Chemistry Questions: Ace Your College Exams
McGraw-Hill's 500 College Physics Questions: Ace Your College Exams
McGraw-Hill's 500 Differential Equations Questions: Ace Your College Exams
McGraw-Hill's 500 European History Questions: Ace Your College Exams
McGraw-Hill's 500 French Questions: Ace Your College Exams
McGraw-Hill's 500 Linear Algebra Questions: Ace Your College Exams
McGraw-Hill's 500 Macroeconomics Questions: Ace Your College Exams
McGraw-Hill's 500 Organic Chemistry Questions: Ace Your College Exams
McGraw-Hill's 500 Philosophy Questions: Ace Your College Exams
McGraw-Hill's 500 Physical Chemistry Questions: Ace Your College Exams
McGraw-Hill's 500 Precalculus Questions: Ace Your College Exams
McGraw-Hill's 500 Psychology Questions: Ace Your College Exams
McGraw-Hill's 500 Spanish Questions: Ace Your College Exams
McGraw-Hill's 500 U.S. History Questions, Volume 1: Ace Your College Exams
McGraw-Hill's 500 U.S. History Questions, Volume 2: Ace Your College Exams
McGraw-Hill's 500 World History Questions, Volume 1: Ace Your College Exams
McGraw-Hill's 500 World History Questions, Volume 2: Ace Your College Exams
McGraw-Hill's 500 MCAT Biology Questions to Know by Test Day
McGraw-Hill's 500 MCAT General Chemistry Questions to Know by Test Day
McGraw-Hill's 500 MCAT Organic Chemistry Questions to Know by Test Day
McGraw-Hill's 500 MCAT Physics Questions to Know by Test Day

McGraw-Hill's

500

Microeconomics Questions

Ace Your College Exams

Eric R. Dodge, PhD, and Melanie E. Fox, PhD

New York   Chicago   San Francisco   Lisbon   London   Madrid   Mexico City
Milan   New Delhi   San Juan   Seoul   Singapore   Sydney   Toronto

Chapter 14 **Externalities** **137**
Questions 418–447

Chapter 15 **Public and Private Goods** **147**
Questions 448–477

Chapter 16 **Income Inequality and Poverty, and Taxes** **155**
Questions 478–500

Answers **163**

INTRODUCTION

Congratulations! You've taken a big step toward achieving your best grade by purchasing *McGraw-Hill's 500 Microeconomics Questions*. We are here to help you improve your grades on classroom, midterm, and final exams. These 500 questions will help you study more effectively, use your preparation time wisely, and get the final grade you want.

This book gives you 500 multiple-choice questions that cover the most essential course material. Each question has a detailed answer explanation. These questions give you valuable independent practice to supplement your regular textbook and the groundwork you are already doing in the classroom.

You might be the kind of student who needs to study extra questions a few weeks before a big exam for a final review. Or you might be the kind of student who puts off preparing until right before a midterm or final. No matter what your preparation style is, you will surely benefit from reviewing these 500 questions that closely parallel the content, format, and degree of difficulty of the questions found in typical college-level exams. These questions and their answer explanations are the ideal last-minute study tool for those final days before the test.

Remember the old saying "Practice makes perfect." If you practice with all the questions and answers in this book, we are certain that you will build the skills and confidence that are needed to ace your exams. Good luck!

—*Editors of McGraw-Hill Education*

CHAPTER 1

Basic Economic Concepts

1. Which of the following would be the best definition of the study of economics?

   (A) Economics is the study of how the stock market operates.
   (B) Economics is the study of money.
   (C) Economics is the study of how scarce resources are allocated to unlimited wants.
   (D) Economics is the study of how firms decide to make hiring decisions.
   (E) Economics is the study of how governments set production goals.

2. Which of the following best describes a microeconomic question?

   (A) What is the value of the US dollar in terms of other foreign currencies?
   (B) Should a particular firm enter a market?
   (C) Is the economy of Japan in a recession?
   (D) What is the value of the goods and services that the United States produces every year?
   (E) What is the aggregate price level in an economy?

3. Sally is asked by her teacher to write a paper based on a macroeconomic topic. Which of the following titles would be appropriate for a macro-economics paper?

   (A) Are Inflation and Unemployment Related?
   (B) Women's Labor Force Decisions Following Marriage
   (C) Does a Mother's Level of Education Influence Purchasing Decisions?
   (D) How Did Households Make Housing Decisions During the Great Depression?
   (E) How Do Families Decide How Much Health Insurance to Purchase?

4. The idea of _____ in economics is that we have unlimited wants but limited resources.

(A) opportunity costs
(B) scarcity
(C) marginal analysis
(D) specialization
(E) normative economics

5. Consumers, firms, and governments face _____ because we are faced with the problem of _____.

(A) marginal analysis; scarcity
(B) specialization and trade; normative economics
(C) trade-offs; specialization
(D) trade-offs; scarcity
(E) marginal analysis; trade-offs

6. Normative analysis can best be shortened to _____, while positive analysis is best shortened to _____.

(A) the next best alternative; the way things should be
(B) the way things should be; the way things are
(C) the way things should be; the next best alternative
(D) the way things are; the next best alternative
(E) the way things are; the way things should be

7. What is the best definition of the term *marginal*?

(A) Instead of
(B) The additional one
(C) The average one
(D) The cheapest one
(E) The most expensive one

8. Jim is at an all-you-can-eat buffet and is considering whether or not to get another plateful of food. What type of analysis should he be doing if he is thinking rationally?

(A) Marginal analysis
(B) Positive analysis
(C) Normative analysis
(D) Free-market analysis
(E) Collective analysis

9. A centrally planned system would be characterized by which of the following?
   (A) Prices effectively allocate resources.
   (B) Private ownership of resources ensures that they are distributed equally.
   (C) Firms have the ultimate choice on what and how much they produce.
   (D) Government decides the best allocation of resources.
   (E) There are no economic resources.

10. The nation of Maxistan is moving from a centralized planning system to a market-based economy. Which of the following will be part of their transition?
    (A) Resources will move toward being rationed by prices rather than by a central government.
    (B) Resources will no longer be rationed, because there is no more scarcity.
    (C) Maxistan will move toward public ownership of resources.
    (D) Maxistan will increase government involvement in production decisions.
    (E) Firms will begin to consult government agencies for which resources they should use in production.

11. The *rationing function of prices* implies that prices do which of the following?
    (A) All individuals get exactly what they need.
    (B) If prices for goods exist, rationing is not necessary since scarcity no longer exists.
    (C) Goods are allocated based on the ability and willingness to pay for a good.
    (D) Individuals are free to pay whatever they wish for an item, regardless of how much it costs to produce.
    (E) Private ownership of goods means that prices aren't necessary to ration goods.

12. Which of the following would be counted in the category of resources called *capital*?
    (A) Money raised by firms through issuing stock
    (B) The time it takes for an invention to get a patent
    (C) The ability of a business owner to combine resources
    (D) The common stock that a family owns in a firm
    (E) The factory that a firm uses to produce goods

13. The four economic resources are
    (A) land, labor, capital, money
    (B) natural resources, capital, land, money
    (C) land, entrepreneurial ability, capital, labor
    (D) land, income, capital, entrepreneurial ability
    (E) income, inflation, capital, land

14. In the production of cookies, which of the following would be considered the economic resource of land?
    (A) The wheat flour used in the cookie dough
    (B) The bowl you use to mix the cookie dough
    (C) The work of the person mixing the cookie dough
    (D) The recipe to mix the cookie dough
    (E) The rack to cool the finished cookies

15. Suppose a café owner wants to increase the number of people she can serve lunch to and is considering whether to put in more tables or hire another server. Which two resources is the owner considering as substitutes in production?
    (A) Labor and land
    (B) Labor and entrepreneurial ability
    (C) Labor and capital
    (D) Capital and entrepreneurial ability
    (E) Capital and land

16. Which of the following categories of economic resources would describe heating oil for a home furnace?
    (A) Entrepreneurship
    (B) Land
    (C) Investment
    (D) Capital
    (E) Labor

17. Max is considering going to culinary school to become a chef. Which of the following considerations captures the idea of his implicit opportunity costs?
    (A) How much money he can borrow to pay tuition
    (B) How many hours per week he will work as a chef once he graduates
    (C) How much tuition he will have to pay
    (D) How many years it will take him to graduate
    (E) How much income he will forego when he quits his current job

18. Eli is deciding whether or not to provide his employees with a retirement plan. Which of the following statements would be considered normative?

(A) Employees may have more incentive to work harder if he provides a retirement plan.

(B) Employees may save more on their own if he provides a retirement plan.

(C) Employers have a moral obligation to provide employees with retirement plans.

(D) Employees may be less likely to quit their jobs for another position if he provides a retirement plan.

(E) The retirement plan will cost him at least $500,000 per year.

19. Joe is a college football player considering whether to attend another year of college or to enter the NFL draft and become a professional football player. Which of the following thoughts reflects the concept of marginal analysis?

(A) Another year of college football will make me better prepared in the future, but I risk getting injured if I do so.

(B) I should have a college degree.

(C) If I continue in college, I will give up $405,000 in income.

(D) I played on average 10 games per year as a college player and will play an average of 15 games per year in the NFL.

(E) If I continue in college, I will give up a salary as well as potential income from endorsing products.

20. Amanda gets an additional $20 in income for working an additional hour, but she has to pay $25 in child care costs. Based on this information, we can say that Amanda should _____ because _____.

(A) work more hours; marginal costs exceed marginal benefits

(B) work fewer hours; marginal costs exceed marginal benefits

(C) work more hours; the opportunity cost of working is $45

(D) work fewer hours; the opportunity cost of working is $45

(E) continue working the same amount; the opportunity cost of not working exceeds the opportunity cost of working

21. The opportunity cost of a choice X is best described as the

(A) combined value of all alternatives that are more valuable than choice X

(B) combined value of all alternatives that are inferior to choice X

(C) total cost, including the cost of the next best alternative to choice X

(D) cost of scarcity

(E) cost of a free market system

22. Suppose Marjorie currently values a pair of shoes at $50, and the price of a pair of shoes is $40. What is Marjorie's best course of action?
    (A) Stop consuming shoes, since she is saving money.
    (B) Increase her consumption of shoes until her income is spent.
    (C) Increase her consumption of shoes until they cost $50 for all pairs of shoes.
    (D) Increase her consumption of shoes until the price of the last pair of shoes she buys equals her value of them.
    (E) Decrease her consumption of shoes.

23. Sue is a college president considering several construction projects: build a gym, a dormitory, or a science building. Construction costs for each building are the same. If she builds a gym, the college will earn an additional $120,000. If she builds a dormitory, the college will earn an additional $120,000. If she builds a science building, the college will earn an additional $100,000. What is the opportunity cost of building a dormitory?
    (A) $120,000, the foregone earnings from the gym
    (B) $120,000, the foregone earnings from the science building
    (C) $220,000, the foregone earnings from the science building and the gym
    (D) $20,000, the foregone earnings from the gym less the earnings from the science building
    (E) There is no opportunity cost.

24. Suppose a state-operated pizza parlor set the price and quantity of pizza produced in an economy. Which of the following might result?
      I. Price may not reflect the true cost of production.
     II. The manager of the pizza parlor may not be motivated to seek better ways to produce.
    III. An inefficient amount of pizza may be produced.
    (A) I only
    (B) II only
    (C) I and III only
    (D) II and III only
    (E) I, II, and III

CHAPTER 2

Production Possibilities

25. In a production possibilities frontier, which of the following would describe the location of an efficient point of production?

(A) Just on the inside of the curve or line

(B) On the inside of a curve, but not on the inside of a straight line

(C) Just on the outside of either a curve or a line

(D) On a line or a curve

(E) On a line, but not on a curve

26. If there is an increase in the quantity of one of the economic resources that is used to make both good A and good B on a production possibilities frontier, which of the following would be true?

(A) A point that had previously been inefficient will now be efficient.

(B) A point that had previously been efficient will now be unattainable.

(C) A point that had previously been unattainable will now be efficient.

(D) You can increase the production of good A only.

(E) You can increase the production of good B only.

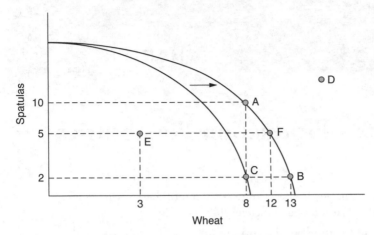

Figure 2.1

27. Refer to Figure 2.1. Suppose a nation wanted to move from producing a combination of spatulas and wheat represented by point E to production represented by point C. Which of the following is true?

   (A) An economy currently producing at a point represented by point E could not move to point C unless it experienced economic growth.
   (B) An economy currently producing at point E is already producing an unattainable amount and will have to decrease the production of either wheat or spatulas.
   (C) An economy currently producing at point E could produce more of both goods and increase production to point C.
   (D) An economy currently producing at point E would need to reduce the amount of spatulas it produced in order to produce more wheat to get to point C.
   (E) An economy currently producing at point E would need to reduce the amount of wheat it produced in order to produce more spatulas to get to point C.

28. According to Figure 2.1, what would be necessary for this economy to shift from producing at point C to point F?

   (A) The country would need to become better at producing only spatulas.
   (B) The country would need to become better at producing only wheat.
   (C) The country would need to become better at producing both goods.
   (D) The country would need to reallocate resources away from producing spatulas to producing wheat.
   (E) The country would need to reallocate resources away from producing wheat to producing spatulas.

29. According to Figure 2.1, what is the opportunity cost of going from production point E to production point F, assuming that F is attainable?

(A) 0 units of spatulas per unit of wheat
(B) 2 units of spatulas per unit of wheat
(C) 3 units of wheat per spatula
(D) 8 units of spatulas per unit of wheat
(E) 5 units of spatula per unit of wheat

30. Which of the following could explain the shift of the production possibilities curve in Figure 2.1?

(A) An increase in the stock of a resource used to produce both wheat and spatulas
(B) An increase in the stock of a resource used to produce wheat, but not spatulas
(C) An increase in the stock of a resource used to produce spatulas, but not wheat
(D) A decrease in an economic resource
(E) A decrease in the stock of labor

31. If the production possibilities frontier of a nation has shifted as shown in Figure 2.1, which of the following is true?

(A) Points A, F, and B are allocatively efficient.
(B) Points A, B, and C are productively efficient.
(C) Points A, F, and B are productively efficient.
(D) Points A, B, and C are allocatively efficient.
(E) All points would be productively efficient, but not allocatively efficient.

32. In Figure 2.1, what information would we need to have to determine whether point A or point F is allocatively efficient?

(A) None—since point A is roughly halfway between the two axes, we know it is allocatively efficient.
(B) The dollar price of each good
(C) Whether or not we could move from point A to point F without a loss of productive efficiency
(D) Whether or not the marginal benefit of wheat exceeded the marginal cost of wheat at point A or point F
(E) Whether or not the marginal cost of wheat is equal to the marginal benefit of wheat at point A or point F

33. What can we say about the costs of production in the production possibility frontier in Figure 2.1?
    (A) This production exhibits constant costs.
    (B) This production exhibits increasing costs.
    (C) This production exhibits decreasing costs.
    (D) This production is costless.
    (E) This production is technology intensive.

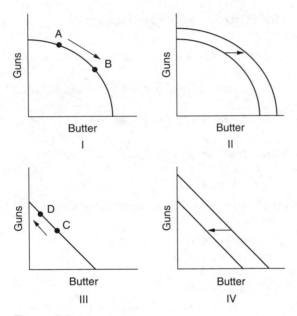

Figure 2.2

34. In Figure 2.2, which of the production possibilities frontiers demonstrates economic growth?
    (A) I only
    (B) IV only
    (C) II only
    (D) I and II only
    (E) II and IV only

35. In Figure 2.2, which of the production possibilities frontiers shows a reallocation of resources?

(A) I only
(B) III only
(C) I and III only
(D) I and II only
(E) II and IV only

36. In Figure 2.2, which of the production possibilities frontiers exhibits increasing costs?

(A) I only
(B) I and II only
(C) II and III only
(D) II and IV only
(E) III and IV only

37. Which of the following best describes absolute advantage?

(A) The ability to produce more of all goods and services given the same resources
(B) The ability to produce a good or service at a lower opportunity cost than another producer
(C) The ability to produce more of all goods and services at a lower opportunity cost than another producer
(D) The ability to produce more goods and services with more resources
(E) The ability to produce at an efficient level when another producer cannot

38. For two producers to both experience gains from trade, which of the following must be true?

(A) The trading price of a good must be higher than the opportunity cost for both producers.
(B) The trading price of a good must be lower than the opportunity cost for only one producer.
(C) The trading price of a good must be lower than the opportunity cost for both producers.
(D) The trading price must lie between the opportunity cost for only one good and one producer.
(E) The trading price must lie between the opportunity cost for all producers and all goods.

39. Elistan can produce either 5 monster trucks or 10 cans of silly string in a day. What is the opportunity cost of one can of silly string?

(A) 5

(B) ½

(C) ½ monster truck

(D) 2 cans of silly string

(E) 5 monster trucks

40. In a single day, Maxistan can produce 8 cheesecakes or 10 prime ribs. In a single day, Elistan can produce 10 cheesecakes or 10 prime ribs. Who has absolute advantage in producing what good?

(A) Elistan has absolute advantage in cheesecakes, but nobody has absolute advantage in producing prime ribs.

(B) Elistan has absolute advantage in producing both goods.

(C) Maxistan has absolute advantage in producing cheesecakes, and Elistan has absolute advantage in producing prime ribs.

(D) Maxistan has absolute advantage in producing prime ribs, and Elistan has absolute advantage in producing cheesecakes.

(E) Neither country has absolute advantage in producing either good.

41. In a single day, Xela can produce 15 fish tanks or 5 butterfly nets. Their potential trading partner, Nire, can produce 15 fish tanks or 3 butterfly nets. Who has the comparative advantage in producing what?

(A) Nire has comparative advantage in producing butterfly nets, and Xela has comparative advantage in producing fish tanks.

(B) Nire has comparative advantage in producing both goods, and Xela has comparative advantage in producing both goods.

(C) Nire has comparative advantage in producing fish tanks, and Xela has comparative advantage in producing butterfly nets.

(D) Nobody has comparative advantage in producing either good.

(E) Nire has comparative advantage in producing butterfly nets, but neither country has comparative advantage in producing fish tanks.

42. Lilly and Kylie are stranded together on a desert island. In a single day Kylie can make either 2 straw shelters or catch 10 fish. Lilly can make 4 straw shelters or catch 8 fish in a day. Which of the following is the correct reason that Kylie should specialize in producing fish?

(A) Kylie should specialize in producing fish because she has absolute advantage in producing fish.

(B) Kylie should specialize in producing fish because she has comparative advantage in producing fish.

(C) Kylie should specialize in producing fish because Lilly has absolute advantage in producing fish.

(D) Kylie should specialize in producing fish because Lilly has comparative advantage in producing fish.

(E) Kylie should specialize in producing fish some of the time, and Lilly should specialize in producing fish some of the time.

43. Megan can bake 5 cakes or 10 pies in an hour, and Matthew can bake 3 cakes or 15 pies in an hour. Which of the following statements regarding the possibility for trade between Megan and Matthew is true?

(A) Megan should specialize in making cakes, Matthew should specialize in making pies, and they would both be willing to trade at a price of 4 pies for every cake.

(B) Megan should specialize in making cakes, Matthew should specialize in making pies, and they would both be willing to trade at a price of 6 pies for every cake.

(C) Megan should specialize in making pies, Matthew should specialize in making cakes, and they would both be willing to trade at a price of 4 pies for every cake.

(D) Megan should specialize in making pies, Matthew should specialize in making cakes, and they would both be willing to trade at a price of 6 pies for every cake.

(E) They should not specialize and trade, since Matthew has absolute advantage in producing pies.

44. Annie can grow 100 bales of cotton or 50 tons of lumber on her land. Will can grow 120 bales of cotton or 80 tons of lumber on his land. What terms of trade would both agree to if they specialize and trade?

(A) They will trade 1 bale of cotton for ⅔ of a ton of lumber.

(B) They will trade 3 bales of cotton for 1 ton of lumber.

(C) They will trade 1 bale of cotton for ¼ of a ton of lumber.

(D) They will trade 1 bale of cotton for ⅝ of a ton of lumber.

(E) No terms of trade can be agreed on, since Will has absolute advantage in producing both goods.

45. Which of the following describes a situation in which there would be potential for gains from trade?
    I. Two potential trading partners having identical opportunity costs
    II. A trading price that is greater than the opportunity cost for both of the potential trading partners
    III. One of the trading partners having absolute advantage in producing both goods
    (A) I only
    (B) II only
    (C) III only
    (D) I and II only
    (E) II and III only

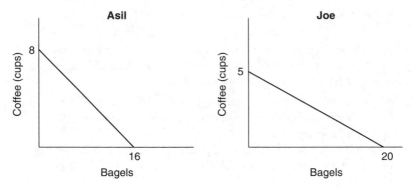

Figure 2.3

46. Refer to Figure 2.3. Which of the following would be an efficient level of production for Asil?
    I. 8 cups of coffee and 0 bagels
    II. 5 cups of coffee and 6 bagels
    III. 4 cups of coffee and 12 bagels
    (A) I only
    (B) II only
    (C) III only
    (D) I and II only
    (E) II and III only

47. Refer to Figure 2.3. What is Asil's opportunity cost of bagels?
    (A) 1 cup of coffee
    (B) ½ cup of coffee
    (C) 2 cups of coffee
    (D) 8 cups of coffee
    (E) ¼ cup of coffee

48. Refer to Figure 2.3. Which of the following trading terms would both Joe and Asil find acceptable?

(A) 1 bagel trades for ⅕ of a cup of coffee.
(B) 1 bagel trades for ⅛ of a cup of coffee.
(C) 1 bagel trades for 3 cups of coffee.
(D) 1 bagel trades for ⅓ of a cup of coffee.
(E) 1 bagel trades for 1 cup of coffee.

49. Refer to Figure 2.3. Joe and Asil currently split their time equally between producing coffee and bagels. If the trading price is 1 bagel for ⅜ of a cup of coffee, which of the following describes the result of specialization and trade?

(A) Joe would be unwilling to trade at this price, so there would be no gains from trade.
(B) Asil will specialize in bagels, and Joe will specialize in coffee. Asil could sell 3 cups of coffee for 8 bagels produced by Joe. Asil will end up with 4 cups of coffee and 8 bagels, and Joe will end up with 3 cups of coffee and 12 bagels.
(C) Asil will specialize in coffee, and Joe will specialize in bagels. Asil could sell 3 cups of coffee for 8 bagels produced by Joe. Asil will end up with 4 cups of coffee and 8 bagels, and Joe will end up with 3 cups of coffee and 8 bagels.
(D) Asil will specialize in coffee, and Joe will specialize in bagels. Asil could sell 3 cups of coffee for 8 bagels produced by Joe. Asil will end up with 5 cups of coffee and 8 bagels, and Joe will end up with 3 cups of coffee and 12 bagels.
(E) Asil will be unwilling to trade at this price, so there would be no gains from trade.

50. Refer to Figure 2.3. Joe has absolute advantage in producing _____, and Asil has comparative advantage in producing _____.

(A) bagels; coffee
(B) neither good; bagels
(C) both goods; bagels
(D) bagels; neither good
(E) both goods; neither good

51. Refer to Figure 2.3. Every time Joe produces a cup of coffee, he gives up making _____ bagels.
(A) 4
(B) 2
(C) ¼
(D) 20
(E) 5

52. Refer to Figure 2.3. Suppose Joe wanted to consume 4 bagels and 5 cups of coffee. Which of the following could allow that to occur?
   I. Joe gets better at producing bagels but not coffee.
  II. Joe gets better at producing both goods.
 III. Joe trades with Asil.

(A) I only
(B) II only
(C) III only
(D) I and III only
(E) II and III only

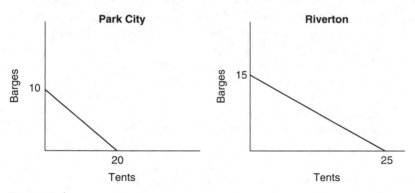

Figure 2.4

53. Refer to Figure 2.4. Park City has absolute advantage in _____ and comparative advantage in _____.
(A) neither good; tents
(B) neither good; neither good
(C) both goods; tents
(D) both goods; barges
(E) both goods; both goods

54. Refer to Figure 2.4. The city of _____ should specialize in making barges because they have _____ in that good.
   (A)   Riverton; absolute advantage
   (B)   Park City; absolute advantage
   (C)   Park City; comparative advantage
   (D)   Riverton; comparative advantage
   (E)   Riverton; total advantage

55. Refer to Figure 2.4. Which of the following is true about the trading situation for Riverton and Park City?
   I.   We cannot know what the final terms of trade will be for certain.
   II.   Riverton should be willing to trade with Park City at a price of 6 barges for 11 tents.
   III.   Riverton should be willing to trade with Park City at a price of 9 barges for 16 tents.
   (A)   I only
   (B)   II only
   (C)   III only
   (D)   II and III only
   (E)   I, II, and III

56. It takes Jo-Jo 10 minutes to grade a homework question and 15 minutes to grade an essay question. What is the opportunity cost of essay questions for Jo-Jo?
   (A)   1½ homework questions
   (B)   1½ minutes
   (C)   3 homework questions
   (D)   ⅔ homework question
   (E)   ⅔ minute

57. It takes Jo-Jo 10 minutes to grade a homework question and 15 minutes to grade an essay question. It takes Karl 20 minutes to grade a homework question and 10 minutes to grade an essay question. Who has comparative advantage in grading homework, and what is their opportunity cost?
   (A)   Karl, 3 essay questions
   (B)   Jo-Jo, ⅔ essay question
   (C)   Jo-Jo, 1½ essay questions
   (D)   Jo-Jo, 2 minutes
   (E)   Karl, 2 minutes

58. In 2005 Jason produced 200 bottles of cabernet and 120 bottles of pinot noir. In 2007 Jason produced 180 bottles of cabernet and 160 bottles of pinot noir. In 2008 Jason made 220 bottles of cabernet. Assuming that Jason is efficient in all years and his resources have not changed in this constant-cost industry, how much pinot noir did he make in 2008?

(A) 20
(B) 80
(C) 200
(D) 120
(E) 160

59. In 2005 Jason produced 200 bottles of cabernet and 120 bottles of pinot noir. In 2007 Jason produced 180 bottles of cabernet and 160 bottles of pinot noir. In 2008 Jason made 220 bottles of cabernet. Which of the following combinations would be efficient production in this constant-cost industry?

  I. 260 bottles of cabernet and 0 bottles of pinot noir
 II. 140 bottles of cabernet and 200 bottles of pinot noir
III. 120 bottles of cabernet and 220 bottles of pinot noir

(A) I only
(B) II only
(C) III only
(D) I and II only
(E) I and III only

60. On Monday Max baked 3 loaves of bread and 18 cupcakes. On Tuesday Max baked 4 loaves of bread and 18 cupcakes. Assuming Max is efficient and has constant costs, which of the following statements is true about what changed between Monday and Tuesday?

  I. Max has more resources to produce both goods.
 II. Max has moved along his production possibilities frontier.
III. Max's production possibilities frontier has rotated out.

(A) I only
(B) II only
(C) III only
(D) I and II only
(E) I and III only

61. Steve is always efficient and has constant costs. On Friday Steve edited 10 papers and had 4 meetings. On Thursday Steve edited 5 papers and attended 6 meetings. Which of the following statements is true about Steve?

   I. Steve would be willing to go to 2 meetings for Patti if she edits 6 papers for him.

  II. Steve can attend 10 meetings in a day.

 III. Steve can attend 3 meetings and edit 10 papers in a day.

(A) I only

(B) II only

(C) III only

(D) I and III only

(E) II and III only

62. Country A has 200 workers, and country B has 400 workers. In country A, each worker can make 20 pairs of socks or 30 picture frames in a year. In country B, each worker can also make 20 pairs of socks or 30 picture frames in a year. Who has comparative advantage in producing which good?

(A) Neither country has comparative advantage in producing socks, since they have identical opportunity costs.

(B) Country A has comparative advantage in producing socks, and country B has comparative advantage in producing picture frames.

(C) Country B has comparative advantage in producing socks, and country A has comparative advantage in producing picture frames.

(D) Country A has comparative advantage in producing both goods.

(E) Country B has comparative advantage in producing both goods.

CHAPTER 3

Supply and Demand

63. The demand for hot dogs will increase if

- (A) the price of hot dogs decreases
- (B) the population increases
- (C) the price of hot dog buns increases
- (D) the supply of hot dogs increases
- (E) the price of hamburgers decreases

64. The demand for airplane tickets will decrease if

- (A) the supply of airplane tickets decreases
- (B) the price of jet fuel increases
- (C) the price of an airplane ticket increases
- (D) the price of hotel rooms decreases
- (E) consumers believe air travel is becoming unsafe

65. Which of the following is a demand determinant for chocolate milk?

- (A) the price of regular milk, which is often used instead of chocolate milk
- (B) the price of chocolate milk
- (C) the cost of the corn that feeds the dairy cows that produce the milk
- (D) the number of milk producers in the market
- (E) the price of the land used to raise the dairy cows

66. Suppose we are told that no matter the price of a 3-D television, more 3-D televisions have been purchased. One explanation for this trend may be that
    (A) consumers have a stronger preference for 3-D televisions
    (B) the number of consumers in the market has decreased
    (C) the cost of producing 3-D televisions has increased
    (D) the number of firms that produce 3-D televisions has decreased
    (E) the number of stores that sell 3-D televisions has decreased

67. Select the choice that would cause a leftward shift in the demand for good X.
    (A) a higher price of good X
    (B) stronger consumer tastes and preferences for good X
    (C) improved technology used to produce good X
    (D) a higher price of an input used in the production of good X
    (E) fewer consumers in the market

68. Which of the following statements are correct?
      I. If the price of milk falls, the demand for milk will shift to the right.
     II. If the price of milk rises, the quantity of milk demanded will fall along the demand curve.
    III. If the price of milk rises, the demand for milk will shift to the left.
    (A) I only
    (B) II only
    (C) III only
    (D) I and III only
    (E) I, II, and III

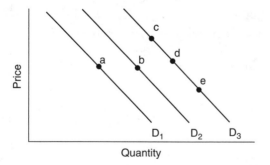

Figure 3.1

69. Refer to Figure 3.1. Which movement between points is consistent with the law of demand?

(A) a to b
(B) b to a
(C) b to c
(D) c to d
(E) d to b

70. Three demand curves for hamburgers are shown in Figure 3.1. Of the following choices, what would cause a movement from point b to point a?

(A) The price of hamburgers increased.
(B) The price of a substitute good decreased.
(C) The price of a complementary good decreased.
(D) Consumer preferences for hamburgers became stronger.
(E) The consumer population increased.

71. Which of the following goods is most likely an inferior good?

(A) used furniture
(B) gold earrings
(C) safari tickets
(D) laptop computers
(E) digital cameras

72. The demand for chocolate cake will increase if

(A) income increases and chocolate cake is a normal good
(B) income increases and chocolate cake is an inferior good
(C) the price of chocolate used to make the cake increases
(D) the medical community reveals that chocolate cake is extremely bad for our health
(E) the price of chocolate cake rises

73. Demand for an inferior good

(A) is vertical
(B) decreases when income decreases
(C) depends on the price of related goods
(D) increases when income increases
(E) increases when income decreases

74. We can determine that apples and bananas are _____ goods because when the price of apples _____, the demand for bananas _____.

(A) complementary; rises; rises
(B) substitute; rises; falls
(C) complementary; falls; falls
(D) substitute; rises; rises
(E) substitute; falls; rises

75. If winter hats and winter mittens are complementary goods, then we expect

(A) the demand for mittens to increase when the price of hats increases
(B) the demand for hats to increase when the price of mittens increases
(C) the demand for mittens to increase when the price of hats decreases
(D) the demand for mittens to decrease when the price of hats decreases
(E) the demand for hats to decrease when the price of mittens decreases

76. The supply of houses is likely to increase if

(A) the number of home builders decreases
(B) the price of houses decreases
(C) consumer incomes increase
(D) the cost of building materials decreases
(E) the wages paid to carpenters increases

77. If the supply curve for good Z is known to have shifted to the left, we might conclude that

(A) consumer tastes for good Z have diminished
(B) the technology used in producing good Z has improved
(C) there are fewer producers of good Z
(D) the price of good Z has fallen
(E) the cost of producing good Z has fallen

78. Which of the following is considered a determinant of supply curves?

(A) consumer income
(B) tastes and preferences
(C) the number of consumers
(D) consumer income expectations
(E) production technology

79. Suppose that many producers of footwear can produce both hiking boots and running shoes. All else equal, if running becomes a more popular activity and the price of running shoes begins to increase, what would we expect to happen in the market for running shoes and the market for hiking boots?

	Market for Running Shoes	Market for Hiking Boots
(A)	An increase in supply	An increase in supply
(B)	An increase in quantity supplied	A decrease in supply
(C)	An increase in quantity supplied	An increase in quantity supplied
(D)	An increase in supply	A decrease in supply
(E)	A decrease in quantity supplied	An increase in supply

80. Which of the following would likely increase the current supply of cars?
    (A) The price of gasoline has decreased.
    (B) The cost of the robotics used to produced cars has increased.
    (C) Car producers expect future car prices to increase.
    (D) The technology used to produce cars has improved.
    (E) The price of new cars has increased.

81. The law of supply is most consistent with which of the following statements?
    (A) When the price of wool increased, sheep ranchers sheared more sheep for market.
    (B) When the cost of steel decreased, car companies were able to produce more cars.
    (C) When one coffee shop in town closed, fewer cups of coffee were sold.
    (D) When the price of lumber decreased, more lumber was purchased at the hardware store.
    (E) When the government subsidized public education, more students received their college degrees at public universities.

82. The law of supply states that, holding all other factors constant, when the price of a good _____, the quantity of that good supplied will _____.
    (A) falls; rise
    (B) remains constant; rise
    (C) rises; fall
    (D) rises; remain constant
    (E) rises; rise

Use Table 3.1 for questions 83–85.

Table 3.1

Price per Pound	Quantity Demanded (pounds)	Quantity Supplied (pounds)
$1	2,500	750
$2	2,300	900
$3	2,100	1,050
$4	1,900	1,200
$5	1,700	1,350
$6	1,500	1,500
$7	1,300	1,650
$8	1,100	1,800
$9	900	1,950

83. Table 3.1 shows the quantity of beef demanded and supplied at a variety of prices. If the market is in equilibrium, the price would be _____ per pound and _____ pounds would be exchanged.
    (A) $4; 1,900
    (B) $5; 350
    (C) $6; 1,500
    (D) $7; 350
    (E) $6; 3,000

84. Table 3.1 shows the quantity of beef demanded and supplied at a variety of prices. Suppose the price of beef is $8 per pound. At this price, there exists a _____ equal to _____ pounds of beef.
    (A) surplus; 800
    (B) surplus; 2,900
    (C) shortage; 700
    (D) shortage; 1,100
    (E) surplus; 700

85. Table 3.1 shows the quantity of beef demanded and supplied at a variety of prices. Suppose the price of beef is $4 per pound. At this price, there exists a _____ equal to _____ pounds of beef.
    (A) surplus; 700
    (B) surplus; 1,900
    (C) shortage; 700
    (D) shortage; 1,900
    (E) shortage; 1,200

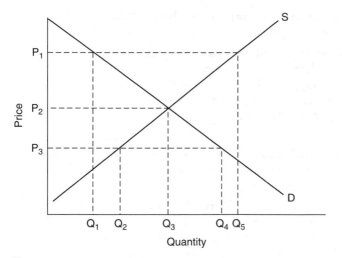

Figure 3.2

86. Figure 3.2 shows the market for a good. If this market reaches equilibrium, the price and quantity will be
    (A) P_1 and Q_1
    (B) P_1 and Q_5
    (C) P_3 and Q_2
    (D) P_2 and Q_3
    (E) P_3 and Q_4

87. Figure 3.2 shows the market for a good. If the current price is P_3, there exists a _____ in the market equal to _____ units of the good.
    (A) surplus; $Q_5 - Q_1$
    (B) shortage; $Q_4 - Q_2$
    (C) surplus; $Q_5 - Q_3$
    (D) shortage; $Q_5 - Q_1$
    (E) surplus; $Q_4 - Q_2$

88. Figure 3.2 shows a market currently in equilibrium. What might cause the market to move to a price of P_1 and quantity of Q_5?
    (A) An increase in supply with no change in demand
    (B) A decrease in demand with no change in supply
    (C) A decrease in supply with no change in demand
    (D) A decrease in supply with a decrease in demand
    (E) An increase in demand with no change in supply

89. Figure 3.2 shows a market currently in equilibrium. What might cause the market to move to a price of P_3 and quantity of Q_4?

    (A) An increase in supply with no change in demand
    (B) A decrease in demand with no change in supply
    (C) A decrease in supply with no change in demand
    (D) A decrease in supply with a decrease in demand
    (E) An increase in demand with no change in supply

90. Figure 3.2 shows a market currently in equilibrium. What might cause the market to move to a price of P_1 and quantity of Q_1?

    (A) An increase in supply with no change in demand
    (B) A decrease in demand with no change in supply
    (C) A decrease in supply with no change in demand
    (D) A decrease in supply with a decrease in demand
    (E) An increase in demand with no change in supply

91. The market for cheese is currently in equilibrium. If the demand for cheese increases, what will happen to the market price and quantity of cheese?

	Market Price	Market Quantity
(A)	Decreases	Decreases
(B)	Decreases	Increases
(C)	Increases	Remains constant
(D)	Increases	Increases
(E)	Increases	Decreases

92. The market for gasoline is currently in equilibrium. If the demand for gasoline decreases, what will happen to the market price and quantity of gasoline?

	Market Price	Market Quantity
(A)	Decreases	Decreases
(B)	Decreases	Increases
(C)	Increases	Remains constant
(D)	Increases	Increases
(E)	Increases	Decreases

93. You are told that the market price of coffee has increased and more coffee is being purchased in the market. Of the following choices, which is the most likely cause of these changes in the coffee market?

   (A) Supply of coffee increased.
   (B) Demand for coffee increased.
   (C) Demand for coffee decreased.
   (D) Supply of coffee decreased.
   (E) The demand for coffee and the supply of coffee both decreased.

94. You are told that the market price of steel has decreased and less steel is being purchased in the market. Of the following choices, which is the most likely cause of these changes in the steel market?

   (A) Supply of steel increased.
   (B) Demand for steel increased.
   (C) Demand for steel decreased.
   (D) Supply of steel decreased.
   (E) The demand for steel and the supply of steel both decreased.

95. You are told that the market price of applesauce has decreased and more applesauce is being sold in the market. Of the following choices, which is the most likely cause of these changes in the applesauce market?

   (A) Supply of applesauce increased.
   (B) Demand for applesauce increased.
   (C) Demand for applesauce decreased.
   (D) Supply of applesauce decreased.
   (E) The demand for applesauce and the supply of applesauce both decreased.

96. You are told that the market price of milk has increased and less milk is being purchased in the market. Of the following choices, which is the most likely cause of these changes in the milk market?

   (A) Supply of milk increased.
   (B) Demand for milk increased.
   (C) Demand for milk decreased.
   (D) Supply of milk decreased.
   (E) The demand for milk and the supply of milk both increased.

97. The market for wine is currently in equilibrium. If the supply of wine increases, what will happen to the market price and quantity of wine?

	Market Price	**Market Quantity**
(A)	Decreases	Decreases
(B)	Decreases	Increases
(C)	Increases	Remains constant
(D)	Increases	Increases
(E)	Increases	Decreases

98. The market for rental housing is currently in equilibrium. If the demand for rental housing increases and the supply of rental housing also increases, what will happen to the market price and quantity of rental housing?

	Market Price	**Market Quantity**
(A)	Uncertain change	Decreases
(B)	Decreases	Uncertain change
(C)	Increases	Uncertain change
(D)	Uncertain change	Increases
(E)	Increases	Increases

99. The market for lumber is currently in equilibrium. If the demand for lumber decreases and the supply of lumber increases, what will happen to the market price and quantity of lumber?

	Market Price	**Market Quantity**
(A)	Uncertain change	Decreases
(B)	Decreases	Uncertain change
(C)	Increases	Uncertain change
(D)	Uncertain change	Increases
(E)	Increases	Increases

100. You are informed that the demand for a good has increased and the supply of that good has decreased. You know that the market price must have _____, while the market quantity could have _____ if the change in demand was _____ than the change in supply.

(A) decreased; increased; greater
(B) increased; increased; less
(C) increased; increased; greater
(D) decreased; increased; less
(E) increased; decreased; greater

101. You are informed that the demand for a good has increased and the supply of that good has also increased. You know that the market quantity must have _____, while the market price could have _____ if the change in demand was _____ than the change in supply.

(A) decreased; increased; greater
(B) increased; increased; less
(C) increased; decreased; greater
(D) decreased; increased; less
(E) increased; decreased; less

102. The market for toys is currently in equilibrium. If the demand for toys decreases and the supply of toys decreases, what will happen to the market price and quantity of toys?

	Market Price	Market Quantity
(A)	Increases	Uncertain change
(B)	Decreases	Uncertain change
(C)	Increases	Decreases
(D)	Uncertain change	Increases
(E)	Uncertain change	Decreases

CHAPTER **4**

Elasticity

103. The price elasticity of supply of good X is

  (A) the percentage change in quantity of X demanded divided by the percentage change in the price of X
  (B) the percentage change in quantity of X supplied plus the percentage change in the price of X
  (C) the percentage change in the price of X divided by the percentage change in quantity of X supplied
  (D) the percentage change in quantity of X supplied divided by the percentage change in the price of X
  (E) the percentage change in quantity of X supplied multiplied by the percentage change in the price of X

104. Suppose the price of eggplant decreases by 4% and eggplant producers reduce the quantity of eggplant supplied by 20%. The price elasticity of supply is equal to

  (A) −4
  (B) .25
  (C) 4
  (D) −5
  (E) 5

105. If we know that the price elasticity of supply of eggnog is 3 and that the price of eggnog has doubled, we predict that

  (A) quantity of eggnog supplied will increase 300%
  (B) quantity of eggnog supplied will also double
  (C) quantity of eggnog supplied will increase 200%
  (D) quantity of eggnog supplied will increase 33.3%
  (E) quantity of eggnog supplied will increase 3,000%

106. In the long run, the price elasticity of supply is _____ the short-run price elasticity of supply because producers have _____ time to adjust to changes in the price.

(A) greater than; more
(B) greater than; less
(C) smaller than; more
(D) equal to; the same amount of
(E) smaller than; less

107. Jason is a seller of Klonks. He has seen the price of a Klonk rise from $10 to $14, and he has responded by increasing his daily production from 100 units to 140 units. Using the midpoint formula, compute Jason's price elasticity of supply between these two prices.

(A) 2
(B) 1
(C) 3
(D) 4
(E) .25

108. Which of the following choices is an accurate formula for the absolute value of the price elasticity of demand (E_d)?

(A) $E_d = (\%\Delta P) \div (\%\Delta Q_d)$
(B) $E_d = (\%\Delta P) \div (\%\Delta I)$
(C) $E_d = (\%\Delta Q_d) \div (\%\Delta P)$
(D) $E_d = (\%\Delta Q_d) \div (\%\Delta I)$
(E) $E_d = (\%\Delta P) \times (\%\Delta Q_d)$

109. If demand for a product is said to be inelastic, it must be the case that the absolute value of the price elasticity of demand (E_d) is

(A) greater than 1
(B) equal to 1
(C) greater than 0 but less than 1
(D) infinitely large
(E) greater than 1, but less than 5

110. Suppose the price elasticity of demand for apples is equal to .75. If the price of apples rises by 10%, we expect a _____ in apple consumption.

    (A) .75% decrease
    (B) 7.5% increase
    (C) 75% increase
    (D) 3.33% decrease
    (E) 7.5% decrease

111. The price of a gizmo has increased. Which of the following would be a reason to expect that there would be an elastic response to this price increase?

    (A) There are very few available substitutes for a gizmo.
    (B) Consumers consider gizmos to be a luxury item.
    (C) Consumers have almost no time to respond to the price increase.
    (D) Gizmos represent a very small share of consumer spending.
    (E) The demand curve for gizmos is approximately vertical in shape.

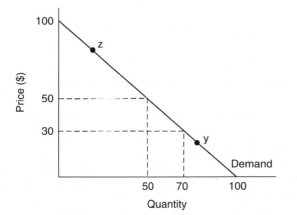

Figure 4.1

112. Referring to the demand curve in Figure 4.1, use the midpoint formula to compute the price elasticity of demand between the prices of $50 and $30.

    (A) 1
    (B) 1.5
    (C) 2
    (D) .67
    (E) 0

113. Refer to Figure 4.1. Consider point z on the demand curve. For a small change in the price at point z, we can say that the price elasticity of demand is

(A) elastic
(B) perfectly inelastic
(C) inelastic
(D) infinitely elastic
(E) equal to zero

114. Refer to Figure 4.1. Beginning at point y on the demand curve, suppose the price is lowered by a small percentage change. We know that total consumer dollars spent on this good will _____ because demand is _____ at this point.

(A) remain constant; unit elastic
(B) decrease; elastic
(C) decrease; inelastic
(D) increase; elastic
(E) increase; inelastic

115. Ruby knows that demand for her clothing is quite price elastic. If she increases her price by even a small percentage, her total revenue dollars will _____ because _____

(A) decrease; the percentage change in quantity demanded will exceed the percentage change in price
(B) remain unchanged; the percentage change in quantity demanded will equal the percentage change in price
(C) decrease; the percentage change in price will exceed the percentage change in quantity demanded
(D) increase; the percentage change in quantity demanded will exceed the percentage change in price
(E) increase; the percentage change in price will exceed the percentage change in quantity demanded

116. After some research, you discover that the income elasticity of demand for a zerk is equal to +2. This tells you that a zerk is a(n) _____ good.

(A) inferior
(B) foreign
(C) complementary
(D) Giffen
(E) normal

117. Among the following choices, identify the inferior good based on the income elasticity (E_I) given.

(A) $E_I = 0$
(B) $E_I = 2$
(C) $E_I = 1$
(D) $E_I = -1$
(E) $E_I = ½$

118. Suppose purchases of notebooks increase by 3% when income increases by 5%. Given this, the income elasticity (E_I) for notebooks is equal to

(A) 15
(B) 2
(C) .60
(D) 1.67
(E) −.33

119. Suppose that when income decreases by 4%, the quantity of margarine demanded rises by 1%. Knowing this, the income elasticity (E_I) for margarine is

(A) $E_I = .25$
(B) $E_I = -¼$
(C) $E_I = -4$
(D) $E_I = -3$
(E) $E_I = 3$

120. If the income elasticity of demand for coffee is .40, then a 6% increase in consumer income would cause consumption of coffee to _____ by _____ .

(A) decrease; 4.2%
(B) increase; .067%
(C) increase; 2.4%
(D) increase; 4%
(E) increase; 3%

121. Of the following choices, select the one most likely to have a negative income elasticity of demand.

(A) 2% milk
(B) Granola
(C) Airplane tickets
(D) Televisions
(E) City bus tickets

122. Luxury goods are often identified as those for which any percentage increase in income is followed by an even larger percentage increase in consumption. Given this, which of the following income elasticity (E_I) measures would identify a luxury good?

(A) $E_I = \frac{1}{2}$
(B) $E_I = -2$
(C) $E_I = 0$
(D) $E_I = 3.5$
(E) $E_I = 1$

123. We know that two goods X and Y are considered substitutes if

(A) the income elasticity is positive for both good X and good Y
(B) the cross-price elasticity is negative between goods X and Y
(C) the price elasticity of demand for good X is greater than 1, and the price elasticity of demand for good Y is less than 1
(D) the cross-price elasticity is positive between goods X and Y
(E) the income elasticity is positive for good X and negative for good Y

124. The following choices show the cross-price elasticity of demand between goods A and B ($E_{A,B}$). Which of the following identifies goods A and B as complementary goods?

(A) $E_{A,B} = 0$
(B) $E_{A,B} = \frac{1}{4}$
(C) $E_{A,B} = -1$
(D) $E_{A,B} = 1.5$
(E) $E_{A,B} = 1$

125. When the price of Diet Coke increases by 2%, the quantity of Diet Pepsi demanded increases by 4%. The cross-price elasticity of demand for Diet Pepsi with respect to the price of Diet Coke is

(A) 2
(B) $\frac{1}{2}$
(C) -2
(D) $-\frac{1}{2}$
(E) 8

126. The cross-price elasticity of demand for Frosted Flakes with respect to the price of Cocoa Puffs is 1.5. This measure tells us that these two breakfast cereal brands are

(A) complementary goods
(B) substitute goods
(C) inferior goods
(D) normal goods
(E) inelastic goods

127. The cross-price elasticity of demand for bacon with respect to the price of eggs is $-.5$. If the price of eggs were to rise by 3%, we predict that the quantity of bacon demanded will _____ by _____.

(A) increase; 3%
(B) decrease; 1.5%
(C) decrease; 3.5%
(D) decrease; 2.5%
(E) decrease; .5%

128. The following choices show the cross-price elasticity of demand between goods A and B ($E_{A,B}$). Which of the following identifies goods A and B as substitute goods?

(A) $E_{A,B} = 0$
(B) $E_{A,B} = \frac{1}{4}$
(C) $E_{A,B} = -1$
(D) $E_{A,B} = -1.5$
(E) $E_{A,B} = -\frac{1}{2}$

129. You are told that the cross-price elasticity of demand for salmon with respect to the price of catfish is .45. Which of the following is an accurate interpretation of this measure?

(A) A 10% increase in the price of catfish will cause a 4.5% decrease in the quantity of salmon demanded.
(B) A 10% increase in the price of catfish will cause a 45% increase in the quantity of salmon demanded.
(C) A 10% decrease in the price of catfish will cause a 4.5% increase in the quantity of salmon demanded.
(D) A 10% increase in the price of salmon will cause a 4.5% increase in the quantity of catfish demanded.
(E) A 10% increase in the price of catfish will cause a 4.5% increase in the quantity of salmon demanded.

CHAPTER 5

Consumer and Producer Surplus

130. When we subtract the price of a good from the price that Jack is willing to pay for that good, we have calculated

- (A) Jack's consumer surplus
- (B) Jack's producer surplus
- (C) Jack's deadweight loss
- (D) Jack's total welfare
- (E) Jack's total utility

131. Ellen enjoys eating muffins. She is willing to pay $10 for her first muffin, $8 for her second, $6 for her third, $4 for her fourth, and $2 for her fifth. If the price of a muffin is $3, how many muffins will Ellen purchase and how much consumer surplus will she receive?

	# Muffins Purchased	Consumer Surplus
(A)	1	$7
(B)	2	$8
(C)	3	$9
(D)	4	$16
(E)	5	$15

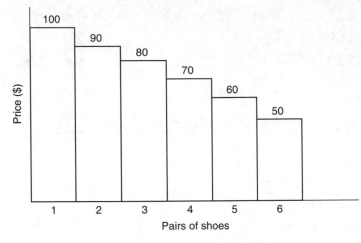

Figure 5.1

132. Refer to Figure 5.1. The graph shows Melanie's willingness to pay for pairs of shoes. If the price of a pair of shoes is $60, Melanie will purchase _____ pairs of shoes and receive _____ of consumer surplus.
    (A) 4; $100
    (B) 5; $100
    (C) 5; $400
    (D) 6; $360
    (E) 4; $90

133. Suppose a consumer purchased a new DVD player. His consumer surplus from this purchase would be found by
    (A) determining how much utility he gained from the purchase of the DVD player
    (B) adding the price he paid for the DVD player to the marginal utility he received from purchasing it
    (C) subtracting the marginal cost of producing the DVD player from the price he paid for it
    (D) subtracting the price he paid for the DVD player from the maximum price he would have paid for it
    (E) dividing the price he paid for the DVD player by the number of years he expects to own it

Use Table 5.1 for question 134.

Table 5.1

Quantities of Cookies	Eli's Willingness to Pay	Max's Willingness to Pay
1	$2.00	$2.50
2	$1.75	$2.00
3	$1.50	$1.50
4	$1.25	$1.00
5	$1.00	$0.50

134. Table 5.1 describes the willingness to pay of two consumers, Eli and Max, for an increasing number of cookies. If the price of a cookie is $1, how many cookies will Eli buy, how many cookies will Max buy, and how much total consumer surplus will be earned?

	# Cookies for Eli	# Cookies for Max	Total Consumer Surplus
(A)	4	5	$5
(B)	5	4	$15
(C)	5	5	$10
(D)	4	3	$5.50
(E)	5	4	$5.50

135. Terrell is a barber who can perform a shave and a haircut to a customer at a constant marginal cost of $4. If Terrell charges each customer $10 and serves seven customers, how much producer surplus has he earned?
    (A) $60
    (B) $84
    (C) $24
    (D) $48
    (E) $42

136. When computing producer surplus for a product that has been sold, we must subtract the _____ from the _____.
    (A) total revenue earned; total cost incurred
    (B) price paid; utility received
    (C) price paid; willingness to pay
    (D) marginal cost incurred; price received
    (E) deadweight loss; consumer surplus

137. The Taco Bus sells tacos at a price of $4 each. The marginal cost of the first taco is $1, the marginal cost of the second is $2, the marginal cost of the third is $3, and the marginal cost of the fourth is $4. If the Taco Bus sells four tacos, how much producer surplus will the firm earn?

(A) $6
(B) $16
(C) $10
(D) $5
(E) $4

138. If we subtract the marginal cost of producing a good from the price received when it is sold, we have calculated

(A) total surplus
(B) producer surplus
(C) marginal revenue
(D) profit
(E) consumer surplus

Use Table 5.2 for question 139.

Table 5.2

Quantity of Kebabs Sold	Ali's Marginal Cost of a Kebab Sold	Rahul's Marginal Cost of a Kebab Sold
1	$0.50	$0.50
2	$1.00	$0.75
3	$1.50	$1.00
4	$2.00	$1.25
5	$2.50	$1.50
6	$3.00	$1.75
7	$3.50	$2.00

139. Table 5.2 shows the marginal costs for two vendors of kebabs at a local food festival. If kebabs are sold at the price of $1.50, Ali will sell _____ kebabs, Rahul will sell _____ kebabs, and combined total producer surplus equals _____.

(A) 2; 4; $4
(B) 3; 5; $4
(C) 3; 5; $12
(D) 5; 5; $2.50
(E) 3; 6; $3.75

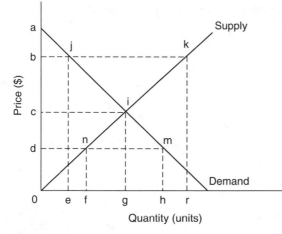

Figure 5.2

140. In Figure 5.2, when the market is in equilibrium, the area of consumer surplus is given by
    (A) a0i
    (B) c0i
    (C) aci
    (D) c0gi
    (E) abj

141. In Figure 5.2, when the market is in equilibrium, the area of producer surplus is given by
    (A) a0i
    (B) c0i
    (C) aci
    (D) c0gi
    (E) abj

142. Which of the following choices would represent the height of an effective price floor in the market shown in Figure 5.2?
    (A) 0b
    (B) 0e
    (C) 0c
    (D) 0d
    (E) 0i

143. Which of the following choices would be an effective price ceiling in the market shown in Figure 5.2?

(A) 0b
(B) 0e
(C) 0c
(D) 0d
(E) 0i

144. Suppose that an effective price ceiling has been imposed on the market portrayed in Figure 5.2. This price ceiling will create a _____ equal to _____.

(A) surplus; (i − e) units
(B) shortage; (i − g) units
(C) shortage; (h − f) units
(D) surplus; (h − f) units
(E) deadweight loss; area nmi

145. Suppose an effective price floor has been imposed on the market portrayed in Figure 5.2. This price floor will create a _____ equal to _____.

(A) surplus; (r − e) units
(B) shortage; (r − e) units
(C) shortage; (h − f) units
(D) surplus; (h − f) units
(E) deadweight loss; area jki

146. Market equilibrium is considered efficient because the sum of _____ and _____ is maximized.

(A) consumer utility; producer profit
(B) consumer willingness to pay; supplier marginal cost
(C) market price; market output
(D) consumer surplus; government tax revenue
(E) consumer surplus; producer surplus

147. If a government policy or other external force moves a competitive market away from the equilibrium level of output, it will create inefficiency known as

(A) economic growth
(B) monopoly profit
(C) price discrimination
(D) deadweight loss
(E) tax revenue

148. Which of the following statements are correct?
    I. When the competitive market is in equilibrium, there is no deadweight loss.
    II. When the competitive market is in equilibrium, the sum of consumer and producer surplus is maximized.
    III. When the competitive market is in equilibrium, resources in this market are allocated efficiently.

(A) I only
(B) II only
(C) III only
(D) I and II only
(E) I, II, and III

Use Table 5.3 for questions 149–151.

Table 5.3

Servings of Oatmeal	Wilford's Willingness to Pay	Rosemary's Marginal Cost
1	$8.00	$2.00
2	$7.00	$2.50
3	$6.00	$3.00
4	$5.00	$3.50
5	$4.00	$4.00
6	$3.00	$4.50
7	$2.00	$5.00

149. Refer to Table 5.3. Assume that there is only one consumer of oatmeal (Wilford) and only one producer of oatmeal (Rosemary). Table 5.3 shows Wilford's willingness to pay and Rosemary's marginal cost at various servings of oatmeal. What is the efficient quantity of oatmeal that would be exchanged in the market?

(A) 3
(B) 4
(C) 5
(D) 6
(E) 7

150. Refer to Table 5.3. Assume that there is only one consumer of oatmeal (Wilford) and only one producer of oatmeal (Rosemary). Table 5.3 shows Wilford's willingness to pay and Rosemary's marginal cost at various servings of oatmeal. Suppose a minimum price of $6 is imposed in the oatmeal market. How many servings will be exchanged and how much deadweight loss will be created?

	Servings of Oatmeal	**Deadweight Loss Created**
(A)	6	$5
(B)	3	$2
(C)	3	$1.50
(D)	5	$0
(E)	3	$1

151. Refer to Table 5.3. Assume that there is only one consumer of oatmeal (Wilford) and only one producer of oatmeal (Rosemary). Table 5.3 shows Wilford's willingness to pay and Rosemary's marginal cost at various servings of oatmeal. Suppose a maximum price of $3 is imposed in the oatmeal market. How many servings will be exchanged, and how much deadweight loss will be created?

	Servings of Oatmeal	**Deadweight Loss Created**
(A)	1	$1.50
(B)	6	$2
(C)	7	$1.50
(D)	4	$2.50
(E)	3	$1.50

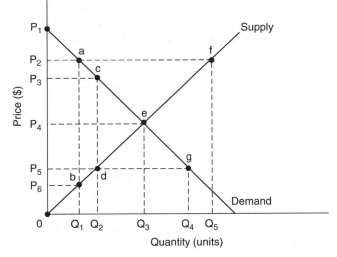

Figure 5.3

152. If the market in Figure 5.3 is in equilibrium, the sum of consumer and producer surplus is equal to the area bounded by points
    (A) P_1eP_4
    (B) P_4e0
    (C) aef
    (D) P_1e0
    (E) cde

153. Suppose that a price floor is set at P_2 in the market shown in Figure 5.3. The area of deadweight loss that results is equal to the area bounded by points
    (A) P_2aQ_10
    (B) aef
    (C) deg
    (D) abe
    (E) P_1aP

154. Suppose that a price floor is set at P_2 in the market shown in Figure 5.3. As a result of the price floor, consumer surplus falls by the area bounded by points _____. Remaining consumer surplus is the area bounded by points _____.

(A) P_2aeP_4; P_1aP_2
(B) P_1eP_4; P_1aP_2
(C) P_4ebP_6; P_6b0
(D) abe; P_1aP_2
(E) P_3cdP_5; P_1aP_2

155. Suppose that a price ceiling is set at P_5 in the market shown in Figure 5.3. The area of deadweight loss that results is equal to the area bounded by points

(A) cde
(B) aef
(C) deg
(D) abe
(E) P_1aP_2

156. Suppose that a price ceiling is set at P_5 in the market shown in Figure 5.3. As a result of the price floor, producer surplus falls by the area bounded by points _____. Remaining producer surplus is the area bounded by points _____.

(A) cde; P_5d0
(B) cde; P_4e0
(C) P_4edP_5; P_5d0
(D) P_2aeP_4; P_1aP_2
(E) P_4e0; P_5d0

157. When an effective price floor is imposed in a competitive market, what typically happens to consumer surplus, producer surplus, and deadweight loss?

	Consumer Surplus	**Producer Surplus**	**Deadweight Loss**
(A)	Falls	Falls	No change
(B)	Falls	Rises	Rises
(C)	Rises	Falls	Rises
(D)	Falls	Rises	Falls
(E)	Falls	Falls	Falls

158. When an effective price ceiling is imposed in a competitive market, what typically happens to consumer surplus, producer surplus, and deadweight loss?

	Consumer Surplus	**Producer Surplus**	**Deadweight Loss**
(A)	Rises	Rises	Rises
(B)	Falls	Rises	Falls
(C)	Rises	Falls	Falls
(D)	Falls	Falls	No change
(E)	Rises	Falls	Rises

159. All else equal, the _____ a price ceiling is set _____ the equilibrium price, the _____ deadweight loss is created by the policy.

(A) further; below; less
(B) further; below; more
(C) further; above; more
(D) closer; above; less
(E) closer; below; more

160. A competitive market produces the equilibrium quantity that maximizes total surplus because for the last unit exchanged, the _____ is equal to the _____.

(A) total utility consumers receive; total profit producers earn
(B) total revenue producers earn; total cost producers incur
(C) marginal utility consumers receive; price consumers pay
(D) price consumers are willing to pay; marginal cost producers incur
(E) consumer surplus; producer surplus

161. When competitive markets are freely allowed to come to equilibrium, _____ is achieved.

(A) allocative efficiency
(B) deadweight loss
(C) price maximization
(D) productive efficiency
(E) price-control efficiency

162. Which of the following statements are correct?
    I. Price controls create deadweight loss because for the last unit exchanged, willingness to pay exceeds marginal cost.
    II. A competitive market produces an equilibrium price that efficiently allocates resources to the market.
    III. Price controls are the only source of deadweight loss in markets.

    (A) I only
    (B) II only
    (C) III only
    (D) I and II only
    (E) II and III only

CHAPTER 6

The Effects of Taxation

163. An excise tax is a tax that

    (A)   is regressive

    (B)   is progressive

    (C)   taxes each unit of production

    (D)   is a tax placcd on buyers

    (E)   is a tax placed on sellers

164. The term _____ refers to the distribution of a tax burden on buyers and sellers.

    (A)   administrative cost

    (B)   tax incidence

    (C)   tax rate

    (D)   proportional tax

    (E)   excise tax

165. Lump sum taxes are _____, but also more _____ than other taxes such as excise or sales taxes.

    (A)   efficient; inequitable

    (B)   progressive; regressive

    (C)   proportional; efficient

    (D)   inefficient; equitable

    (E)   regressive; inefficient

166. Which of the following statements would be a positive economic definition of a regressive income tax?

    (A) A regressive tax is a tax that is unfair to lower income workers.

    (B) A regressive tax is a tax that is unfair to higher income workers.

    (C) A regressive tax is a tax that will increase by a greater amount than income increases.

    (D) A regressive tax is a tax that will increase by a smaller amount than income increases.

    (E) A regressive tax is a tax that is the same for all income earners.

167. In the nation of Xela, income tax is 10% on the first $10,000 in income earned, 15% on the next $20,000 earned, and 30% on all income earned above that amount. Which of the following could be used to describe the taxes in Xela?

    I. Xela has a marginal tax system

    II. Xela has a progressive income tax

    III. Xela has a regressive income tax

    (A) I only

    (B) II only

    (C) III only

    (D) I and II only

    (E) I and III only

168. As the amount of an excise tax rises, the total amount of tax revenue will

    (A) increase

    (B) decrease

    (C) increase, then decrease

    (D) decrease, then increase

    (E) be constant

169. An excise tax is levied on sellers of televisions. Who will bear the incidence of tax in the market for televisions?

    (A) The entire tax incidence will be paid by sellers regardless of the elasticities of the supply or demand curve.

    (B) The sellers will bear a higher burden of the tax than the buyers if the demand curve is less elastic than the supply curve.

    (C) The sellers will bear a higher burden of the tax than the buyers if the demand curve is more elastic than the supply curve.

    (D) The entire tax incidence will be paid by buyers regardless of the elasticities of the supply or demand curve.

    (E) The tax incidence will be split equally between the buyers and sellers regardless of the elasticities of the supply or demand curves.

170. At a particular quantity, the price elasticity of supply is 3 and the price elasticity of demand is 2. Which of the following is true about the incidence of an excise tax at that quantity?

(A) The tax incidence will depend on whom the tax is levied.
(B) The buyers will pay a higher incidence of the tax.
(C) The sellers will pay a higher incidence of the tax.
(D) The buyers and sellers will have an equal tax burden.
(E) The tax is a regressive tax.

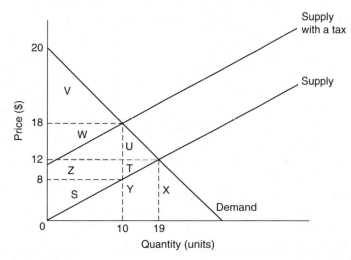

Figure 6.1

171. Refer to Figure 6.1. Which of the following letters corresponds to the total dollar tax incidence paid by demanders?

(A) V
(B) W
(C) X
(D) Y
(E) Z

172. Refer to Figure 6.1. Which of the following refers to the deadweight loss that occurs as a result of demanders changing their behavior in response to the tax?

(A) U
(B) V
(C) W
(D) X
(E) Y

173. Refer to Figure 6.1. We can tell that the _____ is more
_____ because _____.

    (A) demand curve; elastic; buyers pay a higher tax burden
    (B) supply curve; elastic; sellers pay a higher tax burden
    (C) demand curve; inelastic; buyers pay a higher tax burden
    (D) supply curve; inelastic; sellers pay a higher tax burden
    (E) demand curve; inelastic; buyers and sellers have the same tax burden

174. Refer to Figure 6.1. After the excise tax, what is the price that sellers receive (P_s), the price that buyers pay (P_d), and the amount of the tax per unit?

	P_s	P_d	Tax
(A)	20	12	8
(B)	18	12	6
(C)	20	18	2
(D)	8	18	10
(E)	12	8	19

175. Refer to Figure 6.1. What is the total surplus in this market when a tax is imposed?

    (A) S + T + U + V + W + X + Y + Z
    (B) S + T + U + V + Y + Z
    (C) S + T + U + X + Y + Z
    (D) S + V + W + X + Y + Z
    (E) S + V + W + Z

176. Refer to Figure 6.1. What is the tax revenue from this tax?

    I. 100
    II. 180
    III. W + Z

    (A) I only
    (B) II only
    (C) III only
    (D) I and II only
    (E) I and III only

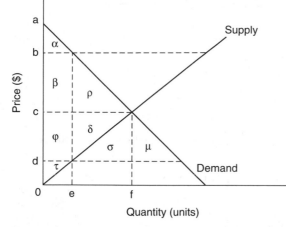

Figure 6.2

177. Refer to Figure 6.2. What is the amount of producer surplus that no longer exists as a result of a tax of (b − d) being imposed?

    (A) β

    (B) μ

    (C) φ

    (D) ρ

    (E) δ

178. Refer to Figure 6.2. Suppose the tax on this market is removed. By what amount will producer surplus increase?

    (A) Producer surplus will increase from φ + δ + τ to α + β + ρ + φ + δ + τ.

    (B) Producer surplus will increase from τ to φ + δ + τ.

    (C) Producer surplus will increase from τ + δ to ρ + α + φ + δ + τ.

    (D) Producer surplus will increase from φ to φ + δ + τ.

    (E) Producer surplus will increase from φ + δ + τ to α + φ + δ + τ.

179. Refer to Figure 6.2. Suppose the elasticity of supply and demand shown here are equal. We could then say for certain which two areas were equal?

    (A) β and φ

    (B) α and τ

    (C) α and β

    (D) β and ρ

    (E) φ and δ

180. Refer to Figure 6.2. What is the amount of inefficiency that exists as a consequence of the tax?

(A) $\alpha + \beta + \delta + \tau$
(B) $\sigma + \mu$
(C) $\rho + \delta$
(D) $\rho + \delta + \sigma + \mu$
(E) $\delta + \sigma$

181. Which of the following is the best explanation of why a lump sum tax is the most efficient form of tax?

(A) It does not alter the incentives of the buyers or the sellers.
(B) It affects only buyers.
(C) It affects only sellers.
(D) It is the most equitable.
(E) It causes the most deadweight loss.

182. Which of the following is caused when you impose a tax on a perfectly functioning market?

(A) Shortage
(B) Surplus
(C) Deadweight loss
(D) Efficiency
(E) Elasticity

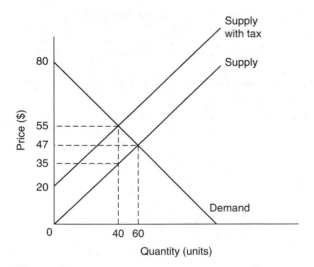

Figure 6.3

183. Refer to Figure 6.3. What is the per unit tax on this good?

    (A) $20

    (B) $8

    (C) $15

    (D) $25

    (E) $47

184. Refer to Figure 6.3. Who bears the greater burden of the tax in this market, and how much of the tax revenue do they pay?

    (A) Sellers, $320 of the tax revenue

    (B) Sellers, $800

    (C) Buyers, $320 of the tax revenue

    (D) Buyers, $480 of the tax revenue

    (E) Sellers, $480 of the tax revenue

185. Suppose the government wanted to impose a tax and wanted the entire burden of the tax to fall on the sellers. What would have to be true of a market for this to be possible?

    (A) The sellers would have to have a perfectly inelastic supply curve, and the buyers would have to have a perfectly inelastic demand curve.

    (B) The buyers would have to have a perfectly elastic demand curve, and the sellers must not have a perfectly elastic supply curve.

    (C) The sellers would have to have a perfectly inelastic supply curve, and buyers must not have a perfectly inelastic demand curve.

    (D) The buyers would have to have a perfectly inelastic demand curve, and the sellers would need to not have a perfectly elastic supply curve.

    (E) Neither buyer nor seller should have perfectly elastic or perfectly inelastic curves.

CHAPTER 7

Consumer Choice

186. Consumers receive happiness from consumption of goods and services. This overall level of happiness is referred to as

(A) marginal utility
(B) a budget constraint
(C) opportunity cost
(D) total utility
(E) a positive externality

187. Jacob enjoys cups of green herbal tea while he works. However, he knows from experience that if he has a fifth cup of tea, he will get a headache and won't be able to concentrate. What does this tell us about Jacob and his utility from cups of green tea?

(A) Jacob cannot afford the fifth cup within his budget constraint.
(B) The marginal utility of the fifth cup is greater than zero, and total utility is rising.
(C) The marginal utility of the fifth cup of tea is less than zero, and total utility is falling.
(D) The total utility of the fourth cup of tea is less than zero.
(E) The marginal utility of the fifth cup of tea is greater than zero, and total utility is equal to zero.

Use Table 7.1 for questions 188–189.

Table 7.1

Hot Dogs	Total Utility from Hot Dogs (utils)
0	0
1	20
2	28
3	34
4	38
5	40
6	41
7	40
8	38

188. A utility-maximizing consumer enjoys eating free hot dogs. Use the data from Table 7.1 to determine how many hot dogs this consumer should eat.

(A) 1
(B) 7
(C) 4
(D) 5
(E) 6

189. A utility-maximizing consumer enjoys eating free hot dogs. Use the data from Table 7.1 to determine the consumer's marginal utility from eating the fifth hot dog.

(A) 2 utils
(B) 1 utils
(C) −1 utils
(D) 40 utils
(E) 8 utils

190. Lucy uses her $48 of weekly income on two items: lipstick and magazines. The price of lipstick is $12 per unit, and the price of magazines is $4 per unit. Which of the following combinations might be a utility-maximizing combination of lipstick and magazines?

(A) 1 lipstick and 9 magazines
(B) 2 lipsticks and 8 magazines
(C) 2 lipsticks and 4 magazines
(D) 4 lipsticks and 1 magazine
(E) 3 lipsticks and 2 magazines

191. Lucy uses her $48 of income on two items: lipstick and magazines. The price of lipstick is $12 per unit, and the price of magazines is $4 per unit. If Lucy is using all of her income, what is the opportunity cost of a lipstick?

(A) $48
(B) 1 magazine
(C) 3 lipsticks
(D) 3 magazines
(E) 4 magazines

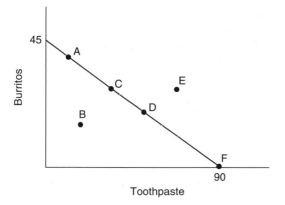

Figure 7.1

192. Mr. Chang uses his income to purchase burritos and toothpaste. The price of a burrito is $6. Based on Figure 7.1, Mr. Chang's income is _____, and the price of toothpaste is _____.

(A) $45; $90
(B) $270; $3
(C) $45; $.50
(D) $270; $90
(E) $7.50; $15

193. Mr. Chang uses his income to purchase burritos and toothpaste. Of the points shown in Figure 7.1, point _____ is unaffordable and point _____ is affordable but cannot maximize Mr. Chang's utility.

(A) E; F
(B) E; A
(C) E; B
(D) C; B
(E) B; F

194. Mr. Chang uses his income to purchase burritos and toothpaste and is currently maximizing his utility at point A in Figure 7.1. If the price of toothpaste falls, which of the following points may represent his new utility-maximizing point?

(A) B
(B) C
(C) D
(D) E
(E) F

195. Mr. Chang uses his income to purchase burritos and toothpaste and is currently maximizing his utility at point C in Figure 7.1. If the price of burritos rises, which of the following points may represent his new utility-maximizing point?

(A) B
(B) A
(C) D
(D) E
(E) F

196. Maddy is currently using all of his income on milk at a price of $4 per unit and on fish at a price of $15 per unit. The marginal utility of the next unit of milk is 40 utils and the marginal utility of the next unit of fish is 100 utils. How can Maddy rearrange his consumption to increase his utility?

(A) He should increase his milk consumption and decrease his fish consumption.
(B) He should decrease his milk consumption and decrease his fish consumption.
(C) He should increase his milk consumption and increase his fish consumption.
(D) He should decrease his milk consumption and increase his fish consumption.
(E) He should do nothing—his utility is already maximized.

197. If a consumer is spending all of her income on two goods, X and Y, she maximizes her utility when

(A) $MU_X \times MU_Y = P_X \times P_Y$
(B) $MU_X + P_X = MU_Y + P_Y$
(C) $MU_X/MU_Y = P_Y/P_X$
(D) $MU_X \times P_X = MU_Y \times P_Y$
(E) $MU_X/P_X = MU_Y/P_Y$

198. Demand curves slope downward because _____ slope downward.

(A) total utility curves
(B) marginal utility curves
(C) supply curves
(D) marginal cost curves
(E) production possibility curves

199. Which of the following statements are correct?
   I. The demand curve for good X slopes downward because marginal utility diminishes as more of good X is consumed.
   II. As the price of good X falls, the marginal utility of good X per dollar rises, prompting more consumption of good X.
   III. As the price of good X falls, the substitution effect prompts the consumer to consume more of good X.

(A) I only
(B) II only
(C) I and II only
(D) I and III only
(E) I, II, and III

200. Julie is currently maximizing her utility by consuming a certain number of units of goods A and B. If the price of good B rises, she will _____ her consumption of good A and _____ her consumption of good B, until _____.

(A) increase; decrease; the marginal utility per dollar is equal for both goods
(B) decrease; decrease; the marginal utility per dollar is equal for both goods
(C) increase; decrease; the marginal utility per dollar is zero for both goods
(D) decrease; increase; the marginal utility per dollar is equal for both goods
(E) decrease; increase; the marginal utility per dollar is zero for both goods

201. Manny considers pizza to be a normal good. When the price of pizza falls, how will the substitution effect and income effect cause his consumption of pizza to change?

	Substitution Effect	**Income Effect**
(A)	More pizza	Same quantity of pizza
(B)	Less pizza	Less pizza
(C)	More pizza	More pizza
(D)	Less pizza	Same quantity of pizza
(E)	Less pizza	More pizza

202. If the price of good Z rises, the quantity of good Z demanded could rise if

(A) good Z is inferior and the income effect is smaller than the substitution effect

(B) good Z is inferior and the income effect is larger than the substitution effect

(C) good Z is inferior and the income effect is equal to the substitution effect

(D) good Z is normal and the income effect is larger than the substitution effect

(E) good Z is normal and the income effect is equal to the substitution effect

203. Suppose that tacos are normal goods. A higher price of tacos will _____ the quantity of tacos demanded due to the substitution effect and _____ the quantity demanded due to the income effect.

(A) increase; decrease

(B) have no impact on; have no impact on

(C) decrease; increase

(D) increase; increase

(E) decrease; decrease

204. Gilligan and Ginger both like to buy coconuts, and both have the same substitution effect for any change in price. However, if the price falls, we observe that Ginger increases her consumption of coconuts by 10, while Gilligan increases his consumption by only 6 coconuts. Which of the following might explain this difference?

(A) Coconuts are inferior goods for Ginger but normal goods for Gilligan.

(B) Coconuts are normal goods for both, but the income effect is stronger for Gilligan.

(C) Coconuts are inferior goods for both, but the income effect is stronger for Ginger.

(D) Coconuts are normal goods for Ginger but inferior goods for Gilligan.

(E) Coconuts are normal goods for both, and the income effect is the same for both.

205. Max has a vertical demand curve for crackers. How would income and substitution effects explain this demand curve?

(A) Crackers are a normal good, and the income effect is equal to the substitution effect.

(B) Crackers are a normal good, and the income effect is greater than the substitution effect.

(C) Crackers are an inferior good, and the income effect is equal to the substitution effect.

(D) Crackers are a normal good, and the income effect is less than the substitution effect.

(E) Crackers are an inferior good, and the income effect is greater than the substitution effect.

CHAPTER 8

Production and Costs

206. A _____ input cannot be changed in the _____ run.

    (A) fixed; long

    (B) fixed; short

    (C) total; long

    (D) variable; short

    (E) variable; long

207. Which of the following costs would be considered a short-run fixed cost for an ice cream shop?

    (A) Wages paid to hourly part-time (or noncontract) employees

    (B) Electricity used to operate the shop and appliances

    (C) Monthly rent paid to the owners of the building under a lease

    (D) Chocolate sauce for sundaes

    (E) Plastic spoons, cones, and other supplies

208. In the short run, when the firm produces zero units of output, which of the following is always equal to zero?

    (A) Total cost

    (B) Total variable cost

    (C) Economic profit

    (D) Total fixed cost

    (E) Economic loss

209. Suppose a firm hires a variable amount of labor to a fixed amount of capital in the short run. The marginal product of labor is

    (A) the change in total cost divided by the change in output

    (B) the change in total output divided by the change in labor employed

    (C) the total output divided by the total cost

    (D) the total output divided by the quantity of labor employed

    (E) the change in total variable cost divided by the change in output

210. The principle of diminishing returns to production is seen graphically as a

(A) total product curve that increases at a decreasing rate as more of a variable input is employed

(B) an average fixed cost curve that declines as more output is produced

(C) a total cost curve that increases at a decreasing rate as more output is produced

(D) a total fixed cost curve that is unchanged as more output is produced

(E) total product curve that increases at a constant rate as more of a variable input is employed

211. Aleks owns a small factory and he has determined that when he employs eight workers that total production is 80 units of output, and when he employs nine workers, production increases to 81 units of output. Based on this information, we can tell that when nine workers are employed, the marginal product of the ninth worker is _____ and the average product of labor is _____.

(A) 10 units; 9 units

(B) 1 unit; 81 units

(C) 1 unit; 9 units

(D) 80 units; 9 units

(E) 1 unit; 8 units

212. Which of the following statements are correct about short-run production functions?

I. When the total product of labor is increasing, the marginal product of labor is negative.

II. When the marginal product of labor is greater than the average product of labor, average product of labor is rising.

III. When the marginal product of labor is falling, the total product of labor is also falling.

(A) I only

(B) II only

(C) III only

(D) II and III only

(E) I, II, and III

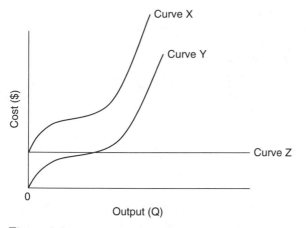

Figure 8.1

213. Short-run cost curves are drawn in Figure 8.1. What function does Curve Y represent in the graph?

(A) Total fixed cost
(B) Total cost
(C) Average total cost
(D) Total variable cost
(E) Marginal cost

214. Short-run cost curves are drawn in Figure 8.1. What function does Curve X represent in the graph?

(A) Total fixed cost
(B) Total cost
(C) Average total cost
(D) Total variable cost
(E) Marginal cost

215. In the short run, which of the following is an accurate description of how to calculate total cost?

(A) Total cost is the sum of total variable cost and marginal cost.
(B) Total cost is the difference between total variable cost and total fixed cost.
(C) Total cost is the sum of average variable cost and average fixed cost.
(D) Total cost is the sum of average variable cost and marginal cost.
(E) Total cost is the sum of total variable cost and total fixed cost.

Use Table 8.1 for questions 216–219.

Table 8.1

Output (Q)	Total Variable Cost (TVC)	Total Cost (TC)
0	$0	$10
1	$5	$15
2	$8	$18
3	$12	$22
4	$17	$27
5	$23	$33
6	$30	$40
7	$38	$48

216. Refer to Table 8.1. What is the marginal cost of producing the *fifth* unit of output for this producer?

(A) $23
(B) $33
(C) $10
(D) $7
(E) $6

217. Refer to Table 8.1. What is the average fixed cost of producing 2 units of output for this producer?

(A) $5
(B) $3
(C) $8
(D) $10
(E) $18

218. Refer to Table 8.1. Which of the following choices best describes the shape of this firm's marginal cost curve?

(A) From units 1 to 2, marginal cost rises, but from units 2 to 7, marginal cost falls.
(B) For all units, marginal cost is constant.
(C) From units 1 to 2, marginal cost falls, but from units 2 to 7, marginal cost rises.
(D) From units 1 to 2, marginal cost is constant, but from units 2 to 7, marginal cost rises.
(E) From units 1 to 2, marginal cost falls, but from units 2 to 7, marginal cost is constant.

219. Refer to Table 8.1. What is the average variable cost of producing 6 units of output for this producer?

(A) $5

(B) $30

(C) $6.67

(D) $10

(E) $40

220. Which of the following statements accurately describes how to compute marginal cost?

(A) Marginal cost is the change in total cost divided by the change in total variable cost.

(B) Marginal cost is the difference between total cost and total variable cost.

(C) Marginal cost is the difference between average total cost and average fixed cost.

(D) Marginal cost is the change in total cost divided by the change in output.

(E) Marginal cost is the change in total fixed cost divided by the change in output.

221. Which of the following is an accurate representation of relationships between short-run costs?

(A) TC = TVC − TFC

(B) ATC = AVC − AFC

(C) AFC = ATC + AVC

(D) ATC = AVC + AFC

(E) AVC = ATC + AFC

222. Of all short-run cost curves, which one has a downward slope for all units of output?

(A) Marginal cost

(B) Average fixed cost

(C) Total variable cost

(D) Average variable cost

(E) Average total cost

223. In the short run, the marginal product of labor is inversely related to
- (A) economic profit
- (B) marginal utility
- (C) average fixed cost
- (D) average product of labor
- (E) marginal cost

224. Suppose that a firm experiences a technological improvement such that the total product of labor curve increases at every quantity of labor employed. How will this affect the marginal product of labor and marginal cost of production in the short run?

	Marginal Product of Labor	Marginal Cost
(A)	Shifts downward	Shifts upward
(B)	No change	No change
(C)	Shifts upward	Shifts downward
(D)	Shifts upward	No change
(E)	No change	Shifts upward

225. Suppose that a firm experiences a technological catastrophe such that the total product of labor curve shifts downward at every quantity of labor employed. How will this affect the average product of labor and average variable cost of production in the short run?

	Average Product of Labor	Average Variable Cost
(A)	Shifts downward	Shifts upward
(B)	No change	No change
(C)	Shifts upward	Shifts downward
(D)	Shifts upward	No change
(E)	No change	Shifts upward

226. All else equal, in the short run as more labor is employed, average product of labor _____, and average variable production cost _____.

- (A) rises then falls; always falls
- (B) falls then rises; always rises
- (C) always falls; always falls
- (D) rises then falls; falls then rises
- (E) falls then rises; rises then falls

227. Total revenue is calculated by

(A) multiplying the number of units sold by the average total cost of producing those units

(B) dividing the total cost of production by the number of units produced

(C) subtracting average total cost from the price at which the units were sold

(D) multiplying the number of units sold by the average variable cost of producing those units

(E) multiplying the number of units sold by the price at which they were sold

228. Fred sells hot dogs at a constant price of $3 and incurs a constant marginal cost of $1. On a typical day he sells 100 hot dogs. What is Fred's daily total revenue from selling hot dogs?

(A) $300

(B) $200

(C) $100

(D) $600

(E) $400

229. A firm produces Zurgs and no matter how many Zurgs are sold, the market price is unaffected. The marginal revenue of the next Zurg sold is equal to

(A) marginal profit

(B) average total cost

(C) price

(D) average variable cost

(E) marginal product

Use Table 8.2 for questions 230–231.

Table 8.2

Price	Quantity Demanded
$1	20
$2	18
$3	16
$4	14
$5	12
$6	10
$7	8

230. Refer to Table 8.2. How much total revenue will the firm receive when the price is set at $5?

    (A) $5
    (B) $60
    (C) $56
    (D) $1
    (E) $12

231. Refer to Table 8.2. What is the marginal revenue associated with a price increase from $3 to $4?

    (A) $8
    (B) $1
    (C) $4
    (D) $56
    (E) $48

232. The difference between economic profit and accounting profit is that economists recognize the _____ costs, while accountants recognize only the _____ costs of operating a business.

    (A) implicit; explicit
    (B) implicit and explicit; implicit
    (C) variable and fixed; sunk
    (D) implicit and explicit; explicit
    (E) variable and fixed; fixed

233. Linda is an artist who would like to open her own gallery. Currently she works at the art museum and earns $19,000 in that position. If Linda wants to earn break-even economic profit with her own gallery, she must earn enough total revenue to cover

(A) her explicit production costs only
(B) her implicit production costs and her forgone salary
(C) her variable and fixed production costs
(D) her explicit production costs and her forgone salary
(E) her sunk costs only

234. To maximize profit, a firm must produce the output where the difference between _____ and _____ is the greatest.

(A) total revenue; total cost
(B) total revenue; total variable cost
(C) total product; marginal product
(D) price; marginal cost
(E) total revenue; average total cost

235. Economists typically assume that the goal of a firm is to

(A) maximize utility
(B) maximize output
(C) maximize sales
(D) maximize profit
(E) maximize revenue

236. A firm is producing the profit-maximizing level of output when

(A) total revenue equals total cost
(B) marginal product equals marginal cost
(C) marginal revenue equals price
(D) price equals average total cost
(E) marginal revenue equals marginal cost

Use Table 8.3 for questions 237–240.

Table 8.3

Output	Total Variable Cost	Total Cost
0	$0	$100
1	$100	$200
2	$140	$240
3	$190	$290
4	$250	$350
5	$320	$420
6	$400	$500
7	$490	$590
8	$590	$690

237. Refer to Table 8.3. If the firm can sell all units of output at a constant price of $70, how many units will be sold to maximize profit?

(A) 0
(B) 5
(C) 6
(D) 7
(E) 2

238. Refer to Table 8.3. Every time the firm sells a unit of output, total revenue rises by $90. If the firm sets output to maximize profit, how many units will be sold?

(A) 0
(B) 5
(C) 7
(D) 6
(E) 8

239. Refer to Table 8.3. Every time the firm sells a unit of output, total revenue rises by $80. If the firm sets output to maximize profit, how much economic profit will the firm earn?

(A) −$20
(B) $480
(C) $400
(D) $80
(E) −$100

240. Refer to Table 8.3. The firm has maximized profit at the output of 8 units. What is the marginal revenue earned from the eighth unit?

(A) $100
(B) $90
(C) $590
(D) $110
(E) $690

241. In the long run, all production costs are

(A) fixed
(B) sunk
(C) variable
(D) marginal
(E) constant

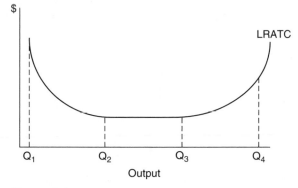

Figure 8.2

242. Refer to Figure 8.2, which shows a firm's long-run average total cost curve. Which range of output corresponds to economies of scale?

(A) Q_2 to Q_3
(B) Q_3 to Q_4
(C) Q_2 to Q_4
(D) Q_1 to Q_4
(E) Q_1 to Q_2

243. Refer to Figure 8.2, which shows a firm's long-run average total cost curve. Which range of output corresponds to diseconomies of scale?

    (A) Q_2 to Q_3
    (B) Q_3 to Q_4
    (C) Q_2 to Q_4
    (D) Q_1 to Q_4
    (E) Q_1 to Q_2

CHAPTER 9

Perfect Competition

244. One of the characteristics of the model of perfect competition is

    (A) asymmetric information
    (B) barriers to entry and exit
    (C) product differentiation
    (D) many buyers and sellers
    (E) high levels of advertising

245. One characteristic of a perfectly competitive market is that

    (A) firms produce a standardized product
    (B) some firms have better market information than others
    (C) there are barriers preventing new firms from entering the market
    (D) the market fails to come to equilibrium without government intervention
    (E) a very small number of firms sell the majority of the products in the market

246. Which of the following describes the behavior of firms in the model of perfect competition?

    (A) Firms engage in heavy spending on advertising.
    (B) Firms have no ability to affect the market price of the product.
    (C) Firms can earn positive economic profit in the long run.
    (D) Firms can create barriers to entry for new firms.
    (E) Firms differentiate their products from other firms.

247. Firms in perfectly competitive markets are often described as

    (A) price setters
    (B) creative advertisers
    (C) price takers
    (D) utility maximizers
    (E) product differentiators

248. In a perfectly competitive market, we expect to see

(A) many firms producing a differentiated product with no ability to affect the market price

(B) many firms producing a differentiated product with some ability to affect the market price

(C) very few firms producing a homogeneous product with some ability to affect the market price

(D) many firms producing a homogeneous product with some ability to affect the market price

(E) many firms producing a homogeneous product with no ability to affect the market price

249. Suppose the market for wheat is perfectly competitive. The demand for any one producer's wheat is

(A) downward sloping

(B) horizontal

(C) perfectly inelastic

(D) upward sloping

(E) vertical

250. If the market for geezums is perfectly competitive, the market demand curve for geezums is _____, while the demand curve for any one firm's output of geezums is _____.

(A) downward sloping; horizontal

(B) downward sloping; downward sloping

(C) horizontal; vertical

(D) horizontal; horizontal

(E) horizontal; downward sloping

251. Assume that the market for beans is perfectly competitive. If the market demand for beans increases, the _____ demand for each perfectly competitive grower of beans will _____.

(A) horizontal; shift downward

(B) horizontal; remain unchanged

(C) horizontal; shift upward

(D) downward sloping; shift upward

(E) downward sloping; shift downward

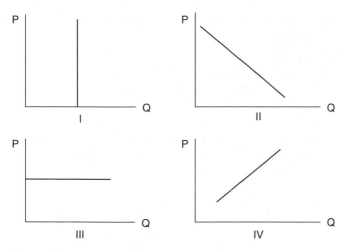

Figure 9.1

252. Refer to Figure 9.1. The graph(s) that best describes the market demand curve in a perfectly competitive market is

(A) I only
(B) II only
(C) III only
(D) II and III only
(E) III and IV only

253. Refer to Figure 9.1. The graph(s) that best describes a firm's demand curve in a perfectly competitive market is

(A) I only
(B) II only
(C) I and III only
(D) III only
(E) IV only

254. In perfect competition, which of the following string of equalities is always true in the short run?

(A) P = MR = ATC
(B) P = MR = MC
(C) P = ATC
(D) P = MC = ATC
(E) P = MR = MC = AVC

255. The short-run supply curve for a perfectly competitive firm is the

(A) average total cost curve

(B) marginal revenue curve

(C) marginal cost curve above average variable cost

(D) average variable cost curve to the right of the marginal cost curve

(E) market price curve

256. Suppose that, in the short run, the price of a key variable input decreases. How will this affect the marginal cost, average total cost, average fixed cost, and average variable cost curves?

	Marginal Cost	Average Total Cost	Average Fixed Cost	Average Variable Cost
(A)	Shifts downward	No change	No change	Shifts downward
(B)	No change	Shifts downward	Shifts downward	Shifts downward
(C)	No change	No change	No change	Shifts downward
(D)	Shifts downward	Shifts downward	Shifts downward	Shifts downward
(E)	Shifts downward	Shifts downward	No change	Shifts downward

257. Suppose that, in the short run, the price of a key fixed input increases. How will this affect the marginal cost, average total cost, average fixed cost, and average variable cost curves?

	Marginal Cost	Average Total Cost	Average Fixed Cost	Average Variable Cost
(A)	Shifts upward	Shifts upward	Shifts upward	No change
(B)	No change	Shifts downward	Shifts upward	No change
(C)	No change	Shifts upward	Shifts upward	No change
(D)	No change	No change	Shifts upward	No change
(E)	No change	No change	No change	No change

258. If a perfectly competitive firm observes the market price rising, the firm will _____ output along the _____ curve.

(A) increase; marginal cost

(B) increase; average total cost

(C) decrease; marginal cost

(D) increase; average variable cost

(E) decrease; average variable cost

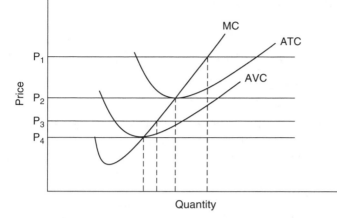

Figure 9.2

259. Refer to Figure 9.2. If the short-run price is _____ the perfectly competitive firm will _____.

    (A) P_1; break even
    (B) P_2; earn negative economic profit
    (C) P_3; earn positive economic profit
    (D) P_1; earn positive economic profit
    (E) P_4; break even

260. Refer to Figure 9.2. If the short-run price is _____, the perfectly competitive firm will _____.

    (A) P_1; break even
    (B) P_2; break even
    (C) P_3; earn positive economic profit
    (D) P_4; earn positive economic profit
    (E) P_2; earn negative economic profit

261. Refer to Figure 9.2. If the short-run price is _____, the perfectly competitive firm will _____.

    (A) P_4; break even
    (B) P_2; earn positive economic profit
    (C) P_3; earn positive economic profit
    (D) P_1; break even
    (E) P_4; earn negative economic profit

262. A firm will shut down in the short run if

(A) TR = TC
(B) P < AVC
(C) P = MC
(D) TR < TC
(E) P < ATC

263. Suppose a firm finds itself in a case where the profit-maximizing decision is to shut down. In this situation, the firm will produce _____ units of output and earn economic profit equal to _____.

(A) zero; −TFC
(B) zero; zero
(C) the most possible; zero
(D) more than zero; −TC
(E) zero; −TVC

264. The shut-down point is located at

(A) a price of zero
(B) the maximum of total revenue
(C) the minimum of average variable cost
(D) the minimum of average total cost
(E) the point where marginal revenue equals marginal cost

265. The short-run profit-maximizing decision in perfect competition is to produce where

(A) P = MC > MR
(B) P = MR = MC = AVC
(C) P = MR = ATC > MC
(D) P = MR = MC > AVC
(E) P > MR = MC

266. You are told that a perfectly competitive firm is maximizing profit in the short run and that economic profits are positive. It must be the case that price is equal to _____ and price must also be _____.

(A) marginal cost; equal to average variable cost
(B) average total cost; greater than marginal cost
(C) marginal cost; less than average total cost
(D) average total cost; greater than average variable cost
(E) marginal cost; greater than average total cost

Table 9.1

Output (Q)	Total Variable Cost (TVC)	Total Cost (TC)
0	$0	$10
1	$5	$15
2	$8	$18
3	$12	$22
4	$17	$27
5	$23	$33
6	$30	$40
7	$38	$48

267. Refer to Table 9.1. If the market price of this price-taking firm's output is $7, economic profit will be

(A) $30
(B) $2
(C) $40
(D) $70
(E) $42

268. Suppose that perfectly competitive firms in the short run are experiencing positive economic profit. In the long run, what will happen to the number of firms in the industry, the market price, and the output of individual firms?

	Number of Firms	**Market Price**	**Individual Firm Output**
(A)	Decrease	Decrease	Decrease
(B)	Increase	Decrease	Increase
(C)	Increase	Decrease	Decrease
(D)	Increase	Increase	Decrease
(E)	Increase	Increase	Increase

269. Suppose that perfectly competitive firms in the short run are experiencing positive economic profit. In the long run, what will happen to the number of firms in the industry, the market level of output, and each firm's economic profit?

	Number of Firms	**Market Output**	**Individual Firm Profit**
(A)	Increase	Decrease	Decrease
(B)	Decrease	Increase	Increase
(C)	Decrease	Decrease	Decrease
(D)	Increase	Increase	Decrease
(E)	Increase	Increase	Increase

270. Suppose that perfectly competitive firms in the short run are experiencing negative economic profit. In the long run, what will happen to the number of firms in the industry, the market price, and the output of individual firms?

	Number of Firms	**Market Price**	**Individual Firm Output**
(A)	Decrease	Decrease	Decrease
(B)	Decrease	Decrease	Increase
(C)	Decrease	Increase	Decrease
(D)	Increase	Increase	Decrease
(E)	Decrease	Increase	Increase

271. When a perfectly competitive firm is in long-run equilibrium, which of the following is true?
(A) P = MR = MC = ATC
(B) P = MR = MC = AVC
(C) P = MR = MC > ATC
(D) P > MR = MC = ATC
(E) P = ATC > MR = MC

272. In perfect competition, short-run economic profits are met by long-run _____ of firms, short-run economic losses are met by long-run _____ of firms, but in either case, economic profits in the long run are _____.
(A) entry; exit; greater than zero
(B) entry; exit; equal to zero
(C) exit; entry; equal to zero
(D) entry; entry; equal to zero
(E) entry; exit; less than zero

273. The model of perfect competition is said to achieve allocative efficiency in the long run because
(A) firms break even
(B) price is equal to minimum average total cost
(C) price is equal to marginal cost
(D) price is equal to marginal revenue
(E) firms shut down

274. In the model of perfectly competitive markets, the market outcome is allocatively efficient because

(A) average total cost is minimized for each firm
(B) all firms break even in the long run
(C) all firms are price takers
(D) economic profits are maximized
(E) the sum of consumer and producer surplus is maximized

275. Which of the following statements correctly describe efficiency in the model of perfect competition?

I. Allocative efficiency is achieved because price is equal to marginal cost.
II. Productive efficiency is achieved because average total cost is minimized.
III. Allocative efficiency is achieved in the short run, but not in the long run.

(A) I only
(B) II only
(C) I and II only
(D) III only
(E) I, II, and III

276. Which of the following choices is an accurate description of efficiency in the model of perfect competition?

(A) Allocative efficiency is achieved in both the short and long run, but productive efficiency is achieved only in the short run.
(B) Allocative efficiency is achieved only in the short run, but productive efficiency is achieved in both the short and the long run.
(C) Allocative efficiency is achieved only in the long run, but productive efficiency is achieved in both the short and the long run.
(D) Allocative efficiency is achieved in both the short and long run, but productive efficiency is achieved only in the long run.
(E) Allocative efficiency is achieved only in the short run, but productive efficiency is achieved only in the long run.

277. Firms in perfect competition are allocatively efficient and productively efficient in the long run because of what conditions?

	Allocatively Efficient	Productively Efficient
(A)	P = MC	P = ATC
(B)	P = MR	P = MC
(C)	P = MR	P = AVC
(D)	P = MC	P = AVC
(E)	P = AVC	P = ATC

278. Of the characteristics of perfect competition, the one most directly responsible for long-run break-even profits is

(A) a homogenous product
(B) no barriers to entry or exit
(C) price-taking behavior
(D) a differentiated product
(E) many small producers

279. If it weren't for the _____ assumption of perfect competition, each firm would be able to advertise the differentiating characteristics of its product to entice consumers.

(A) free entry and exit
(B) many small producers
(C) homogenous product
(D) allocative efficiency
(E) asymmetric information

280. The _____ assumption of the perfectly competitive model ensures that a firm's long-run level of output will be at the minimum of average total cost.

(A) free entry and exit
(B) symmetric information
(C) many small producers
(D) price-taking
(E) differentiated product

281. The fact that perfectly competitive firms have _____ creates a level of output that is allocatively efficient.

    (A) asymmetric information
    (B) a differentiated product
    (C) perfect information
    (D) no ability to set the price
    (E) free entry and exit

282. If perfectly competitive firms had _____, we would likely see firms incurring advertising expenses.

    (A) perfect information
    (B) standardized products
    (C) no ability to set the price
    (D) free entry and exit
    (E) differentiated products

CHAPTER 10

Monopoly

283. A source of market power that exists due to falling long-run average total cost is

(A) patents and copyrights
(B) economies of scale
(C) product differentiation
(D) advertising
(E) trade barriers

284. When a firm creates a new product or a new production technique, it can profit from this by acquiring from the government a(n)

(A) patent
(B) marketing campaign
(C) exclusive control of a raw material
(D) range of declining average total costs
(E) differentiated product

285. Suppose that a lunar mining company discovers a new kryptonite deposit on the moon. This discovery allows it to have monopoly power in the market for kryptonite back on Earth. This source of monopoly power is due to

(A) product differentiation
(B) copyrights
(C) exclusive control of a raw material
(D) diseconomies of scale
(E) trade barriers

286. If a large company can prevent smaller companies from competing on the basis of cost, the large company is using _____ to create market power.

(A) patents and licenses
(B) exclusive control of a raw material
(C) product differentiation
(D) economies of scale
(E) advertising

287. In the city of Montrose, electric regulations allow for only a single public utility to provide electricity to the citizens of Montrose. Which of the following statements is true?

I. The market for electricity in Montrose is a monopoly.
II. The barriers to entry in the electricity market are due to regulation.
III. The electricity company can charge whatever price it desires since it has no competition.

(A) I only
(B) II only
(C) III only
(D) I and II only
(E) I, II, and III

288. Which of the following is a key assumption of the monopoly model?

(A) Barriers to entry
(B) A product with several substitutes
(C) Price-taking behavior
(D) Many identical producers
(E) Interdependence between close rivals

289. Which of the following is a key assumption of the monopoly model?

(A) A product with a few close substitutes
(B) Strategic game playing with close rivals
(C) Price-setting behavior
(D) A few direct competitors
(E) Extensive product differentiation

290. To be considered a pure monopoly, a market must have

(A) mobile resources that freely flow into the market
(B) at least one direct competitor
(C) only one firm with no close competitors
(D) break-even profits in the long run
(E) a perfectly elastic demand curve for the product

291. If a monopolist cannot price discriminate and wants to increase the number of units that it sells, it must

(A) set the market quantity higher and charge the same price
(B) lower the price that it charges for its good
(C) differentiate its good from that of competitors
(D) obtain a patent for the good it produces
(E) agree to set the price of the good with its competitors

292. Which of the following are assumptions of the monopoly model?
   I. Barriers to entry exist.
  II. One firm produces a product with no close substitutes.
 III. The firm sets the market price of the product.

(A) I only
(B) I and II only
(C) II only
(D) I and III only
(E) I, II, and III

293. A monopolist's demand curve slopes downward, while the monopolist's marginal revenue curve

(A) slopes upward and intersects demand
(B) slopes downward and lies below demand
(C) is horizontal and equal to the price
(D) does not exist
(E) slopes downward and lies above demand

294. When a single-price monopolist lowers the price to sell more output, it must lower the price on all units sold. This explains why

(A) the firm's marginal revenue curve is downward sloping and the same as the firm's demand curve
(B) the firm's marginal revenue curve is downward sloping and lies above the firm's demand curve
(C) the firm's marginal revenue curve is downward sloping and lies below the firm's demand curve
(D) the firm's marginal revenue curve is upward sloping and lies below the firm's demand curve
(E) the firm's marginal revenue curve is horizontal and lies below the firm's demand curve

295. A monopolist is currently selling 3 units at a price of $5. If the firm lowers the price to $4, a total of 4 units will be sold. The firm calculates that the marginal revenue of the fourth unit is _____, which is _____ the price of the fourth unit.

(A) $1; less than
(B) $16; greater than
(C) $4; equal to
(D) −$1; less than
(E) $3; less than

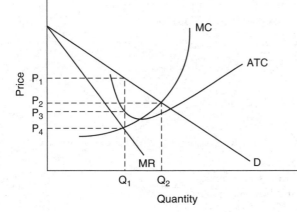

Figure 10.1

296. Refer to Figure 10.1. If the monopolist maximizes profit, how many units of output will be sold and at what price?

	Units of Output	**Price**
(A)	Q_2	P_1
(B)	Q_2	P_2
(C)	Q_1	P_4
(D)	Q_1	P_3
(E)	Q_1	P_1

297. Refer to Figure 10.1. If the monopolist maximizes profit, total profit is equal to:

(A) $Q_2 \times P_2$
(B) $Q_1 \times (P_1 - P_4)$
(C) $Q_1 \times (P_1 - P_2)$
(D) $Q_1 \times (P_1 - P_3)$
(E) $Q_1 \times P_1$

Use Table 10.1 for question 298.

Table 10.1

Price	Quantity Demanded
$12	1
$11	2
$10	3
$9	4
$8	5
$7	6
$6	7
$5	8
$4	9

298. Table 10.1 shows the demand schedule for a monopolist facing a constant marginal cost of $4. Assume that the firm pays no fixed costs. How many units of output will the firm produce, and how much economic profit will be earned?

    (A) 5 units; $8
    (B) 5 units; $40
    (C) 7 units; $36
    (D) 5 units; $20
    (E) 7 units; −$6

299. When we compare monopoly to perfect competition in the long run, we expect the monopoly model to generate an outcome with

    (A) higher prices, break-even profits, and deadweight loss
    (B) higher prices, economic profits, and deadweight loss
    (C) lower prices, economic profits, and deadweight loss
    (D) higher prices, economic profits, and allocative efficiency
    (E) higher prices, break-even profits, and allocative efficiency

300. A monopolist creates _____ because the _____ is greater than the _____.

    (A) economic profit; marginal revenue; marginal cost
    (B) economic profit; price; marginal cost
    (C) deadweight loss; marginal revenue; marginal cost
    (D) deadweight loss; price; average total cost
    (E) deadweight loss; price; marginal cost

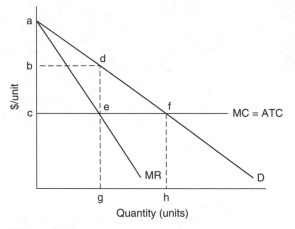

Figure 10.2

301. Refer to Figure 10.2. Using the labels provided in the graph, identify the area of deadweight loss that would exist if this were a monopoly market.

(A) def
(B) abd
(C) acf
(D) bcde
(E) efgh

302. Refer to Figure 10.2. Suppose that the graph initially portrays a competitive market. If the market were to become a monopoly, use the labels in the graph to identify the area of lost consumer surplus.

(A) def
(B) abd
(C) bdfec
(D) bcde
(E) efgh

303. Refer to Figure 10.2. Suppose that the graph portrays a profit-maximizing monopolist. If the market were to become perfectly competitive, use the labels in the graph to identify the area of monopoly profit that would be transferred to consumers as consumer surplus.

(A) def
(B) abd
(C) bdfec
(D) bcde
(E) afc

304. When a firm sells the same product to different consumers and charges the consumers different prices, the firm is said to be engaging in

(A) price utilization
(B) price discrimination
(C) price minimization
(D) predatory pricing
(E) price maximization

305. Blueknighted Airlines flies round trip from Chicago to Houston several times a day. Steve buys a round-trip ticket one month in advance and pays a price of $200. If Julie buys the ticket one day in advance, and sits next to Steve on the plane, she pays a price of $1,000. Such differences in price are known as

(A) utility maximization
(B) revenue exploitation
(C) price discrimination
(D) antitrust pricing
(E) predatory pricing

306. Suppose that a monopolist charges each buyer a price equal to her maximum willingness to pay. In this case of _____, total consumer surplus is equal to _____.

(A) perfect price discrimination; zero
(B) efficiency pricing; monopoly profits
(C) perfect price discrimination; monopoly profits
(D) inelastic price discrimination; zero
(E) bulk pricing; zero

307. Which of the following statements are true?
  I. Price-taking firms and monopolists alike can participate in price discrimination.
  II. Successful price discrimination requires the ability to prevent customers from reselling the product.
  III. Under a system of price discrimination, customers with lower price elasticities of demand tend to pay higher prices than customers with higher price elasticities of demand.

(A) I only
(B) II and III only
(C) II only
(D) III only
(E) I, II, and III

308. Suppose that the only theater in town has successfully had the following pricing system for years: seniors pay $5, children under 12 years old pay $4, local students pay $6, veterans pay $7, and all other adults pay $8. According to price discrimination theory, which group has the greatest price elasticity of demand?

(A) Children under 12 years old
(B) Seniors
(C) Students
(D) Veterans
(E) Adults

309. If one producer can supply the entire market at a lower per-unit cost than if the same market were being supplied by more than one firm, it is referred to as a _____.

(A) full-employment monopoly
(B) monopsony
(C) duopoly
(D) natural monopoly
(E) perfect monopoly

310. A natural monopoly can emerge in a market due to

(A) several firms colluding to act as one firm
(B) one firm acquiring all available patents
(C) sole ownership of an important production resource
(D) free entry and exit of firms
(E) economies of scale over the entire range of market demand

311. A monopolist is able to maintain profits into the long run primarily because

(A) of mutual interdependence
(B) of collusive behavior
(C) barriers to entry exist
(D) of product differentiation
(E) of price-taking behavior

312. The characteristic of monopoly that allows the firm to set the price of the product is that
   (A) there are no close substitutes for the product
   (B) firms are mutually interdependent
   (C) there is extensive product differentiation
   (D) there are no barriers to entry
   (E) the firm experiences diseconomies of scale

313. Because a monopolist has _____, the level of output will be _____ than the competitive level of output.
   (A) diseconomies of scale; less
   (B) price-setting ability; less
   (C) a standardized product; less
   (D) product differentiation; more
   (E) barriers to entry; more

314. In the long run, the monopolist can maintain a price that exceeds average total cost at the quantity produced because
   (A) perfect information exists
   (B) of a differentiated product
   (C) there are barriers to entry
   (D) market demand is downward sloping
   (E) there is mutual interdependence between firms

315. In a monopoly, the price exceeds marginal cost because
   (A) the firm produces a standardized product
   (B) of the extensive economies of scale that exist
   (C) asymmetric information exists
   (D) the firm has the ability to set the price
   (E) of cartel behavior

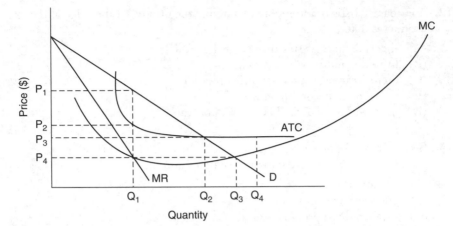

Figure 10.3

316. Using the labeling in Figure 10.3, at what level of output would a regulated monopolist be earning break-even profits? What price would the regulated monopolist charge?

(A) Output = Q_1 Price = P_1
(B) Output = Q_1 Price = P_2
(C) Output = Q_2 Price = P_3
(D) Output = Q_3 Price = P_4
(E) Output = Q_4 Price = P_3

317. Using the labeling in Figure 10.3, if the government wanted to regulate the monopolist to produce the output that was socially efficient, what output would be produced and what price would be charged?

(A) Output = Q_1 Price = P_1
(B) Output = Q_1 Price = P_2
(C) Output = Q_2 Price = P_3
(D) Output = Q_3 Price = P_4
(E) Output = Q_4 Price = P_3

318. Suppose the monopolist in Figure 10.3 is initially unregulated. If the government were to mandate that the firm produce where economic profits are zero, how would output and price change?

Change in Output	Change in Price
(A) Increase by $(Q_2 - Q_1)$ units	Decrease by $(P_1 - P_3)$ dollars
(B) Increase by $(Q_2 - Q_1)$ units	Decrease by $(P_1 - P_2)$ dollars
(C) Increase by $(Q_3 - Q_1)$ units	Decrease by $(P_2 - P_3)$ dollars
(D) Increase by $(Q_4 - Q_1)$ units	Decrease by $(P_2 - P_4)$ dollars
(E) Increase by $(Q_3 - Q_2)$ units	Decrease by $(P_1 - P_4)$ dollars

319. Suppose the monopolist in Figure 10.3 is initially regulated to earn break-even profits. If the government were to mandate that now the firm must produce where there is no deadweight loss to society, how would output and price change?

Change in Output	Change in Price
(A) Increase by $(Q_2 - Q_1)$ units	Decrease by $(P_1 - P_3)$ dollars
(B) Decrease by $(Q_2 - Q_1)$ units	Increase by $(P_1 - P_3)$ dollars
(C) Decrease by $(Q_3 - Q_1)$ units	Increase by $(P_1 - P_3)$ dollars
(D) Increase by $(Q_4 - Q_1)$ units	Increase by $(P_2 - P_4)$ dollars
(E) Increase by $(Q_3 - Q_2)$ units	Decrease by $(P_3 - P_4)$ dollars

320. Suppose the monopolist in Figure 10.3 is initially regulated to produce the socially efficient level of output. If the government were to completely deregulate the market and allow the firm to maximize profit, how would output and price change?

Change in Output	Change in Price
(A) Increase by $(Q_2 - Q_1)$ units	Decrease by $(P_1 - P_3)$ dollars
(B) Decrease by $(Q_2 - Q_1)$ units	Increase by $(P_1 - P_3)$ dollars
(C) Decrease by $(Q_3 - Q_1)$ units	Increase by $(P_1 - P_3)$ dollars
(D) Decrease by $(Q_3 - Q_1)$ units	Increase by $(P_1 - P_4)$ dollars
(E) Increase by $(Q_3 - Q_2)$ units	Decrease by $(P_3 - P_4)$ dollars

CHAPTER 11

Oligopoly

321. Which of the following would definitely be a characteristic of an oligopoly industry?

   (A) A large number of producers each producing a relatively small share of production in an industry

   (B) A large number of producers where a few firms produce most of the output in an industry

   (C) An industry with no barriers to entry

   (D) An industry with differentiated products

   (E) An industry where products are fairly standardized

322. Which of the following characteristics would we expect to see only in an oligopoly industry?

   (A) Advertising

   (B) Patents

   (C) Copyrights

   (D) Interdependent pricing

   (E) Barriers to entry

323. Which of the following characteristics do some oligopolies and all perfectly competitive industries have in common?

   (A) Homogeneous products

   (B) Heterogeneous products

   (C) Barriers to entry

   (D) High concentration ratios

   (E) A small number of firms

324. As long as costs and product demand are the same for all kinds of industry, the quantity that is produced in an oligopoly market will always be _____ market, and the price will always be _____ market.

(A) higher than a monopoly, higher than a monopoly

(B) higher than a monopoly, lower than a perfectly competitive

(C) higher than a monopoly, higher than a perfectly competitive

(D) the same as a monopoly, higher than a perfectly competitive

(E) higher than a perfectly competitive, the same as a perfectly competitive

325. What is the minimum number of firms required for an industry to be an oligopoly?

(A) 1

(B) 2

(C) 3

(D) 100

(E) many

326. Which of the following industries best describes an oligopoly?

(A) A college campus with a single cafeteria

(B) A market for tutoring services where hundreds of college students offer tutoring for hundreds of high school students

(C) A market for babysitting where there are four babysitters

(D) A market for labor in a town with a single employer

(E) A market for water and sewage in a city where there is a single official water supplier

Use Table 11.1 for questions 327–328.

Table 11.1

Firm	Share of the Market
Kerry's Koffee	35%
Monica's Mocha Emporium	25%
Jonathan's Javahaus	11%
Coffee Wonderland	6%
The Last Drop	5%
Central Perk	5%
Java the Coffee Hut	3%
The Daily Grind	3%
Wakey Wakey!	3%
Miss Melly's Coffee and Tea	2%
The Koffee Kart	2%

327. Refer to Table 11.1, which describes the market share of coffee shops in Madison. What is the four-firm concentration ratio of this market?

(A) 77%
(B) 10%
(C) 19.25%
(D) −10%
(E) 0%

328. Refer to Table 11.1, which describes the market share of coffee shops in Madison. What kind of industry is this market likely to be?

(A) Monopoly
(B) Monopsony
(C) Oligopoly
(D) Oligopsony
(E) Competitive

329. A group of firms that agrees to act as a monopoly is called a _____.

(A) Natural monopoly
(B) Increasing cost industry
(C) Cartel
(D) Perfect competition
(E) Nationalized industry

330. Which of the following make it difficult for oligopolies to form cartels in the United States?

   I. Antitrust regulation

  II. The collusion among firms

 III. The self-interest of cartel members

(A) I only

(B) II only

(C) III only

(D) I and II only

(E) I and III only

331. Which of the features of an oligopoly market most directly creates the potential for long-run profits?

(A) Cartels

(B) Barriers to entry

(C) Collusion

(D) Homogeneous products

(E) Interdependent pricing

332. In the market for sushi in a small town, there are three sushi restaurants. When Dan's Sushi Palace sets its prices, its rivals Heather's Sushirama and Sarah's Sushi Parlor follow suit. This practice is called

(A) extortion

(B) price discrimination

(C) overt collusion

(D) price leadership

(E) stabilization pricing

333. One of the defining characteristics of oligopoly markets is the conflict between _____ and _____ in the industry.

(A) the number of firms; antitrust regulation

(B) self-interest; cooperation

(C) antitrust regulation; tax policy

(D) the number of firms; tax policy

(E) choosing price; choosing quantity

334. The market for Gloomps is characterized by the demand curve
$Q = 20 - 2P$, where Q is the market quantity and P is the market price.
If the market for Gloomps is a duopoly, and one firm decides to produce
5 Gloomps and the other firm decides to produce 3 Gloomps, what will
be the market price for Gloomps?

(A) $20
(B) $12
(C) $16
(D) $12
(E) $6

335. The market for Gloomps is characterized by the demand curve
$Q = 20 - 2P$, where Q is the market quantity and P is the market price.
Gloomps can be produced at zero cost. If the market for Gloomps is a
duopoly and the two firms are able to collude, which of the following
quantities would be best for them to collectively choose?

(A) 50
(B) 20
(C) 10
(D) 5
(E) 8

Use Table 11.2 for questions 336–337.

Table 11.2 Market Demand for Purpletts

Q	P	Profit
0	$24	$0
1	$21	$21
2	$18	$36
3	$15	$45
4	$12	$48
5	$9	$45
6	$6	$36
7	$3	$21
8	$0	$0

336. Refer to Table 11.2, which gives the market demand for Purpletts, a good with no cost of production. If this market is a duopoly and firms are able to collude, what price will they choose?

(A) $24
(B) $12
(C) $4
(D) $8
(E) $0

337. Refer to Table 11.2, which gives the market demand for Purpletts, a good with no cost of production. Suppose the two firms in this duopoly market have agreed to set the market quantity at the cartel price and split the quantity sold equally between the two firms. One of the firms is considering breaking the agreement and increasing its production by 1 unit. What is the quantity that this firm is considering producing, their profit if they break the agreement, and their profit if they keep to the agreement instead?

	Quantity the Firm Is Considering Producing	Profit if They Violate the Agreement Between Firms	Profit if They Do Not Violate the Agreement Between Firms
(A)	4	48	24
(B)	2	27	24
(C)	3	24	27
(D)	3	27	24
(E)	2	24	27

338. Despite the existence of antitrust regulation, price or quantity setting may still happen through _____.

(A) price taking

(B) monopoly pricing

(C) price discrimination

(D) overt collusion

(E) tacit collusion

339. Which of the following best describes the reason why game theory is useful for analyzing oligopoly behavior?

(A) In an oligopoly, firms act strategically to increase their market share at the expense of their competitors' market share.

(B) Firms view the ability to beat their rivals as a game to be played and won, regardless of the profit that they have at the end of the game.

(C) A market with only two suppliers cannot be demonstrated with a traditional supply and demand model.

(D) Oligopolies have no costs to produce their goods, so there is never a supply curve for an oligopoly.

(E) Game theory does not account for the strategies of other firms, so it omits information that is not necessary to analyze oligopoly behavior.

340. Which of the following best describes a dominant strategy?

(A) A strategy that is a best response to another player choosing their best response

(B) A strategy that is the best strategy to play, regardless of another player's strategy

(C) A strategy that is never a good strategy to choose, regardless of another player's strategy

(D) A payoff matrix

(E) A strategy that will never be chosen

341. Another term for a Nash equilibrium is a

(A) dominant strategy

(B) dominated strategy

(C) cooperative equilibrium

(D) noncooperative equilibrium

(E) strategy

Use Table 11.3 for questions 342–343.

Table 11.3 Pricing Strategies and Associated Profits for Two Taco Shops

		The Taco Bus	
		Low Price	High Price
The Fajita Wagon	Low Price	Taco Bus: $1,000 Fajita Wagon: $1,000	Taco Bus: $500 Fajita Wagon: $6,000
	High Price	Taco Bus: $6,000 Fajita Wagon: $500	Taco Bus: $4,000 Fajita Wagon: $4,000

342. Refer to Table 11.3, which describes the payoffs to different pricing strategies for a duopoly. Which best describes the best strategy choices for the Fajita Wagon?

(A) The Fajita Wagon should charge low prices only if the Taco Bus charges high prices.

(B) The Fajita Wagon does not have a good way to respond to the Taco Bus choosing a high price.

(C) The Fajita Wagon should charge low prices only if the Taco Bus charges low prices.

(D) The Fajita Wagon should charge high prices only if the Taco Bus charges low prices.

(E) The Fajita Wagon should charge low prices whether or not the Taco Bus charges high prices.

343. Refer to Table 11.3, which describes the payoffs to different pricing strategies for a duopoly. What set of strategies would be the Nash equilibrium for this game?

(A) The Fajita Wagon earns $1,000 profit, and the Taco Bus earns $1,000 profit.

(B) The Fajita Wagon earns $4,000 profit, and the Taco Bus earns $4,000 profit.

(C) There is no Nash equilibrium in this game.

(D) The Fajita Wagon adopts a high price, and the Taco Bus adopts a high price.

(E) The Fajita Wagon adopts a low price, and the Taco Bus adopts a low price.

Use Table 11.4 for questions 344–347.

Table 11.4   A Set of Firm Strategies and Payoffs (Firm 1, Firm 2)

		Firm 2's Choices	
		A	B
Firm 1's Choices	X	($15, $10)	($20, $18)
	Y	($13, $20)	($14, $15)

344. Refer to Table 11.4, which describes the payoffs to different strategies for a duopoly. Why is the Nash equilibrium of this game likely to be what we see in the real world?

   (A) Firms do not have an incentive to alter their strategies from this set of strategies.
   (B) Firms wish to see the other firm do as badly as possible.
   (C) Firms seek to maximize industry profits.
   (D) Firms are prevented by law from colluding.
   (E) Firms are unable to change their strategies.

345. Refer to Table 11.4, which describes the set of strategies and their associated payoffs for two firms. Which of the following describes the noncooperative equilibrium for this game?

	Firm 1's Strategy	Firm 2's Strategy	Firm 1's Payoff	Firm 2's Payoff
(A)	A	B	$15	$20
(B)	X	A	$10	$15
(C)	X	B	$20	$18
(D)	X	A	$15	$10
(E)	X	B	$13	$20

346. Refer to Table 11.4, which describes the set of strategies and their associated payoffs for two firms. Which of the following describes why the strategies {A, Y} are unlikely to be played?

   (A) If Firm 2 plays strategy A, Firm 1's best response is to play strategy X.
   (B) If Firm 1 plays strategy A, Firm 2's best response is to play strategy X.
   (C) If Firm 1 plays strategy Y, Firm 2's best response is to play strategy B.
   (D) If Firm 2 plays strategy A, Firm 1's best response is to play strategy Y.
   (E) If Firm 2 plays strategy A, Firm 1 does not have a good response to this strategy.

347. Refer to Table 11.4, which describes the set of strategies and their associated payoffs for two firms. Which of the following describes each firm's dominant strategy?

(A) Neither firm has a dominant strategy.
(B) Firm 1's dominant strategy is X, and Firm 2 does not have a dominant strategy.
(C) Firm 1's dominant strategy is A, and Firm 2 does not have a dominant strategy.
(D) Firm 2's dominant strategy is B, and Firm 1's dominant strategy is X.
(E) Firm 2's dominant strategy is B, and Firm 1's dominant strategy is Y.

Use Table 11.5 for questions 348–350.

Table 11.5   A Prisoner's Dilemma

		Scott	
		Confess	Don't Confess
Ian	Confess	Scott: −10 Ian: −10	Scott: −20 Ian: 0
	Don't Confess	Scott: 0 Ian: −20	Scott: −2 Ian: −2

348. Refer to Table 11.5, which describes the payoffs for two people who have been accused of a crime and the payoffs, in the form of years in prison (a negative value refers to more time in prison), to confessing or not confessing. Which of the following describes Scott's dominant strategy?

(A) Scott does not have a dominant strategy.
(B) Scott's dominant strategy is to confess only if Ian does not confess.
(C) Scott's dominant strategy is to not confess only if Ian confesses.
(D) Scott's dominant strategy is to confess.
(E) Scott's dominant strategy is to not confess.

349. Refer to Table 11.5, which describes the payoffs for two people who have been accused of a crime and the payoffs, in the form of years in prison (a negative value refers to more time in prison), to confessing or not confessing. What would be a Nash equilibrium in this situation?

(A) There is no Nash equilibrium.
(B) (confess, don't confess)
(C) (confess, confess)
(D) (don't confess, confess)
(E) (don't confess, don't confess)

350. Refer to Table 11.5, which describes the payoffs for two people who have been accused of a crime and the payoffs, in the form of years in prison (a negative value refers to more time in prison), to confessing or not confessing. What is the combination of strategies that would provide the highest payoff for this game?

    (A) There is no optimal set of strategies.

    (B) (confess, don't confess)

    (C) (confess, confess)

    (D) (don't confess, confess)

    (E) (don't confess, don't confess)

351. In a small town there are two pizza restaurants. If neither restaurant advertises, its revenue will not change. If only one firm advertises, the firm that advertises will double its revenue and the firm that doesn't advertise will see a decrease in its revenue, but if both firms advertise, their revenue will not change. What outcome would be predicted by game theory in this market?

    (A) Both restaurants will advertise.

    (B) One restaurant will advertise.

    (C) Neither restaurant will advertise.

    (D) Game theory is only a theory and cannot predict real-world events.

    (E) Game theory would predict that sometimes one restaurant would advertise, and the rest of the time both will advertise.

352. The primary goal of antitrust policy is to ensure that

    (A) consumers can trust the safety and quality of products

    (B) perfectly competitive industries do not behave like oligopolies

    (C) oligopolies do not behave like monopolies

    (D) firms in an industry can act as a cartel to raise prices

    (E) workers can engage in collective bargaining with firms for higher wages

353. Which of the following regulations was designed to prevent collusive and anticompetitive practices by firms?

    (A) The Herfindahl-Hirschman Act of 1949

    (B) The Equal Pay Act of 1963

    (C) The Marketing Act of 1914

    (D) The Fair Trade Act of 1976

    (E) The Sherman Antitrust Act of 1890

354. Which of the following characteristics of oligopoly markets makes it easier for firms to engage in price collusion?

(A) Dissimilar marginal costs across firms
(B) The absence of barriers to entry
(C) The presence of both large and small firms
(D) A small number of firms
(E) Vigilant enforcement of antitrust laws

CHAPTER 12

Monopolistic Competition

355. Which of the following best reflects the profit maximization choice for a monopolistically competitive firm?

(A) P = MC = MR
(B) P < MR = MC
(C) P > MC = MR
(D) P < MR < MC
(E) P > MR > MC

356. Which of the following is the primary way that monopolistically competitive industries differ from perfectly competitive industries?

(A) Perfectly competitive firms have no barriers to entry, but there are barriers to entry in monopolistic competition.
(B) Perfectly competitive firms have identical products, but firms produce products in monopolistic competition that are more diverse.
(C) Perfectly competitive firms exhibit long-run profits, but monopolistically competitive firms do not have profits in the long run.
(D) Perfectly competitive industries have many firms, whereas monopolistically competitive firms are characterized by a small number of firms selling the majority of products in a market.
(E) Perfectly competitive industries have control over the price that they can charge consumers, whereas monopolistically competitive firms cannot individually influence price.

357. The monopolistic aspect of monopolistic competition refers to the fact that

(A) there are legal barriers to producing a good that could compete with firms already in the market

(B) like monopolies, firms in these industries earn positive long-run economic profits

(C) firms in a monopolistically competitive industry choose MR = MC as their profit maximizing choice of quantity, just as monopolists do

(D) like monopolists, monopolistically competitive firms have incentive to advertise

(E) firms in a monopolistically competitive industry have, in a sense, a monopoly over their own good, which is slightly different from other goods in the market

358. The monopolistically competitive industry is most similar to _____ in the number of firms and _____ in their ability to set price.

(A) monopoly, oligopoly

(B) oligopoly, perfect competition

(C) oligopoly, monopoly

(D) monopoly, perfect competition

(E) perfect competition, monopoly

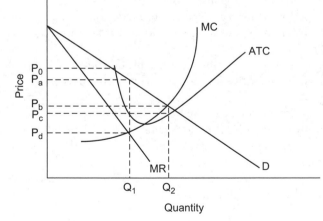

Figure 12.1

359. Refer to Figure 12.1. The monopolistically competitive firm facing the demand and costs curves in the graph would choose a quantity of _____ and a price of _____.

(A) Q_1, whatever was determined in the market
(B) Q_1, P_a
(C) Q_1, P_b
(D) Q_2, whatever was determined in the market
(E) Q_2, P_b

360. Refer to Figure 12.1. The marginal cost of the profit-maximizing choice of quantity is

(A) P_a
(B) P_b
(C) P_c
(D) P_d
(E) P_0

361. Refer to Figure 12.1. The short-run profits that a monopolistically competitive firm would earn are represented by the area

(A) $P_b P_d Q_1$
(B) $(P_a - P_c)Q_1$
(C) $P_b P_c Q_1$
(D) $(P_b - P_c)Q_2$
(E) $0 P_d Q_1$

362. Refer to Figure 12.1. Which of the following could potentially be the long-run price for this firm?

   I. P_a
  II. P_b
 III. P_c

(A) I only
(B) II only
(C) III only
(D) I and II only
(E) II and III only

363. Refer to Figure 12.1. Which of the following best describes how other firms entering this industry would alter this graph?
    (A) The ATC curve would shift down.
    (B) The ATC curve would shift left.
    (C) The demand and marginal revenue curves would shift to the left.
    (D) The MC curve would become downward sloping.
    (E) The MC curve would shift to a new point along the demand curve.

364. Refer to Figure 12.1. Which of the following types of industries could this graph represent?
    (A) Monopoly in the short run, but not the long run
    (B) Monopolistic competition in the short run, but not the long run
    (C) Perfect competition in the short run, but not the long run
    (D) Monopoly in the long run, but not the short run
    (E) Monopolistic competition in the long run, but not the short run

365. Which of these industries has incentive to advertise?
     I. Public goods
    II. Perfect competition
   III. Monopolistic competition
    (A) I only
    (B) II only
    (C) III only
    (D) I and III only
    (E) I, II, and III

366. Which describes the price and quantity that a profit-maximizing monopolistically competitive firm will choose in the long run?
    (A) Produce the quantity where $MC = MR$, and set $P = ATC$.
    (B) Produce the quantity where $MC = MR$, and set $P < ATC$.
    (C) Produce the quantity where $MC < MR$, and set $P =$ minimum ATC.
    (D) Produce the quantity where $MC > MR$, and set $P =$ minimum ATC.
    (E) Produce the quantity where $MC = MR$, and set $P =$ minimum ATC.

367. Which of the following is a kind of positive externality associated with monopolistically competitive industries?

(A) The Cobb-Douglas externality
(B) The business stealing externality
(C) The Lagrange externality
(D) The product variety externality
(E) The advertising externality

368. Which of the following is a kind of negative externality associated with monopolistically competitive industries?

(A) The Cobb-Douglas externality
(B) The business stealing externality
(C) The Lagrange externality
(D) The product variety externality
(E) The advertising externality

369. Which of the following is the best explanation for why monopolistically competitive firms advertise?

(A) Advertising ensures that they will have positive long-run profits.
(B) Advertising makes sure that they produce at the lowest possible cost per unit.
(C) If a monopolistically competitive firm advertises, a firm is able to earn a higher profit by further differentiating their good from others.
(D) Advertising allows a monopolistically competitive firm to produce at a point where price is lower than average variable cost.
(E) If a monopolistically competitive firm advertises, their marginal revenue curve will become a horizontal line.

370. Which of the following characteristics of a monopolistically competitive industry make it the most likely to advertise?

(A) $P > MC$ and $P = MR$
(B) $P > MC$ and barriers to entry
(C) $P = MC$ and barriers to entry
(D) $P > MC$ and no barriers to entry
(E) $P < MC$ and $P = MR$

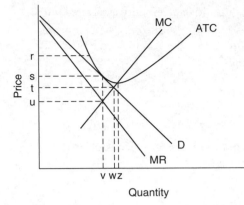

Figure 12.2

371. Refer to Figure 12.2. Which of the four types of industries could this represent?

    (A) A perfectly competitive firm in the long run

    (B) A monopolistically competitive firm in the long run

    (C) A monopolistically competitive firm in the short run

    (D) A perfectly price-discriminating monopolist in the short run

    (E) A perfectly price-discriminating oligopolist in the long run

372. Refer to Figure 12.2. Which of the following is true of this firm in the long run?

    (A) $P = r$, $ATC = s$, $MC = t$

    (B) $P = u$, $ATC = s$, $MC = u$

    (C) $P = s$, $ATC = t$, $MC = t$

    (D) $P = s$, $ATC = t$, $MC = s$

    (E) $P = s$, $ATC = s$, $MC = u$

373. Refer to Figure 12.2. Which of the following is true of the long-run outcome for a monopolistically competitive industry?

   I. The long-run profit-maximizing quantity is not the quantity that minimizes the cost per unit of production.

   II. The long-run profit-maximizing quantity will be a quantity that reduces the amount of deadweight loss that occurs compared to a monopoly.

   III. The long-run profit-maximizing quantity will be at a point where $P < ATC$ and $P > MC$.

  (A) I only
  (B) II only
  (C) III only
  (D) I and II only
  (E) II and III only

374. Refer to Figure 12.2. How much excess capacity does this firm have?

  (A) $z - v$
  (B) $z - w$
  (C) $v - z$
  (D) $w - z$
  (E) $v - z$

375. Refer to Figure 12.2. Which of the following areas represents deadweight loss?

  (A) $(s - u) \times v$
  (B) $u \times v$
  (C) $\frac{1}{2}(t - u) \times (w - v)$
  (D) $(t - u) \times (w - v)$
  (E) $\frac{1}{2}(s - u) \times (w - v)$

376. Which of the following correctly completes the statement about monopolistically competitive industries? Monopolistically competitive industries _____.

  (A) are neither allocatively efficient nor productively efficient in the long run
  (B) have deadweight loss in the long run but not the short run
  (C) have deadweight loss in the short run but not the long run
  (D) have long-run productive efficiency but not short-run productive efficiency
  (E) have no excess capacity in the long run, but do in the short run

377. Excess capacity always occurs when a firm
  (A) makes an economic profit
  (B) makes break-even profits
  (C) produces a quantity below the quantity that minimizes the ATC curve
  (D) produces a quantity above the quantity that minimizes the ATC curve
  (E) has no barriers to entry, flooding the market with firms

378. Which of the following characteristics of a monopolistically competitive firm causes it to make no economic profits in the long run?
  (A) Slightly differentiated products
  (B) Large number of firms
  (C) No barriers to entry
  (D) The ability to price discriminate
  (E) A large number of buyers

379. Which of the following characteristics lead to the price charged by a monopolistically competitive firm to be higher than the price charged by a perfectly competitive firm?
  (A) Slightly differentiated products
  (B) Large number of firms
  (C) No barriers to entry
  (D) The ability to price discriminate
  (E) A large number of buyers

380. Which of the following characteristics of monopolistic competition is likely to lead to firms that spend money on advertising?
  (A) Firms produce a homogenous product.
  (B) Each firm sells a slightly differentiated good.
  (C) Firms are able to perfectly price discriminate.
  (D) There are a relatively small number of sellers.
  (E) There are no barriers to entry.

381. Which of the following characteristics leads to the fact that a monopolistically competitive industry will be associated with deadweight loss?
  (A) The long-run and short-run outcomes are identical.
  (B) Each firm sells a slightly differentiated good.
  (C) Firms are able to perfectly price discriminate.
  (D) There are a relatively small number of sellers.
  (E) There are no barriers to entry.

382. The type of industry that produces the highest quantity is the
_____ because _____.

(A) perfectly competitive industry; there are no barriers to entry
(B) perfectly competitive industry; it has product differentiation
(C) perfectly competitive industry; it has no control over price
(D) oligopoly industry; it has no control over price
(E) monopolistically competitive industry; there are no barriers to entry

383. All else equal, as the number of firms in an industry increases,

(A) the quantity of a monopolistically competitive industry gets closer to the quantity produced by an oligopoly industry
(B) the quantity of a perfectly competitive industry gets closer to the quantity produced by a monopolistically competitive industry
(C) the quantity of an oligopoly industry gets closer to the quantity produced by a monopoly industry
(D) the quantity produced by an oligopoly industry gets closer to the quantity produced by a perfectly competitive industry
(E) the quantity produced by a monopoly industry gets closer to the quantity produced by an oligopoly industry

384. Which of the following industries have the potential for long-run profits?

(A) Monopoly, monopolistic competition, oligopoly, and perfect competition
(B) Monopolistic competition, oligopoly, and perfect competition
(C) Monopoly, oligopoly, and perfect competition
(D) Monopoly and oligopoly
(E) Monopoly and monopolistic competition

385. Which of the following industries would have allocative efficiency?

(A) Oligopoly only
(B) A single-price monopoly and perfect competition
(C) Monopolistic competition and perfect competition
(D) Oligopoly and perfect competition
(E) Perfect competition only

386. The market for published books is characterized by a large number of authors writing and selling books on a variety of topics, such as mysteries, romance novels, comedy, and young adult fiction. Anyone who writes a book can sell that book in a variety of online and print-based formats. There is a great deal of advertising in this market. Which of the following statements is true about the published book industry?

   I. It is monopolistically competitive.

  II. The price of books would be lower if all of the books sold were identical.

 III. Authors can expect to make profits in the long run.

(A) I only

(B) II only

(C) III only

(D) I and II only

(E) I, II, and III

387. Which market structures are the most common market structures in the real world?

(A) Monopoly and perfect competition

(B) Monopolistic competition and oligopoly

(C) Monopolistic competition and perfect competition

(D) Oligopoly and perfect competition

(E) Monopoly, monopolistic competition, and perfect competition

CHAPTER 13

Factor Markets

388. Suppose the demand for peppers is rising. How will this affect the demand for pepper pickers, the wage for pepper pickers, and employment in the pepper picker labor market?

	Demand	**Wage**	**Employment**
(A)	Increase	Increase	Decrease
(B)	Increase	Decrease	Increase
(C)	Increase	Increase	Increase
(D)	Increase	Decrease	Decrease
(E)	Decrease	Increase	Decrease

389. The economy is in a recession, and consumer spending for large appliances (such as refrigerators) has fallen. At the factories that produce these large appliances, we expect the demand for workers to _____ and wages for these workers to _____.

(A) decrease; increase
(B) decrease; decrease
(C) increase; increase
(D) remain unchanged; remain unchanged
(E) increase; decrease

390. Because the demand for labor is a function of the demand for the goods produced by the labor, labor demand is referred to as

(A) a derived demand
(B) a complementary demand
(C) a perfectly elastic demand
(D) an aggregate demand
(E) an investment demand

391. Which of the following would cause both wages and employment in the market for autoworkers to increase?

    (A) A very weak stock market

    (B) An increase in the price of gasoline

    (C) An increased unemployment rate

    (D) A growing size of the labor force

    (E) An increase in the demand for cars

392. If we see that the unemployment rate among carpenters is rising and average wages for carpenters are falling, we might conclude that

    (A) interest rates are falling, making it easier for homebuyers to get an affordable mortgage

    (B) low prices for raw materials like lumber, copper, and cement are causing construction companies to increase building

    (C) tax laws give homeowners an even bigger tax reduction for interest paid on their mortgage

    (D) a recession has caused the demand for new homes to fall

    (E) lower taxes have boosted demand for new construction

393. Which of the following would increase the demand for workers who assemble mobile phones?

    (A) The wage of these assembly workers decreases.

    (B) The demand for mobile phones increases.

    (C) The supply of mobile phones decreases.

    (D) The wage of these assembly workers increases.

    (E) The demand for mobile phones decreases.

Use Table 13.1 for questions 394–396.

Table 13.1

Units of Labor (L)	Marginal Product of Labor (MP$_L$)
1	24
2	21
3	18
4	15
5	12
6	9
7	6
8	3

394. Refer to Table 13.1. If the competitive price of the product produced by the labor is equal to $2, what is the value of the marginal product of the fifth unit of labor?

(A) $12
(B) $2
(C) $24
(D) $6
(E) $10

395. Refer to Table 13.1. Suppose we know that the value of the marginal product of the seventh unit of labor is $15. If the firm operates in a competitive product market, what is the price of the good being produced by this labor?

(A) $2.50
(B) $2
(C) $6
(D) $15
(E) $7

396. Refer to Table 13.1. This firm sells output in a competitive product market at an equilibrium price of $3. If the competitive wage for a unit of labor is $45, how many units of labor will be employed?

(A) 2
(B) 3
(C) 8
(D) 5
(E) 4

397. If a firm hires labor in a competitive labor market and produces in a competitive output market, the firm's demand for labor is _____ and given by the _____.

(A) downward sloping; marginal product of labor curve
(B) upward sloping; value of the marginal product of labor curve
(C) horizontal; wage
(D) downward sloping; value of the marginal product of labor curve
(E) horizontal; market price of output

398. Suppose that Jerry produces crunks and is employing six workers at the current market wage. If market demand for crunks rises and increases the price at which Jerry can sell them, how will this affect Jerry's demand for labor?

(A) The VMP_L curve shifts downward, increasing employment at the current market wage.

(B) The VMP_L curve shifts upward, increasing employment at the current market wage.

(C) The VMP_L curve shifts upward, decreasing employment at the current market wage.

(D) The VMP_L curve shifts downward, decreasing employment at the current market wage.

(E) The VMP_L curve does not shift, so employment does not change at the current market wage.

399. Suppose a firm employs only labor at a market wage of w and capital at a market rate of r. To hire the least-cost combination of labor and capital, which of the following conditions must apply?

(A) $\dfrac{MP_L}{w} = \dfrac{MP_K}{r}$

(B) $\dfrac{MP_L}{r} = \dfrac{MP_K}{w}$

(C) $\dfrac{MP_L}{MP_K} - \dfrac{r}{w}$

(D) $w \times MP_L = r \times MP_K$

(E) $MP_L - MP_K$

400. Sarah employs labor at a wage of $20 and capital at a rate of $10. Currently the marginal product of labor is 5 units and the marginal product of capital is 2 units. Can Sarah adjust her combination of labor and capital to decrease her costs of producing the same level of output?

(A) Yes, she should decrease her employment of both labor and capital.

(B) No, she is already hiring the optimal combination of labor and capital.

(C) Yes, she should increase her employment of labor and decrease her employment of capital.

(D) Yes, she should decrease her employment of labor and increase her employment of capital.

(E) Yes, she should increase her employment of both labor and capital.

401. Ricky has chosen the least-cost combination of labor and capital to produce 1,000 units of output. If the price of capital falls, we expect Ricky to increase his employment of _____, decrease his employment of _____, and see his capital-to-labor ratio (K/L) _____.
  (A) labor; capital; fall
  (B) capital; labor; stay unchanged
  (C) labor; capital; stay unchanged
  (D) capital; labor; rise
  (E) capital; labor; fall

Use Table 13.2 for questions 402–404.

Table 13.2

Hourly Wage	Jeffrey's Hours of Work	Ted's Hours of Work	John's Hours of Work
$10	0	40	40
$20	20	60	40
$30	40	50	40

402. Table 13.2 shows the hours of work three workers would supply to the labor market at three different wages. At any wage, each worker must decide how many hours to devote to work and how many hours to leisure. Assume that these three workers constitute the labor supply for the entire market. If the market wage rises from $20 to $30, total hours of labor supplied will
  (A) rise from 20 to 40 hours
  (B) fall from 60 to 50 hours
  (C) remain constant at 40 hours
  (D) rise from 80 to 130 hours
  (E) rise from 120 hours to 130 hours

403. Table 13.2 shows the hours of work three workers would supply to the labor market at three different wages. At any wage, each worker must decide how many hours to devote to work and how many hours to leisure. Which worker(s) has a backward-bending labor supply curve?
  (A) Jeffrey
  (B) Ted
  (C) John
  (D) Ted and John
  (E) All three

404. Table 13.2 shows the hours of work three workers would supply to the labor market at three different wages. At any wage, each worker must decide how many hours to devote to work and how many hours to leisure. Which of the following statements is true?

    I. Jeffrey's labor supply curve has a downward-sloping range.

   II. Between wages of $10 and $20, Ted's substitution effect between labor and leisure is smaller than the income effect.

  III. John's labor supply curve is the least elastic.

   (A) I only

   (B) II only

   (C) III only

   (D) II and III only

   (E) I and II only

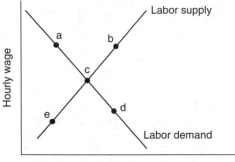

Figure 13.1

405. Figure 13.1 shows a labor market initially in equilibrium. Which of the following would cause a new equilibrium at point a?

   (A) More workers qualify to work in this occupation.

   (B) The government creates a rule making it more difficult for new workers to enter this market.

   (C) Demand weakens for the good being produced by this labor.

   (D) The price of a substitute factor of production rises.

   (E) The price of a complementary factor of production falls.

406. Figure 13.1 shows a labor market initially in equilibrium. Which of the following would cause a new equilibrium at point b?

(A) More workers qualify to work in this occupation.
(B) The government creates a rule making it more difficult for new workers to enter this market.
(C) Demand weakens for the good being produced by this labor.
(D) The price of a substitute factor of production rises.
(E) The price of a complementary factor of production rises.

407. Figure 13.1 shows a labor market initially in equilibrium. Which of the following would cause a new equilibrium at point d?

(A) More workers qualify to work in this occupation.
(B) The government creates a rule making it more difficult for new workers to enter this market.
(C) Demand strengthens for the good being produced by this labor.
(D) The price of a substitute factor of production rises.
(E) The price of a complementary factor of production rises.

408. Figure 13.1 shows a labor market initially in equilibrium. Which of the following would cause a new equilibrium at point e?

(A) More workers qualify to work in this occupation.
(B) The government creates a rule making it more difficult for new workers to enter this market.
(C) Demand weakens for the good being produced by this labor.
(D) The price of a substitute factor of production rises.
(E) The price of a complementary factor of production falls.

409. An effective minimum wage in a competitive labor market creates a _____ of labor because at the minimum wage _____.

(A) surplus; the quantity of labor demanded exceeds the quantity of labor supplied
(B) shortage; the quantity of labor supplied exceeds the quantity of labor demanded
(C) shortage; the quantity of labor demanded exceeds the quantity of labor supplied
(D) surplus; the quantity of labor supplied equals the quantity of labor demanded
(E) surplus; the quantity of labor supplied exceeds the quantity of labor demanded

410. When a factor market has only one demander of labor, the market is labeled a(n)

(A) natural monopoly
(B) labor union
(C) competitive market
(D) monopsony
(E) oligopoly

Use Table 13.3 for questions 411–412.

Table 13.3

Wage	Units of Labor Supplied	Value of the Marginal Product of Labor
$4	1	$16
$5	2	$14
$6	3	$12
$7	4	$10
$8	5	$8
$9	6	$6
$10	7	$4

411. Refer to Table 13.3, which shows how a single employer can hire an increasing quantity of labor, but must pay the labor higher wages. The table also shows the firm's value of the marginal product of labor. What is the firm's marginal factor cost of the seventh unit of labor?

(A) $16
(B) $70
(C) $4
(D) $7
(E) $21

412. Refer to Table 13.3, which shows how a single employer can hire an increasing quantity of labor, but must pay the labor higher wages. The table also shows the firm's value of the marginal product of labor. To maximize profit, how many units of labor will be employed and what wage will be paid?

	Units of Labor Employed	**Wage Paid**
(A)	3	$6
(B)	4	$7
(C)	7	$10
(D)	5	$8
(E)	4	$10

413. Suppose Melanie's Mints is a firm that can hire labor in a perfectly competitive labor market, but sells its mints in a monopoly product market. Compared to a firm that sells mints in a perfectly competitive product market, Melanie will hire _____ units of labor and pay each _____ wage.

(A) fewer; the same
(B) more; a lower
(C) fewer; a lower
(D) more; the same
(E) fewer; a higher

414. The factor market for capital is perfectly competitive and in equilibrium. If the price of labor, a substitute factor of production, falls, we expect

(A) demand for capital to rise, increasing the rental rate and increasing the quantity of capital employed
(B) supply of capital to fall, decreasing the rental rate and decreasing the quantity of capital employed
(C) demand for capital to fall, decreasing the rental rate and decreasing the quantity of capital employed
(D) supply of capital to rise, decreasing the rental rate and increasing the quantity of capital employed
(E) supply of capital to fall, increasing the rental rate and decreasing the quantity of capital employed

415. The factor market for capital is perfectly competitive and in equilibrium. Suppose the government offers firms a subsidy to invest in capital equipment. In the capital market we expect

(A) demand for capital to rise, increasing the rental rate and increasing the quantity of capital employed
(B) supply of capital to fall, decreasing the rental rate and decreasing the quantity of capital employed
(C) demand for capital to fall, decreasing the rental rate and decreasing the quantity of capital employed
(D) demand for capital to rise, increasing the rental rate and decreasing the quantity of capital employed
(E) supply of capital to fall, increasing the rental rate and decreasing the quantity of capital employed

416. The factor market for land is currently in equilibrium. In the production function, capital is a complementary factor with land, and capital and labor are substitutes for each other. If the supply of capital increases, causing a decrease in the rental rate of capital, how will this affect the market for labor and the market for land?

	Market for Labor	**Market for Land**
(A)	Demand increases	Demand increases
(B)	Supply increases	Demand increases
(C)	Demand decreases	Demand decreases
(D)	Demand decreases	Supply increases
(E)	Demand decreases	Demand increases

417. The factor market for land is currently in equilibrium. In the production function, capital is a complementary factor with land, and capital and labor are also complementary with each other. If the supply of capital decreases, how will this affect the market for labor and the market for land?

	Market for Labor	**Market for Land**
(A)	Demand increases	Demand increases
(B)	Supply increases	Demand increases
(C)	Demand decreases	Demand decreases
(D)	Demand decreases	Supply increases
(E)	Demand decreases	Demand increases

CHAPTER 14

Externalities

418. When a transaction between two parties conveys an external benefit to a third party, it is known as a

(A) public good
(B) natural monopoly
(C) positive externality
(D) negative externality
(E) monopsony

419. Jane owns an orange grove. On the other side of the highway from her grove, Ted owns some honeybees and sells the honey. In the process of making honey, Ted's bees fly to Jane's orange grove and pollinate her trees, increasing the productivity of her orange grove. Ted's production of honey is an example of a _____ because Jane is the recipient of a(n) _____.

(A) positive externality; Pigouvian subsidy
(B) positive externality; external benefit
(C) negative externality; external cost
(D) natural monopoly; Pigouvian tax
(E) positive externality; Pigouvian tax

420. A positive externality is generated whenever one person's actions in an exchange provide _____ to others not involved in the exchange.

(A) external benefit
(B) deadweight loss
(C) product differentiation
(D) external cost
(E) a tax

421. Which of the following is most likely providing a positive externality to society?

(A) Cigarette smoking
(B) Coal-burning power plants
(C) Burning piles of leaves and yard debris
(D) Public education
(E) Garbage landfills

422. Steve's mother always takes Steve to the health clinic to get a $10 flu shot for him before he starts another year of elementary school. This flu shot is a positive externality because

(A) it imposes an external cost on his classmates and teachers
(B) it increases the chance his unvaccinated classmates and teachers get the flu
(C) it requires his mother to pay $10 for the flu shot
(D) it reduces the chance that Steve gets the flu
(E) it reduces the chance his unvaccinated classmates and teachers get the flu

423. Houseweyer is a paper mill on the edge of town. In the production of paper, the mill emits a pungent aroma that wafts downwind and has caused property values to decline in affected neighborhoods. This is an example of

(A) a negative externality
(B) a public good
(C) external benefits
(D) a natural monopsony
(E) a common resource

424. When a transaction imposes external costs on third parties, it is referred to as a

(A) public good
(B) private good
(C) negative externality
(D) common resource
(E) natural monopoly

425. A negative externality is generated whenever one person's actions provide
_____ to others.

(A) external benefit
(B) deadweight loss
(C) product differentiation
(D) external cost
(E) a subsidy

426. Jesse has purchased a new $500 stereo that is so loud it causes his neighbor
JJ's windows to rattle and JJ has trouble sleeping. Jesse's actions are an
example of a negative externality because

(A) Jesse had to pay the $500 cost for a stereo
(B) Jesse gets the benefit of the stereo
(C) JJ is incurring a cost from Jesse's use of the stereo
(D) JJ enjoys the music coming from Jesse's stereo
(E) the stereo store received revenue from the sale of the stereo

427. Pollution from a corporation's factory is an example of _____
because it creates _____ the broader society.

(A) a negative externality; external benefits for
(B) a natural monopoly; economies of scale to
(C) an oligopoly; long-run profits for
(D) a public good; external costs for
(E) a negative externality; external costs for

428. If there is a positive externality in a market, the market level of output will
create a situation where

(A) the marginal private benefit exceeds the marginal social benefit
(B) the marginal social benefit exceeds the marginal private benefit
(C) the marginal social cost exceeds the marginal private cost
(D) the marginal social cost exceeds the marginal private benefit
(E) the marginal social cost exceeds the marginal social benefit

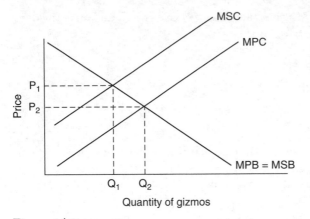

Figure 14.1

429. Refer to Figure 14.1, which shows the market for gizmos. A _____ exists in this market because at the market output, _____.
    (A) negative externality; MSC > MPC
    (B) positive externality; MSC > MSB
    (C) negative externality; MSB > MSC
    (D) negative externality; MSB > MPB
    (E) positive externality; MSC > MPC

430. Figure 14.1 shows the market for gizmos. If the market ignores the externality, what is the equilibrium market output and price? What is the socially efficient output and quantity?

	Market Output	Market Price	Efficient Output	Efficient Price
(A)	Q_1	P_1	Q_2	P_2
(B)	Q_2	P_2	Q_1	P_1
(C)	Q_1	P_2	Q_2	P_1
(D)	Q_2	P_1	Q_1	P_2
(E)	Q_1	P_1	Q_1	P_1

431. Figure 14.1 shows the market for gizmos. If the socially efficient quantity of gizmos was being produced, it would be the case that
    (A) MSC > MPC = MPB > MPC
    (B) MSC = MPC = MPB > MSB
    (C) MSC = MPB = MSB > MPC
    (D) MSC > MPC = MPB = MSB
    (E) MSC = MPC = MPB = MSB

432. The market for education generates external benefits to society. At the market outcome, it is the case that

(A) MSB = MSC
(B) MPC = MSB
(C) MPC > MPB
(D) MSB > MPB
(E) MPB > MSB

433. The market equilibrium price of a goozum is $12, and the equilibrium quantity is 1,000 units. Suppose that every time a goozum is purchased, another citizen's welfare is improved by $1. At the equilibrium quantity, we can tell that

(A) the marginal private benefit of a goozum is $1
(B) the marginal social benefit of a goozum is $1,000
(C) the marginal private benefit of a goozum is $12,000
(D) the marginal social benefit of a goozum is $13
(E) the marginal private cost of a goozum is $1

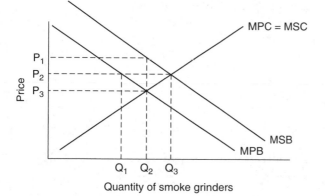

Figure 14.2

434. The market for smoke grinders is shown in Figure 14.2, on the previous page. At the market equilibrium, what can we say about the level of output, the price, and the level of deadweight loss?

	Market Output	Market Price	Deadweight Loss
(A)	Lower than the efficient output	Higher than the efficient price	Exists
(B)	Lower than the efficient output	Lower than the efficient price	Exists
(C)	Higher than the efficient output	Lower than the efficient price	Exists
(D)	Higher than the efficient output	Higher than the efficient price	Exists
(E)	Equal to the efficient output	Equal to the efficient price	Does not exist

435. The market for smoke grinders is shown in Figure 14.2. Which of the following statements is accurate?
  I. Deadweight loss exists because at Q_2 the MSB > MPB.
  II. The socially efficient price of a smoke grinder is P_1.
  III. A negative externality exists in this market.
  IV. The socially efficient output is Q_1.

(A) I only
(B) I and IV only
(C) II only
(D) II and III only
(E) IV only

436. The market for smoke grinders is shown in Figure 14.2. The deadweight loss in the market is equal to

(A) zero
(B) $Q_2 \times (P_1 - P_3)$
(C) $\frac{1}{2} \times (Q_3 - Q_2) \times (P_1 - P_3)$
(D) $Q_1 \times (P_2 - P_3)$
(E) $Q_3 \times P_2$

437. When production of a good generates harmful pollution to the environment, economists recognize a deadweight loss in that market because at the market outcome

(A) the marginal private cost exceeds the marginal social cost
(B) the marginal social benefit exceeds the marginal private cost
(C) the marginal private cost exceeds the marginal private benefit
(D) the marginal private cost exceeds the marginal social benefit
(E) the marginal social cost exceeds the marginal private cost

Use Table 14.1 for questions 438–440.

Table 14.1

Units of Plastics	Marginal Social Benefit = Marginal Private Benefit ($)	Marginal Private Cost ($)	External Cost ($)
1	15	5	4
2	14	6	4
3	13	7	4
4	12	8	4
5	11	9	4
6	10	10	4
7	9	11	4
8	8	12	4
9	7	13	4

438. Refer to Table 14.1. If the market for plastics is in equilibrium, what is the market price of plastics and the market quantity?

	Market Price	**Market Quantity**
(A)	$12	4
(B)	$4	5
(C)	$9	7
(D)	$10	6
(E)	$8	8

439. Refer to Table 14.1. If the market for plastics were producing at the socially efficient point, what is the efficient price of plastics and the efficient quantity?

	Market Price	Market Quantity
(A)	$12	4
(B)	$4	4
(C)	$9	7
(D)	$10	6
(E)	$12	8

440. Refer to Table 14.1. The government wishes to impose a Pigouvian tax on plastics producers to eliminate the externality. How large should the tax be to move the output from the market outcome to the efficient outcome?

(A) $12

(B) $4

(C) $8

(D) $10

(E) $2

441. During heavy rains the sewage treatment plant in town cannot handle the extreme volume of water that enters the facility, and it must release untreated sewage into the river that flows past Danielle's Day Care. The occasional aroma of sewage has caused Danielle to lose some customers, and her profits are falling. If we used the Coase theorem to remedy this situation, we might recommend

(A) a law requiring the sewage treatment plant to improve its handling of raw sewage

(B) a direct payment from Danielle to the sewage treatment plant to compensate the plant for her lost profits

(C) a direct payment from the sewage treatment plant to Danielle to compensate her for lost profits

(D) a per-unit tax on the sewage treatment plant equal to Danielle's lost profits

(E) a per-unit subsidy to the sewage treatment plant equal to Danielle's lost profits

442. Suppose that Killdeer Chemical has been a heavy polluter of the environment by releasing 500 tons of sludge every year. The government has dictated to Killdeer that they can emit only 250 tons or face steep penalties. This type of policy for the external costs of pollution is called

(A) a Pigouvian tax
(B) the Coase theorem
(C) tradable emissions permits
(D) command-and-control standards
(E) a Pigouvian subsidy

443. The idea that externalities can be eliminated if the affected parties negotiate a settlement between themselves is the premise of

(A) a command-and-control standard
(B) a per-unit tax
(C) a Pigouvian subsidy
(D) tradable pollution permits
(E) the Coase theorem

444. When people get the flu shot, their actions provide external benefits to the rest of us. These external benefits are not recognized by the market for flu shots. Of the following choices, which is the most direct way to achieve the socially efficient quantity of flu shots?

(A) Provide a per-unit subsidy to buyers of flu shots.
(B) Impose a per-unit tax on the providers of flu shots.
(C) Impose a per-unit tax on the buyers of flu shots.
(D) Require buyers and sellers to negotiate a fair price between themselves.
(E) Impose a price floor in the market for flu shots.

445. Because of the free-rider effect, a market will _____ a public good, requiring that _____ provide it.

(A) underproduce; firms
(B) efficiently produce; firms
(C) underproduce; the government
(D) underproduce; foreign consumers
(E) overproduce; charities

446. If a negative production externality is present in a market,

(A) the marginal social cost exceeds the marginal private cost at the equilibrium output

(B) the marginal social cost is less than the marginal private benefit at the equilibrium output

(C) the marginal social cost is equal to the marginal private cost at the equilibrium output

(D) the marginal social benefit exceeds the marginal social cost at the equilibrium output

(E) the marginal social cost is less than the marginal private cost at the equilibrium output

447. Positive externalities exist in market X when

(A) consumers in market X receive spillover benefits from market X transactions

(B) other third parties receive spillover benefits from market X transactions

(C) producers in market X receive spillover benefits from market X transactions

(D) third parties receive spillover costs from market X transactions

(E) third parties are taxed by the government because of market X transactions

CHAPTER 15

Public and Private Goods

448. Which of the following is most likely a private good?

(A) A compact car
(B) Air pollution
(C) Local police departments
(D) Cancer research
(E) Space exploration

449. Which of the following is most likely a public good?

(A) A pair of sandals
(B) A mobile phone
(C) A television
(D) A jet engine
(E) Space exploration

450. The characteristic of private goods that describes how the good is distributed to those willing and able to pay for it is called

(A) the commons
(B) excludability
(C) rivalry
(D) efficiency
(E) inefficiency

451. A gallon of gasoline is a private good because it has the characteristic of _____.

(A) homogeneity
(B) nonrivalry
(C) inefficiency
(D) efficiency
(E) excludability

452. There are twelve freshly baked apple pies at Dottie's bakery. While there are many people in town who would enjoy an apple pie, only those who are willing and able to pay the $10 price for a pie will receive a pie. This characteristic of apple pies is referred to as

(A) excludability
(B) the commons
(C) efficiency
(D) rivalry
(E) inefficiency

453. There are twelve freshly baked apple pies at Dottie's bakery. When Jason buys the very last apple pie, the next customer, Jennifer, finds there are no more pies and she must wait until tomorrow when more pies are ready for sale. Jennifer's situation is why apple pies have the characteristic of private goods known as

(A) excludability
(B) inefficiency
(C) efficiency
(D) rivalry
(E) the commons

454. When economists say that a private good has the characteristic of excludability, it means that

(A) the government must provide the good to all, even if they are unwilling and unable to pay the price
(B) the same unit of a good cannot be consumed by more than one consumer at a time
(C) sellers prevent buyers from buying the good if they are unwilling or unable to pay the price
(D) access to the good is open for all to use and consume
(E) the government cannot produce the good and sell to consumers

455. A gallon of milk is a private good because it has the characteristic of _____.

(A) nonexcludability
(B) rivalry
(C) a common resource
(D) efficiency
(E) homogeneity

456. When economists say that a private good has the characteristic of rivalry, this means that

(A) the government must provide the good to all, even if they are unwilling and unable to pay the price

(B) the government cannot produce the good and sell to consumers

(C) sellers prevent buyers from buying the good if they are unwilling and unable to pay the price

(D) the same unit of a good cannot be consumed by more than one consumer at a time

(E) access to the good is open for all to use and consume

457. Stan bought a can of soda for $1 at a vending machine. Which of the following demonstrates how cans of soda have the rivalry characteristic of private goods?

(A) Sharon wants to buy a soda but can't find $1 in her desk; so she goes without.

(B) Sharon doesn't like soda, so she doesn't buy any from the vending machine.

(C) The office manager has removed the vending machine so nobody can buy sodas.

(D) The office manager has a never-ending supply of sodas and provides one to any thirsty employee at no cost.

(E) Sharon goes to buy a soda but discovers that Stan has drunk the last one.

458. Which of the following are private goods?

   I. A leather coat

  II. A city fire hydrant

 III. The county sheriff's policing

 IV. A pair of sunglasses

(A) I only

(B) II and III only

(C) I, II, and IV only

(D) I and IV only

(E) III only

459. A meatball sub sandwich is a private good because it is

(A) nonrival and nonexcludable

(B) rival and nonexcludable

(C) rival and excludable

(D) nonrival and excludable

(E) inefficient and unprofitable

460. Which of the following is unlikely to be efficiently exchanged in a market?

(A) Streetlights
(B) Gasoline
(C) Apples
(D) Paintbrushes
(E) Picasso paintings

461. Stoplights in a neighborhood are public goods because they are

(A) nonrival and nonexcludable
(B) rival and nonexcludable
(C) rival and excludable
(D) nonrival and excludable
(E) efficient and rival

462. Which of the following are public goods?

   I. A NASA mission to Mars
  II. A city fire department
 III. A city park
 IV. A pair of pants

(A) I only
(B) I, II, and III only
(C) I and II only
(D) II and III only
(E) IV only

463. If a city installs a new art sculpture in the center of the city park, the sculpture is considered a public good because

(A) the city, not a corporation, hired a sculptor to create the artwork
(B) one person's enjoyment does not prevent another person from enjoying it
(C) the sculptor charged $25,000 to create the artwork
(D) the first person to visit the park prevents other visitors from seeing the sculpture
(E) the city will profit from charging each person viewing the artwork $2 for the pleasure to do so

464. A common resource, like wild mushrooms growing in a public forest, is

(A) nonrival and nonexcludable
(B) rival and nonexcludable
(C) efficient and excludable
(D) nonrival and excludable
(E) efficient and rival

465. When common resources, such as schools of fish in the ocean, are
_____ and _____, they tend to be _____.

- (A) nonrival; nonexcludable; overharvested
- (B) nonrival; excludable; overharvested
- (C) rival; nonexcludable; overharvested
- (D) rival; excludable; underharvested
- (E) rival; nonexcludable; underharvested

466. Suppose that a stand of old-growth forest is on public property and
nobody can claim ownership of the trees. The trees and the lumber that
they would provide are referred to as a

- (A) private good
- (B) public good
- (C) negative externality
- (D) common resource
- (E) artificially scarce good

467. Which of the following best fits the description of a common resource?

- (A) A new house
- (B) National defense
- (C) Space exploration
- (D) A manicure
- (E) Lobsters off the coast of New England

468. When a commonly held resource is overexploited because of a lack of
property rights, it is referred to as a(n)

- (A) natural monopoly
- (B) tragedy of the commons
- (C) positive externality
- (D) spillover benefit
- (E) economic growth

469. The city of Madison has a very large fireworks show to celebrate
Independence Day. The city knows that it cannot successfully charge
an admission fee for the show, because people can easily view the fireworks
from their homes without paying. This behavior is known as the

- (A) private good problem
- (B) government bureaucracy problem
- (C) free-rider problem
- (D) tragedy of the commons
- (E) negative spillover costs

470. George, Elaine, and Jerry are working on a group project for their statistics class. The professor will give each student the same grade, no matter how much effort each student puts forth. George knows that Jerry and Elaine will work tirelessly to make the best grade on the project, so George puts forth minimal effort. Economists describe George's behavior as

(A) free riding
(B) the tragedy of the commons
(C) positive spillover benefits
(D) irrational
(E) a private good

471. Suppose a public art museum charges no admission fee, but asks for voluntary contributions from those who attend the museum. Economists would expect that contributions would be _____ because of _____ behavior.

(A) low; irrational
(B) high; free-riding
(C) low; inefficient
(D) high; rational
(E) low; free-riding

472. A pay-per-view movie costs $10 for a cable TV subscriber, but many thousands of households can simultaneously view the movie. This movie's characteristics would be described as

(A) rival and nonexcludable
(B) efficient and nonrival
(C) nonrival and excludable
(D) rival and excludable
(E) inefficient and excludable

473. Which of the following goods would be considered nonrival and excludable?

(A) A gallon of gasoline
(B) Local police departments
(C) Scientific research
(D) Satellite television programming
(E) A laptop computer

474. A large state forest charges an annual fee for a pass, but people with the pass can hike in state forest as much as they like. The state forest is

(A) excludable and nonrival
(B) excludable and rival
(C) nonexcludable and rival
(D) inefficient and rival
(E) nonexcludable and nonrival

475. Which of the following examples is most likely a common resource?

(A) Cans of soup
(B) Pay-per-view wrestling matches
(C) Tickets to the World Cup
(D) Oysters in Chesapeake Bay
(E) National defense

476. Which of the following is the best example of a tragedy of the commons?

(A) A huge crop of rice causes prices to fall.
(B) Rough streets causes the city to pave the potholes.
(C) Unlimited duck hunting causes the duck population to decline.
(D) A sale on lawn furniture causes the store to run out.
(E) A hurricane wipes out the coffee crop in Hawaii.

477. Which of the following is most likely to be exchanged in a market?

(A) Climate change research
(B) City police
(C) Fire hydrants
(D) National defense
(E) Apartments

CHAPTER 16

Income Inequality and Poverty, and Taxes

478. A poverty line is best described as which of the following?

(A) A line describing proportional income below which people struggle to survive

(B) An amount of income below which survival is impossible

(C) A level of income that is set by a government or other agency beneath which people are described as being "in poverty"

(D) A line that represents unequal proportions of income, below which people are described as being "in poverty"

(E) An absolute level of income that always describes people as being poor

479. In the United States, the poverty line is equal to approximately:

(A) $10,000 for a family of 4

(B) Three times the amount of income required to have an adequate diet

(C) The amount of income it takes to rent a one-bedroom apartment and feed a family of four

(D) The minimum level of income that is required to survive

(E) The dollar amount of income that is required to be considered middle class

480. Which of the following is a potential source of income inequality?
  I. Differences in ability
 II. Differences in age
III. Differences in education and training

(A) I only
(B) II only
(C) III only
(D) I and III only
(E) I, II, and III

481. Which of the following is a justification for income equality that is based on positive analysis?

(A) It is unfair that some people earn more than others.
(B) The marginal benefit of wealth is lower at higher levels of wealth and higher at lower levels of wealth.
(C) Guaranteeing income equality may alter incentives to make harder work more attractive.
(D) Unequal incomes are illegal.
(E) Unequal income always reflects discrimination against the poor.

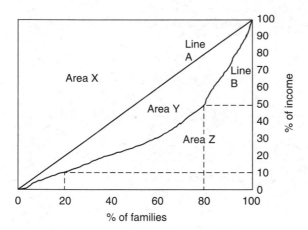

Figure 16.1

482. Refer to Figure 16.1. What does Line A represent?

(A) The poverty line
(B) The line of equality of income
(C) The Lorenz curve
(D) The quintile line
(E) The line of income inequality

483. Refer to Figure 16.1. What does Line B represent?

(A) The poverty line
(B) The line of equality of income
(C) The Lorenz curve
(D) The quintile line
(E) The decile line

484. Refer to Figure 16.1. Which of the following statements is true?

(A) The farther away the Lorenz curve is from the line of equality, the greater the amount of income inequality.
(B) The closer the Lorenz curve is to the line of equality, the greater the amount of income inequality.
(C) The more vertical Line A is, the greater the degree of income inequality.
(D) The less vertical Line A is, the greater the degree of income inequality.
(E) The higher Line B is above Line A, the greater the degree of income inequality.

485. Refer to Figure 16.1. Which of the following areas is needed to calculate the Gini coefficient?

I. X
II. Y
III. Z

(A) I and III only
(B) I and II only
(C) I only
(D) I, II, and III
(E) II and III only

486. Refer to Figure 16.1. How is the Gini coefficient calculated?

(A) Line B − Line A
(B) Line A − Line A
(C) Area X/Area Y
(D) Area X/(Area Y + Area Z)
(E) Area Y/(Area Y + Area Z)

487. Refer to Figure 16.1. Which of the following statements is true?

(A) 10% of families earn $20,000 in income each.
(B) 20% of families each make 10% of all income earned in the country.
(C) 20% of families earn a total of 10% of the income earned in the country.
(D) 60% of families earn 50% of the income in the country.
(E) Income is distributed equally in this country.

488. Which of the following is true of a Gini coefficient?

 I. The closer the Gini coefficient is to 1, the greater the degree of income inequality.
 II. The Gini coefficient is a good measure of poverty.
III. The closer the Gini coefficient is to 0, the greater the degree of income inequality.

(A) I only
(B) II only
(C) III only
(D) I and II only
(E) II and III only

489. Jenny earns an income of $10,000, and Samford earns an income of $40,000. If they each earn another $1,000 of income, Jenny will pay $100 in tax and Samford will pay an additional $400 in tax. Which of the following statements is true?

(A) Samford has a lower average tax rate than Jenny.
(B) Samford has a lower marginal tax rate than Jenny.
(C) Samford has a higher marginal tax rate than Jenny.
(D) Samford and Jenny pay the same marginal tax rate.
(E) Samform and Jenny both pay a proportional tax.

490. Jenny earns an income of $10,000, and Samford earns an income of $40,000. If they each earn another $1,000 of income, Jenny will pay $100 in tax and Samford will pay an additional $400 in tax. Which of the following best describes the type of tax system that Jenny and Samford are in?

(A) Flat tax
(B) Progressive tax
(C) Regressive tax
(D) Capital gains tax
(E) Sales tax

491. Charles earns $20,000 per year and spends about 10% of his income on food. Prodigy earns $30,000 per year and spends about 8% of his income on food. If a tax rate on food of 3% is imposed, what kind of tax is this?

(A) Flat tax
(B) Progressive tax
(C) Regressive tax
(D) Capital gains tax
(E) Negative income tax

492. If the labor supply curve is more _____, then redistributive wealth policies will lead to _____ incentive to work.

(A) elastic, no change in
(B) inelastic, no change in
(C) elastic, an increased
(D) inelastic, a decreased
(E) elastic, a decreased

493. Which of the following pairs of income tax policy and labor supply would be associated with the smallest efficiency loss?

(A) Elastic labor supply, flat tax
(B) Elastic labor supply, highly progressive tax
(C) Elastic labor supply, highly regressive tax
(D) Elastic labor supply, negative income tax
(E) Inelastic labor supply, flat tax

494. If a policy maker was most concerned with equity issues, which of the following taxes would that policy maker likely propose?

(A) Regressive income tax
(B) Progressive income tax
(C) Flat income tax
(D) Flat sales tax
(E) Lump sum tax

495. Which of the following is the most appropriate measure to determine the actual share of taxes that an individual pays?

(A) Average tax rate
(B) Marginal tax rate
(C) Efficient tax rate
(D) Mandatory tax rate
(E) Equity tax rate

496. Which of the following statements best describes the idea behind the equity and efficiency trade-off?

(A) In order to make a few people better off, you will have to make the vast majority of people worse off.

(B) The most efficient way for a corporation to pay a tax is to pass it along to the shareholders.

(C) The most efficient tax rate is one that taxes everyone at the same rate (i.e., an equitable tax rate).

(D) To achieve a more equitable income distribution through tax policy, the result may also be a higher amount of deadweight loss.

(E) Equity cannot be achieved, but efficiency can be achieved.

497. Marjorie earns $100,000 per year and pays an average tax rate of 25%, Randi earns $80,000 per year and pays an average tax rate of 15%, and Renee earns $45,000 per year and pays no income tax, but receives a tax refund due to tax credits of $4,500 per year. Which of the following features does this tax system include?

(A) Progressive taxes, regressive taxes, and flat taxes

(B) Regressive taxes and flat taxes

(C) Regressive taxes and income taxes

(D) Progressive taxes and lump sum taxes

(E) Negative income tax and progressive taxes

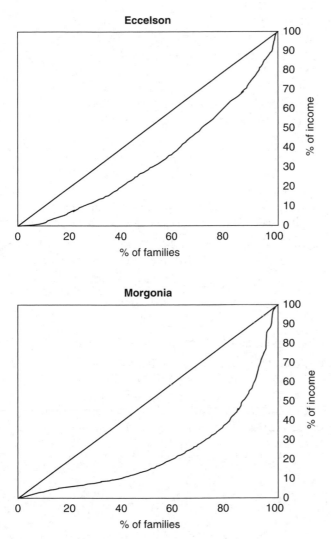

Figure 16.2

498. Refer to Figure 16.2, on the previous page. Which of the following statements can be made based on the information in the figures?

(A) Eccelson has a higher degree of poverty than Morgonia.
(B) Morgonia has a higher degree of poverty and inequality than Eccelson.
(C) Morgonia has a higher degree of inequality than Eccelson.
(D) Morgonia has a higher tax rate than Eccelson, which has caused greater inequality.
(E) Morgonia has a higher level of inequality caused by educational disparities.

499. Which of the following Gini coefficients is closest to the Gini coefficient that represents income inequality in the United States since the year 2000?

(A) 0
(B) 1
(C) .95
(D) .30
(E) .45

500. Which of the following regions has the highest Gini coefficients?

(A) Southern Europe (countries such as Greece, Italy, and Spain)
(B) Southern Africa (countries such as Botswana, Namibia, and South Africa)
(C) Northern Europe (countries such as Finland, Norway, and Sweden)
(D) The Middle East (countries such as Iran, Israel, and Yemen)
(E) Australia

ANSWERS

Chapter 1: Basic Economic Concepts

1. (C) Economics is the study of how individuals, households, firms, and entire societies choose to allocate scarce resources. Societies face unlimited wants, but because resources are scarce, decisions must be made on how to best allocate them. Resources might be allocated in markets, by using money, or by a central planning agency in the government. Therefore, all choices besides C represent parts of the study of economics, but not the definition of the field itself.

2. (B) Microeconomics is a combination of *micro*, meaning small, and *economics*. Therefore, microeconomics is "small" decision-making about how to allocate scarce resources. Microeconomics focuses on economic decision-making of households, firms, and individuals. All of the other choices reflect questions that may arise in the study of macroeconomics, which focuses on problems and questions that face an economy as a whole rather than an individual decision-maker. For instance, typical microeconomics questions involve individual firm decisions on production and hiring, and individual and household decisions on purchasing and whether or not to work.

3. (A) Macroeconomics is a combination of *macro*, meaning large, and *economics*. Therefore, macroeconomics is about "large" decision-making, not on how individuals choose to allocate scarce resources, but on how these resources are allocated for an economy as a whole. All of the other choices reflect problems that a microeconomist would consider. Macroeconomics tends to be concerned with issues such as unemployment in a society, rather than at an individual level. Other macroeconomics issues include aggregate production in an economy (as opposed to the production of a firm or a single industry) and a raise in the general price level (as opposed to an increase in a single price).

4. (B) In economics, the term *scarcity* refers to the fact that all of the economic resources (land, labor, capital, and entrepreneurial ability) are limited. Scarcity is an important concept because if it were not for scarcity, economics would not be a particularly important field of study. If society was faced with unlimited wants but also had unlimited resources, we could satisfy the unlimited wants without having to make trade-offs.

5. (D) Scarcity means that every time a decision is made to allocate a resource toward a particular use, we are also deciding to divert that resource from another use. Trade-offs occur because we cannot allocate resources to every one of our desires. We refer to the costs of these trade-offs as opportunity costs. Marginal analysis is the decision-making process that a rational decision-maker uses to decide how to make those trade-offs.

6. (B) Normative analysis, sometimes called normative economics, is prescriptive. It says what should happen and is a recommendation for what should happen. An easy way to remember this is to think of social norms—the way we think people should behave in society. An example of a normative economic statement would be something like "income should be equitably distributed" or "taxes should be lower." On the other hand, positive economics, sometimes called positive analysis, is descriptive. It says how things are or how the economy actually works rather than how it should work. An example of a positive economic statement would be something like "an increase in income will result in more goods being purchased" or "an increase in the price of a good will lead to higher profits for a firm."

7. (B) A shortcut way of remembering what the term *marginal* means in economics is "the last" or "the next" one. For instance, in marginal decision-making, an agent is deciding on whether or not to use one more or one less, based on the additional benefit from the last one (marginal benefit) and the additional cost of the last one (marginal cost). Common mistakes that students make in economics are focusing on the cheapest unit, the most expensive unit, or the average.

8. (A) Marginal analysis is decision making based on the marginal benefit and marginal cost of a decision. In this case, Jim is deciding whether the marginal (next) plate of food from the buffet will be worth the cost that would be associated with that additional plate of food, such as any monetary cost, additional exercise he might have to do later, or physical discomfort from eating more. According to marginal analysis, as long as the benefit he receives from *one more* plate of food is more than the cost of eating *one more* plate of food, he will continue to eat. He will stop eating when he believes that the marginal cost will exceed the marginal benefit from the next plate of food.

9. (D) The characteristics of a free market economy are that prices allocate resources in a market setting with minimal government intervention and established property rights. In a centrally planned system, resources are allocated by a central planning authority (usually a government), which decides what and how much is produced, who enjoys the production, and how much of the production each individual is entitled to. Since governments do the allocation, rather than prices, any price that exists in a centrally planned economy will not carry very much information and may be arbitrarily set. Firms may have little, if any, decision-making ability, as the production has been dictated by the central planning authority.

10. (A) In going from a centrally planned economy to a market-based economy, Maxistan is moving from a centralized rationing system to a decentralized rationing system, namely, prices. Scarcity still exists, so some sort of rationing function is still necessary to allocate scarce resources. In moving to a market economy, Maxistan will need to shift to freedom of individuals to acquire resources to produce goods and services and to choose which of their resources to sell to others, private ownership of those resources, an economy driven by self-interest, competition, and prices for goods that are determined by markets with no (or minimal) government intervention.

11. (C) The rationing function of prices refers to the fact that in a competitive market, prices send signals to both buyers and sellers. Price indicates to sellers the willingness and ability of consumers to pay for a good, and price indicates to buyers the cost of producing a good. The goods are then allocated (i.e., rationing) to those most willing and able to pay for the good. In other words, prices coordinate the market in a market-based system in the way that a government might coordinate the allocation of goods in a non-market-based economy.

12. (E) Capital, which is frequently abbreviated as K in economics, is a good that is produced and is in turn used to produce other goods. A factory is produced in the sense that it is constructed from other resources, using labor and land (including the natural resources that are included in land, like cement and energy), and then is used to produce goods. Students often confuse the colloquial use of the word *capital* in finance. Firms may "raise capital," which usually means gathering money through issuing bonds or stocks, or other financial strategies. Usually, this money is then used to purchase capital such as equipment or machinery, or to construct a production facility.

13. (C) The four resources are land (usually abbreviated lowercase l), labor (L), capital (K), and entrepreneurial ability (which has various abbreviations). Contrary to the assumptions of many students, money is not an economic resource. Money is merely a tool that is used to facilitate the exchange of resources, goods, and services.

14. (A) Included under the category of land are natural resources, such as actual land, energy, the production of the land (primary products such as agriculture), and minerals. A bowl or a cooling rack would be considered capital because it is produced. The work of the person mixing the dough would be considered labor, since it is the work of a person.

15. (C) To some degree, all of the economic resources are substitutable. In this case, the café owner wants to increase production (the number of meals served), which can be done in one of two ways. The café can either increase the capital investment by buying and installing more tables, which would enable more people to be seated in the café at any given time. Alternatively, the café could hire another server, which would enable more people at any given time to be served. In either case, the total number of meals served in the café would increase.

16. (B) Land is a catchall phrase in economics that refers not just to actual land that you can stand on, but any natural resource. One of the critical natural resources that is included in this category is any resource that produces energy. Heating oil, which is a petroleum product, would be considered land even though it is not the colloquial use of the word *land*.

17. (E) Opportunity cost refers to the value of the next best alternative. Opportunity costs are different from explicit costs such as tuition or books. If he goes to school, he will not be able to work at all or at minimum, he will not be able to work as much as when he is not in school. Therefore, the income that he will lose when he goes to school would be considered an opportunity cost.

18. (C) A normative statement is prescriptive, describing what should be done rather than the way things are, which would be a positive statement. For instance, a positive statement would be, "Employees may be less likely to quit," because it is a probable response rather than prescriptive. When evaluating whether a statement is normative or positive, the word *should* (explicit or implied) is a giveaway that the statement is normative.

19. (A) Marginal analysis involves evaluating the additional cost and additional benefit of a decision. Whether or not one should have a college degree is normative analysis. The foregone income of playing an additional year in college is an opportunity cost that should be part of a marginal analysis, but is not a marginal analysis in itself. Choice D is just a statement of the trade-off that Joe is facing, rather than an analysis of his choices. However, choice A evaluates the benefits of one more year of college (being a better prepared, and ostensibly better paid, player in the future) as well as the costs of one more year (the risk of a career-ending injury).

20. (B) A rational person consumes to the point where marginal cost is equal to marginal benefit. In this case, the marginal cost (MC) of working another hour, $25 dollars, exceeds the marginal benefit (MB) of an additional $20 in income. When MC > MB, you should decrease consumption of the good in question. This is a general rule in economics. If MC < MB, increase consumption. If MC > MB, decrease consumption. If MC = MB, this is the optimal amount of consumption.

21. (C) When there are no explicit, or out-of-pocket, costs, opportunity costs are the value of the single next best alternative. For instance, suppose you have the choice of working as a babysitter at $8 per hour, restaurant cashier at $9 per hour, landscaper at $10 per hour, or dog walker at $11 per hour. The opportunity cost of being a dog walker is $10, because the next best alternative is being a landscaper.

22. (D) The optimal consumption point is where the marginal benefit (MB) equals the marginal cost (MC). Since Marjorie values shoes at $50, her optimal decision is to continue to buy shoes until the value she places on the last pair is equal to the $40 price tag. For now, since she is only paying $40, it would be optimal, assuming that she is still within her budget constraint, for Marjorie to buy more shoes.

23. (A) Opportunity cost is the cost of the next best alternative, and the next best alternative to building a dormitory, which earns $120,000, is building a gym, which also earns $120,000. Note that it would not be correct to add up all of the next best alternatives. It would also be incorrect to subtract the value of the next best alternative, which would yield zero opportunity cost.

24. (E) In a command economy, the price that is set by the government would not necessarily reflect the true cost of production of a good, as it would in a market-based economy. This is because in the long run a producer in a market-based economy would not be willing to produce at a loss, whereas in a command-and-control economy, the producer may not have a choice. Similarly, since producers in a command-and-control economy will not be the beneficiaries of any improvements in production, they will have little incentive to innovate and find more efficient ways to produce. As a result, more or less may be produced than both producers and consumers would otherwise like.

Chapter 2: Production Possibilities

25. (D) A production possibilities frontier (frequently abbreviated as *PPF*) shows all of the efficient combinations of production of two goods. It is called a frontier because it shows the limit of possibilities given the available resources. A PPF may be a straight line or bowed outward. All the points that lie on the PPF are efficient. All the points that lie outside the PPF are unattainable given the current available resources. All points that lie inside the PPF are inefficient, meaning that not all of the resources are being used in production.

26. (C) If there is an increase in an economic resource that is used to make both good A and good B, then the production possibilities frontier will shift out. That means that the intersection points on both the A axis and B axis will be at higher levels of production: you could produce more of good A, more of good B, or more of both good A and good B. With more resources, a point that was previously unattainable will now be efficient.

27. (D) Point E is an inefficient combination of production. This means that this economy could increase production given its current resources because it is not currently allocating its resources efficiently, or many of the nation's resources are idle and producing neither spatulas nor wheat. To produce point C, this economy would have to reduce its production of spatulas and reallocate those resources, and the idle resources, to the production of wheat.

28. (B) Point F is on a production possibilities frontier (PPF) that has rotated outward. Notice that even after this rotation of the PPF, if this country devotes all of its resources to producing spatulas, the amount of spatulas it can make doesn't change. But if it devotes all of its resources to producing wheat, it can now produce more wheat. Therefore, this rotation must have occurred because it now has more economic resources or better technology used in the production of wheat.

29. (A) Point E, producing 5 units of spatulas and 3 units of wheat, is an inefficient level of production because it lies inside the production possibilities frontier. If the economy moves to point F, it would now be producing 5 units of spatulas and 12 units of wheat. Therefore, the economy would not be giving up anything to reach this combination of production. Note that when an economy is producing at an inefficient level, it is either because resources are not being used efficiently and can be reallocated, or that resources are not being used at all. In this case, moving from point E to point F would not be reallocating resources away from the production of spatulas toward the production of wheat (as would happen in a move from point E to point C). This would indicate that there were resources going unused that could have been used for making wheat.

30. (B) The shift shown in Figure 2.1 shows an increase in the ability to make one of the two goods if all resources were devoted to making that good (wheat), but not an increase in the production of the other good if all resources were devoted to making that good (spatulas). This means that some resource used to make only wheat has increased: for instance, an increase in agricultural labor, an increase in capital used to grow wheat but not spatulas, or an increase in wheat-growing technology.

31. (C) Productive efficiency is producing at a point that is on the production possibilities frontier, meaning that all resources are being put to their best productive use. Allocative efficiency is when the combination of production occurring is the amount that an economy would best like. On any given production possibilities frontier (some books and teachers call it a production possibilities curve, or PPC) only one point is allocatively efficient. Without more information, we cannot tell if any of these points are allocatively efficient. However, since A, F, and B are all on the same production possibilities frontier, we can tell that for an economy with that production possibilities frontier, all three of these points would be productively efficient.

32. (E) A rational society will consume at the point where the marginal cost of consumption is equal to the marginal benefit. We do not need prices to figure out marginal cost in this case, since we can determine the cost of one good in terms of the units of the other good that is given up. A common mistake that students make is that the best choice is to have equal consumption of the two goods and assume that point A would be the best choice of consumption. This is not a correct assumption, since it is possible that this society highly values wheat and doesn't get much value out of spatulas. In this case, a consumption point such as F more likely would be allocatively efficient than point A. To draw any conclusions, we need to know how a society values these goods in terms of marginal benefit.

33. (B) The production possibilities frontier shown in Figure 2.1 is bowed out, which means that it exhibits increasing costs. For instance, suppose the economy is initially producing at point A. As it moves from point A to point F to point B, it gives up increasing amounts of spatulas to get each additional unit of wheat. This indicates that there are different opportunity costs of production at various levels of production. When a production possibilities frontier is bowed out, the opportunity cost will vary at each point on the curve. But with a straight line, the opportunity cost is the same at every point along the curve.

34. (C) Economic growth is the ability to produce more goods and services. Economic growth is illustrated in a production possibilities frontier (PPF) by an outward shift. In the PPF shown in I, there is only a reallocation of production, rather than an ability to make more of both goods. In the PPF shown in IV, there is actually a decrease in the ability to produce both goods. Only II shows an outward shift.

35. (C) A reallocation of resources is a movement along a single curve. Both I and III show an economy reallocating productive resources away from one good and toward the other good. A shift of a production possibilities frontier as shown in either II or IV doesn't actually tell us how an economy is currently producing. Rather, II tells us that for any particular allocation of resources, you could produce more of either good, and IV tells us that this economy can now produce less of either good.

36. (B) Anytime you see a production possibility frontier that is bowed outward, as is shown in I and II, this indicates that the economy has increasing costs. Anytime you see a production possibility frontier that is a straight line, as is shown in III and IV, this indicates that the economy has constant costs.

37. (A) Absolute advantage is the ability to produce more goods and services given the same quantity of resources than another producer. Stated another way, absolute advantage is the ability to produce the same quantity of goods and services with fewer inputs than another producer. Note that you can have absolute advantage in one or more goods. For instance, if Melanie can produce 10 lunches or 12 dinners in a day, and Eric can produce 8 lunches or 10 dinners in a day, Melanie has absolute advantage in producing both goods because using the same level of inputs (a single day) she can produce more lunches or more dinners.

38. (E) Gains from trade occur when producers specialize in what they have comparative advantage in and then trade at a price that falls between the opportunity costs for each producer. The logic behind this is simple. Suppose you can produce two goods, A and B, and every time you produce 1 unit of good A, you give up 2 units of good B. If another producer comes along and offers to sell you 1 unit of good A, but it will cost you 3 units of good B, you would be unwilling to trade, because you can make good A more cheaply yourself. Likewise, your trading partner will only be willing to sell you a good for more than it costs that partner to produce. Therefore, to trade, the price must fall between the costs for both producers and for all goods.

39. (C) To translate the production possibilities curve into an equation, let M stand for monster trucks and S stand for silly string. For Elistan, 1 day = 5M or 1 day = 10S. Since 1 day = 1 day, we can rearrange this to be 5M = 1 day = 10S, or 5M = 10S. To find the opportunity cost of monster trucks, we simply need to solve this for M by dividing both sides of the equation by 5, which gives us M = 2S. If we translate this into words, we are saying producing 1 monster truck requires the equivalent time to produce 2 cans of silly string. So every time Elistan produces 1 monster truck, it gives up 2 cans of silly string, and when it produces 1 can of silly string, it gives up ½ a monster truck. Note that choices A and B are incorrect because opportunity costs are expressed in terms of another good. By saying just "5" or "½," it is unclear what is being talked about . . . it could be 5 eggplants for all we know.

40. (A) Absolute advantage is the ability to produce more goods given the same inputs. Here, the input is time. In one day, Elistan can produce 10 cheesecakes, but Maxistan can produce only 8 cheesecakes, so Elistan has absolute advantage in producing cheesecakes. In one day Elistan can produce 10 prime ribs and Maxistan can produce 10 prime ribs, so neither has absolute advantage in producing prime ribs.

41. (C) Comparative advantage is having the lower opportunity cost of producing a good. So to solve this, we need to find out what the opportunity cost for each good is for each producer. For Xela, they can use all of their resources to produce 15 fish tanks (F) or 5 butterfly nets (B), so mathematically, resources = 15F or resources = 5B, which we can rearrange to get 15F = 5B. Solving for F gets F = ⅓B, and solving for B gets 3F = B. So a fish tank equals ⅓ of a butterfly net, and a butterfly net equals 3 fish tanks. For Nire, 15F = 3B, so F = ⅕B and 5F = B. Since Nire gives up less butterfly nets for each fish tank, Nire has comparative advantage in producing fish tanks. Xela gives up less fish tanks to produce butterfly nets, so Xela has comparative advantage in producing butterfly nets.

42. (B) The basis for specialization and trade is comparative advantage. Whoever has comparative advantage in producing a good (they can produce a good at a lower opportunity cost) should specialize in producing that good. In this case, Kylie has comparative advantage in producing fish as her opportunity cost for producing fish is ⅕ of a shelter, rather than ½ of a shelter. Lilly has comparative advantage in producing shelter as her opportunity cost of producing shelter is only 2 fish as opposed to the 5 fish Kylie gives up whenever she builds a shelter. Therefore, Kylie should specialize in producing fish and Lilly should specialize in producing shelter.

43. (A) Matthew has comparative advantage in producing pies because his opportunity cost of a pie is only ⅕ of a cake, as opposed to the ½ cake that Megan gives up every time she bakes a pie. Megan has comparative advantage in producing cakes because she gives up only 2 pies for each cake, but Matthew gives up 5 pies for each cake he makes. When two agents specialize and trade, they will be willing to trade if the trading price lies between the two opportunity costs for each trader. If Megan produces 5 cakes and trades 2 of those cakes, she will in return get 8 pies, leaving her with 3 cakes and 8 pies. This combination of goods is outside of her production possibilities without trade (it might help to draw her production possibilities frontier to demonstrate this). Likewise, if Matthew produces 15 pies and trades 8 of those for 2 cakes, he is left with 2 cakes and 7 pies, which is also outside of his original production possibilities. Because each person can consume outside of his or her original production possibilities, they are said to both "gain from trade."

44. (D) Annie and Will won't agree to trade unless the trading price makes them at least better off than they would be without trading. Suppose Will currently uses ⅓ of his land to produce cotton and the rest to produce lumber, which yields him 40 bales of cotton and 26⅓ tons of lumber, and Annie splits her land between cotton and lumber, which gives her 50 bales of cotton and 25 tons of lumber. If they specialize in what they have comparative advantage in, Annie can produce 100 bales of cotton, and Will can produce 80 tons lumber. At a trading price of ⅝ of a ton of lumber for each bale of cotton, Annie can trade 50 of those bales for 31.25 tons of lumber (50 × ⅝ = 31.25), so she now has 50 bales of cotton and 31.25 tons of lumber, leaving her better off. Will now has 50 bales of cotton and 48.75 tons of lumber. Therefore, since the trading price was between the opportunity costs for each trader, both are left better off and would be willing to specialize and trade.

45. (C) For there to be gains from trade, three conditions must be met. First, the two parties must have different opportunity costs. Second, each party should specialize in what they have comparative advantage in. Third, the trading price must lie between the opportunity costs for each producer and each good. Note that even if one of the trading partners has absolute advantage in both goods, as long as the other conditions are met, there is still the possibility for gains from trade.

46. (D) Any level of production that lies on Asil's production possibility frontier (PPF) would be an efficient level of production. The first choice, 8 cups of coffee and 0 bagels, clearly lies on her PPF. According to Figure 2.3, Asil's production possibilities could be described as 8C = 16B. Solving for C and B, we get C = 2B and ½C = B. So every time she makes a bagel, she gives up half a cup of coffee. If she moved from making 8 cups of coffee to 5, she would give up 3 cups of coffee and get 6 bagels (3 × C = 3 × 2B, so 3C = 6B), so the second choice is also efficient. However, if she gave up 1 more cup of coffee, she would not gain 6 more bagels, so choice III is unattainable.

47. (B) To find Asil's opportunity cost of making bagels, we can use the information given in Figure 2.3. If she devoted all of her resources to making coffee, she will make 8 cups of coffee, so 8C = resources. If she devoted all of her resources to making bagels, she would make 16 bagels, so 16B = resources. Putting this together, we get 8C = 16B. We then solve for B to get her opportunity cost of making bagels, which yields ½C = B. Therefore, her opportunity cost of a bagel is half a cup of coffee.

48. (D) For Asil and Joe to be willing to trade, the trading price must lie between both of their opportunity costs. For Asil, 8C = 16B, so C = 2B and ½C = B. For Joe, 5C = 20B, so C = 4B and ¼C = B. Therefore, any trading price for a bagel would have to be between ½ and ¼ of a cup of coffee.

49. (D) If Joe splits his time between making coffee and bagels, then ⁵⁄₂C = 2½ cups of coffee and ²⁰⁄₂B = 10 bagels. If Asil splits her time, then ⁸⁄₂C = 4 cups of coffee and ¹⁶⁄₂B = 8 bagels. Asil has the comparative advantage in producing coffee (her opportunity cost is C = 2B), and Joe has the comparative advantage in producing bagels (his opportunity cost is C = 4B). If they each specialized, Asil would have 8 cups of coffee and Joe 20 bagels before trade. A trade price of ⅜ of a cup for a bagel would be between ½ and ¼ of a cup of coffee, and both would be willing to trade. Asil could sell 3 cups of coffee and get 8 bagels for that, leaving her with 5 cups of coffee and 8 bagels. Joe would then have 3 cups of coffee, for which he sold 8 bagels to get, leaving him with 3 cups of coffee and 12 bagels. Both are better off as a result of specializing and trading.

50. (A) Since Joe can make 20 bagels using the same resources and Asil can make only 16, he has absolute advantage in making bagels. Since Asil has the lower opportunity cost of producing coffee, she has comparative advantage in producing coffee. Note that it is just a coincidence that she also has absolute advantage in producing coffee.

51. (A) This question is asking you to find the opportunity cost of coffee for Joe. In a single day he can produce either 5 cups of coffee or 20 bagels, so 5C = 20B. Solving for coffee yields C = 4B. Therefore, every time he gives up a cup of coffee, he gives up making 4 bagels.

52. (E) If Joe is consuming 5 cups of coffee, there is no way he could also produce 4 bagels, according to the production possibilities frontier in Figure 2.3. If he became better at producing only bagels, then the only way he could still consume 5 cups of coffee is if he spent all of his time producing coffee, so I is not a correct choice. However, if he improved at producing both goods, his production possibilities frontier could shift out and he could consume that amount. Alternatively, the other way to consume at a point beyond his production possibilities is to specialize and trade with Asil.

53. (A) If they devoted all of their resources to making barges, Riverton could make more barges than Park City. If they devoted all of their resources to making tents, Riverton could make more tents than Park City. Therefore, Riverton has absolute advantage in making both goods. To find the opportunity cost for barges for Park City, $10B = 20T$, so $B = 2T$ and $\frac{1}{2}B = T$. For Riverton, $15B = 25T$, so $B = \frac{5}{3}T$ and $\frac{3}{5}B = T$. Since $\frac{1}{2} < \frac{3}{5}$, Park City has comparative advantage in making tents.

54. (D) Each city should specialize in the good in which they have comparative advantage. Since Riverton has comparative advantage in making barges, Riverton should specialize in making barges. Since Park City has comparative advantage in making tents, Park City should specialize in making tents.

55. (E) Since we know that the two cities have different opportunity costs, we know that there is potential for gains. However, the exact amount of trade that will occur will depend on the price that is negotiated between the two cities. As long as the price of a tent is between $\frac{1}{2}$ and $\frac{3}{5}$ of a barge, as it is in II and III, both cities will be willing to trade because they will be relatively better off than without trade.

56. (A) If it takes Jo-Jo 10 minutes to grade a homework question and 15 minutes to grade an essay question, then in a single hour he can grade either 6 homework questions or 4 essay questions, which would give us $6HW = 4E$, or $1\frac{1}{2}HW = E$. Recall that the opportunity cost is the cost of the next best alternative. Here, the next best alternative is grading the other type of question. Note that time is an input to production here, not something of value itself.

57. (B) If it takes Jo-Jo 10 minutes to grade a homework question and 15 minutes to grade an essay question, then in a single hour he can grade either 6 homework questions or 4 essay questions, which would give us $6HW = 4E$, or $HW = \frac{2}{3}E$. If it takes Karl 20 minutes to grade a homework question and 10 minutes to grade an essay question, then in a single hour he can grade either 3 homework questions or 6 essay questions, which would give us $3HW = 6E$, or $HW = 2E$. Since Jo-Jo has a lower opportunity cost of grading homework questions, he has comparative advantage in grading homework questions.

58. (B) Here we are given two points that lie on Jason's linear (straight line) production possibilities frontier (PPF). To find the opportunity cost of one good in terms of another with a linear PPF, we need to find the slope of that straight line. To find the slope of a linear curve, we find the rise/run. Suppose we plotted the units of cabernet on the horizontal axis and pinot noir on the vertical axis. Here the rise is the change between 2005 and 2007 in pinot noir, so $120 - 160 = -40$. The run is the change between 2005 and 2007 in cabernet production, which would be $200 - 180 = 20$. To find the opportunity cost of cabernet in terms of pinot, $-40/20 = -2$. Therefore, every time he makes a bottle of cabernet, he gives up 2 bottles of pinot noir. If he went from 200 bottles of cabernet to 220, he must give up 2 bottles of pinot noir for each of the 20 bottles of cabernet, bringing him from 120 bottles of pinot noir to 80.

59. (A) For this type of question it would be useful to create a figure. We are given two points on Jason's production possibilities frontier (PPF): (120 pinot noir, 200 cabernet) and (160 pinot noir, 180 cabernet), which we can use to find the slope of the PPF. Assuming we put cabernet on the x-axis, the slope is -2. So if he produces 260 bottles of cabernet, he would not be able to produce any pinot noir. If he produced 140 bottles of cabernet, he would be able to produce 240 bottles of pinot noir, so II would not be efficient. III would also be inefficient.

60. (E) Suppose Max was being efficient both days, was making the same amount of one good but more of the other good, and was able to make more of one good without having to give up the other. In this case, Max could not only make 18 cupcakes, but also make an additional loaf of bread; so he must be able to produce at least more bread and possibly more cupcakes. Therefore, his production possibilities frontier has either shifted or rotated out.

61. (A) Here we are given two points on a linear production possibilities frontier and we are told that Steve is always efficient. We can use this to determine that every time he goes to 2 meetings, he gives up editing 5 papers. So if he is going to 6 meetings, he can edit 5 papers; if he goes to 8 meetings, he can edit 0 papers, and after that there is nothing more to give up, so II is incorrect. Similarly, if he goes from 4 meetings to 3 meetings, he will be able to edit 12.5 papers, so III would be inefficient. Steve's opportunity cost indicates that when he goes to 2 meetings, he gives up editing 5 papers. So if Patti will exchange 6 papers for 2 meetings, he would be better off.

62. (A) If country A has 200 workers who each produce 20 socks (S) or 30 picture frames (PF) in a year, then in a single year country A can produce $20 \times 200 = 4,000$ socks or $30 \times 200 = 6,000$ picture frames in a year. So for country A, $4,000S = 6,000PF$ and $S = \frac{3}{2}PF$ and $\frac{2}{3}S = PF$. If country B has 400 workers who each produce 20 socks or 30 picture frames, then country B can produce $20 \times 400 = 8,000$ socks or $30 \times 400 = 12,000$ picture frames. This becomes $8,000S = 12,000PF$, or $S = \frac{3}{2}PF$ and $\frac{2}{3}S = PF$. Neither country has comparative advantage in producing both goods. Note that no matter what the opportunity costs had turned out to be, it is mathematically impossible to have comparative advantage in both goods, and this can never be a correct answer.

Chapter 3: Supply and Demand

63. (B) A larger population results in more consumers for almost all goods, especially food items. The number of consumers in the market is a demand determinant, or factor that will shift demand curves to the right or left. Simply having more bodies will increase the demand for goods like hot dogs. A decrease in the price of hot dogs will decrease the quantity demanded of hot dogs (a movement along the demand curve), but would not decrease demand (a shift of the entire demand curve). Hot dog buns are a complement to hot dogs, and if the price of hot dog buns increases, the demand for hot dogs will decrease. If the price of hamburgers, a substitute for hot dogs, goes down, then the demand for hot dogs will decrease.

64. (E) Consumers' tastes and preferences are also a determinant of demand. If a product, like air travel, is deemed unsafe, consumers will have a weaker preference for the product, thus shifting the demand for it to the left. The price of jet fuel, an input into the production of air travel, would affect supply. If the price of an airplane ticket increases, this would decrease the *quantity demanded*, rather than decrease demand. If the price of hotel rooms, a complement for air travel, decreases, then the demand for airplane tickets would increase.

65. (A) A change in the price of regular milk will affect the demand for chocolate milk because regular milk is a substitute good for chocolate milk. A lower price of regular milk would increase the quantity of regular milk demanded, but would shift the demand for chocolate milk to the left because at any given price of chocolate milk it is now relatively more expensive than regular milk. A determinant of demand is a factor that will fundamentally affect (shift) the demand curve. A change in the price results in a movement along the fixed demand curve, not a shift. This is a distinction that, if you're not careful, can often result in points being lost on an exam. Choices C, D, and E are all determinants of supply; they would shift the supply of chocolate milk, but not affect the demand for it.

66. (A) If we are told that no matter the price, more 3-D televisions are being purchased, it is an indicator that the demand has increased, or shifted to the right. If you draw a graph where a demand curve has increased or shifted to the right, you can see that at every possible quantity the price that consumers are willing and able to pay has increased. A stronger taste or preference for these products would result in such a shift of demand. The cost of producing televisions and number of firms or stores involved in selling televisions are all factors that would affect the supply curve rather than the demand curve.

67. (E) A change in the technology used to produce good X or the price of a production input would cause a shift in the supply of good X rather than a shift in demand. A change in the price of good X would cause a movement only along the fixed demand curve, but fewer consumers would reduce (or shift leftward) demand for the product. The determinants of demand are consumer income, the price of complements and substitutes, tastes and preferences, consumer expectations about price, and the number of consumers.

68. (B) This statement restates the law of demand using milk as an example. The other two choices, I and III, are incorrectly stating that a change in the price will cause a shift in demand. The demand for a good will never change in response to a change in the price of that good. Rather, the *quantity demanded* for a good will change when its price changes.

69. (D) The law of demand says that all else equal, when the price of a good increases, the quantity of that good demanded will decrease. The movement from point c to point d tells us that as the price increased, quantity demand decreased along the fixed demand curve. All other choices reflect shifts in demand. If the choice of "d to e" had been available, this would have also described the law of demand, because the law of demand also implies that when the price of a good decreases, the quantity demanded of a good will increase.

70. (B) The movement from point b to point a is going to be the result of something that decreases the demand for hamburgers. If the price of a substitute good (like pizza) falls, more pizza will be consumed and the demand for hamburgers shifts to the left. An increase in the price of hamburgers would cause a movement along a single curve, such as a movement from point d to point c.

71. (A) An inferior good is something that has stronger demand when consumer incomes fall and weaker demand when consumer incomes increase. When considering all choices, a good such as used furniture best fits that description. When people see increased income, they usually choose to buy more new furniture and less used furniture.

72. (A) If chocolate cake is a normal good, then demand for it will increase with higher incomes and decrease with lower incomes. Demand for all normal goods moves in the same direction as income. A change in the price of chocolate, an input to the production of chocolate cakes, would change the supply of chocolate cakes.

73. (E) Demand for an inferior good moves in the opposite direction from a change in income. If incomes decrease, then demand increases. Note that an inferior good also cannot have a vertical demand curve. A vertical curve is perfectly inelastic, which is only possible if a good has no substitutes. Many normal goods and inferior goods are substitutes for each other. A good example of this is new cars (normal) and used cars (inferior).

74. (D) The demand for apples depends upon the price of substitute goods. If bananas are substitutes, then a decrease in the price of apples results in more apples being consumed and a decreased demand for bananas. This also works in reverse: if bananas become more expensive, the demand for apples shifts to the right. Remember that for substitute goods, when the price of one good increases, the demand for the substitute also increases.

75. (C) The demand for mittens depends upon the price of complementary goods, like hats. If these goods are used together, a decrease in the price of mittens will cause more mittens to be consumed and an increase in demand for the hats that go with them. If the price of hats were to increase, fewer hats would be consumed and the demand for mittens would decrease. For complementary goods, it is important to remember that when the price of one good increases, the demand for its complement decreases.

76. (D) Like demand curves, supply curves are also affected by external variables (the determinants of supply) that shift the curve to the right or left. The supply of any good will increase if one of these determinants, the price of factors of production, or inputs, decreases. When it becomes less costly to build a house, the supply of houses will shift to the right. This is because for any given quantity of houses, it will cost the producer less to make that quantity and the producer therefore would be willing to accept a lower price for that quantity.

77. (C) The number of suppliers is also a determinant of supply. If there are fewer suppliers of good Z, the supply curve will shift to the left. Consider a market with 20 suppliers, each willing to supply 5 units of Z when the price of Z is $10 and 8 units of Z when the price is $12. This would inform us that there is a market supply of 100 units of Z when p = $10 and a market supply of 160 when p = $12. If for some reason one of those suppliers left the market, then all else equal, the market supply would be 95 units when the price is $10 and 155 units when the price is $12. Thus at any given price, the market supply will be lower when a supplier exits this market.

78. (E) Production technology will affect (or shift) the supply curve. If producers acquire better technology, they can produce more output with the same amount of inputs. This translates into a supply curve that lies farther to the right; more output is produced at any price. Consumer income, tastes and preferences, the number of consumers, and consumer income expectations are all demand determinants but do not affect the supply curve.

79. (B) If a producer can produce more of a good that fetches a higher price, they will do so. Because running shoes are selling at higher prices, the supplier will increase quantity of running shoes supplied along the supply curve for running shoes. This is the law of supply in action—responding to a higher price of a good by increasing the quantity supplied of that good. However, this new production plan would require a decrease in the supply of hiking boots. The price of an alternative product, the running shoes, is a determinant in the supply of hiking boots.

80. (D) Better production technology shifts supply curves to the right. This is because better technology would allow the same quantity of production at a cheaper price (or looking at it slightly differently, a higher quantity of production at the same price), which would make a supplier willing to accept a lower price for any given quantity. While it might be tempting to choose choice C, if producers expect future car prices to be higher, they will reduce the current supply of cars while they wait for those higher prices to occur, which would actually decrease supply (or shift the supply curve to the left).

81. (A) The law of supply states that all else equal, when the price of a good increases, firms will increase the quantity of that good supplied. If the price of wool is rising, there will be an increase in the quantity of wool supplied. Recall that as more is produced, resource scarcity means that most production is done with increasing costs. Consider a producer who was willing to supply 5 pounds of wool when the price of wool was $7 a pound. The producer was willing to supply this amount because this was the point for him that the marginal cost equaled the marginal benefit. If the marginal benefit (the price per pound) increased, now MB > MC, he should increase his quantity supplied.

82. (E) This is simply a restatement of the law of supply: all else equal, the quantity supplied of a good will rise when the price of a good rises. It is important to know both this and the law of demand inside and out. Students frequently confuse increases and decreases in supply and demand with changes in quantities supplied or demanded. The law of supply and the law of demand always refer to changes in the quantity supplied and the quantity demanded, respectively. Another way to restate these laws is to remember that for the law of demand, there is an inverse relationship between price and quantity demanded, and for the law of supply, there is a positive relationship between price and quantity supplied.

83. (C) Equilibrium occurs at the only price where the quantity demanded equals the quantity supplied. At this price, all units that are produced by sellers are purchased by buyers. Just as in physics, the term *equilibrium* refers to a state of balance—the balance between opposing forces. Note that it is *not* where "supply equals demand." To say that "supply equals demand" is saying that these two opposing forces are the same. Graphically, that would mean the two curves were the same curve! Rather, equilibrium refers to a price that makes the *quantity supplied* equal to the *quantity demanded.*

84. (E) At prices that exceed the equilibrium price, quantity supplied will exceed quantity demanded. Sellers enjoy higher prices, so they will increase production when the price rises. Buyers do not enjoy higher prices, so they will reduce consumption when the price rises. This disparity gives us a surplus (or excess supply) equal to the difference between quantity supplied and quantity demanded.

85. (C) At prices below the equilibrium price, quantity demanded will exceed quantity supplied. For instance, if the market price were $2, then buyers would want to buy 2,300 pounds, but sellers would be willing to sell only 900 pounds at that price. When there are fewer units supplied than consumers wish to buy, a shortage (or excess demand) exists and it is equal to the difference between the quantity demanded and the quantity supplied.

86. (D) When supply and demand are combined in a graph, the equilibrium point is found at the intersection of the supply curve and the demand curve. The quantity point on the demand curve that corresponds to a price of P_2 is Q_3. The quantity point on the supply curve that corresponds to a price of P_2 is Q_3. Thus at the price of P_2, quantity demanded is equal to quantity supplied at quantity Q_3.

87. (B) The price P_3 is below the equilibrium price of P_2 that brings the quantity supplied and quantity demanded into balance. This low price creates a shortage because the quantity demanded exceeds the quantity supplied: quantity demanded at P_3 is Q_4 and quantity supplied at P_3 is Q_2. The size of the shortage is equal to $Q_4 - Q_2$.

88. (E) The equilibrium price in this market is P_2, and the equilibrium quantity in this market is Q_3. A new price of P_1 would mean a higher price, and a new quantity of Q_5 would be a higher quantity. The point that corresponds to P_1 and Q_5 would therefore result from an increase in the demand curve. Starting at the equilibrium point, this rightward shift in demand would increase both price and quantity. To demonstrate this, try re-creating this graph and show what happens if supply increases.

89. (A) The equilibrium in this market is a price of P_2 and a quantity of Q_3, so if price is now P_3 and quantity is Q_4, then the price has fallen but market quantity has risen. Since we know the change in both price and quantity, we can tell for sure that only one curve has shifted. Likewise, since price and quantity have moved in opposite directions, we can tell that it is the supply curve that changed. The point that corresponds to P_3 and Q_4 must be the result of a rightward shift in supply. Starting in equilibrium, when the supply curve increases, it creates a temporary surplus because the new quantity supplied exceeds the original quantity demanded. This surplus is eliminated by a falling price, and the new equilibrium quantity is greater than before. When a supply curve increases, quantity also increases, but the price decreases.

90. (C) The point that corresponds to P_1 and Q_1 must be the result of a leftward shift in supply. Starting in equilibrium, when the supply curve decreases, it creates a temporary shortage because the new quantity supplied is less than the original quantity demanded. This shortage is eliminated by a rising price, and the new equilibrium quantity is less than before. When a supply curve decreases, quantity also decreases, but the price increases.

91. (D) If we start at a point where a market is in equilibrium, an increase in demand will create a temporary shortage of cheese. This is because the new quantity demanded exceeds the original quantity supplied at the original price. As the market adjusts to a new equilibrium, the price rises to eliminate the shortage and more cheese is exchanged in the market. Therefore, when demand curves increase, price and quantity both increase.

92. (A) If we start at a point where a market is in equilibrium, a decrease in demand will create a temporary surplus of gasoline. This is because the new quantity demanded is less than the original quantity supplied at the original price, due to the fact that when demand decreases, people are willing to buy less of a good at any given price. As the market adjusts to a new equilibrium, the price falls to eliminate the surplus and less gasoline is exchanged in the market. Therefore, when demand curves decrease, price and quantity both decrease.

93. (B) If you know that both the price and quantity have increased in the coffee market, it is most likely that the demand for coffee has increased. An increase in demand places an upward pressure on both prices and quantity. Recall that a change in supply will yield opposite effects on price and quantity (one will increase and one will decrease). If both supply and demand were changing at the same time, we would be able to tell whether either price or quantity had increased, but the effect on at least either price or quantity would be ambiguous. When in doubt, draw a quick graph in the margin of your test book and you can see the impact of an increase in demand.

94. (C) Whenever you see a situation in which you can tell the effect on both price and quantity, you know for certain that only supply has changed or only demand has changed. Recall that whenever you see price and quantity moving in the same direction, whether both price and quantity are rising or both price and quantity are falling, you know that demand has to be changing. Price and quantity move in different directions when supply changes. In this case you know that both the price and quantity of steel have decreased in the market for steel. This is a clear sign that the demand for steel has decreased.

95. (A) The decreased price of applesauce while the quantity has increased is a clear sign that supply has increased. First of all, if we know both a new price and quantity with no ambiguity, then we know for certain that only one curve has shifted. The change in quantity is always in the same direction as the change in supply, while the price moves in the opposite direction.

96. (D) We know that the price of milk has increased but the quantity has decreased, so a new price and quantity are both known and the new price and quantity moved in different directions. A decrease in supply would cause these changes. Again, a quick sketch of the milk market would confirm that decreased supply is the correct answer and the other choices are incorrect.

97. (B) Because quantity always moves in the same direction as the change in supply, you can quickly focus on the choices that state quantity of wine is going to increase. And because an increase in supply causes a surplus, and because a surplus is eliminated by falling prices, look for the choice that also includes a decreased price of wine.

98. (D) When both curves are shifting in a market, it is helpful to analyze each shift one at a time. An increase in demand will increase both the price and quantity of rental housing. An increase in supply will increase the quantity but decrease the price. Therefore, we know for sure that quantity is going to increase, but there are competing effects on the price of rental housing. The only thing we can say about the new price is that it is uncertain or it would depend upon which effect (upward from demand versus downward from supply) is strongest.

99. (B) When the demand for lumber decreases, it will decrease both the price and quantity of lumber. When the supply increases, it will cause a greater quantity but a lower price of lumber. Therefore, we know that the price of lumber will be lower, but there is an uncertain change in the new quantity of lumber. Because the two market forces, supply and demand, are exerting opposite and opposing forces on quantity, we cannot determine which side of the market will exert more force.

100. (C) When the demand for a good increases, both price and quantity will increase. When the supply of a good decreases, the price will increase and the quantity will decrease. We can say for sure that the price is going to be higher. The new quantity will increase if the demand shift is greater than the supply shift. The new quantity will decrease if the supply shift is stronger than the demand shift.

101. (E) When the demand for a good increases, both price and quantity will increase. When the supply of a good increases, the price will decrease and the quantity will increase. We can say for sure that the quantity is going to rise. The new price will increase if the demand shift is greater than the supply shift. The new price will decrease if the supply shift is stronger than the demand shift.

102. (E) A decreased demand for toys will decrease both the price and quantity. The decreased supply of toys will also decrease quantity but will increase price. Therefore the quantity is certainly going to decrease, but the change in the price is uncertain. When you are figuring out these types of questions, it might be useful to abbreviate using arrows. Here, D: p↓ and S: p↑, and D: q↓ and S: q↓. If the arrows are pointing in the same direction, you can tell with certainty what the effect will be. Since the arrows for price go in opposite directions, the effect on the price will be ambiguous. Students are often tempted to conclude, especially when using graphs to work through the reasoning on these types of questions, that there is no change in price. *This is not correct!* We simply cannot say for certain what has happened to price. This is a common "trap" that is sometimes put in exam question choices . . . don't fall for it!

Chapter 4: Elasticity

103. (D) The price elasticity of supply measures how responsive producers are to a change in the price. We know that a higher price will almost always prompt these firms to increase the quantity of output they supply, but we don't know if that response will be large (relative to the change in price) or small. By dividing the percentage change in quantity supplied by the percentage change in price, we can measure this response. Note: for all elasticity measures, the percentage change in quantity (the response) is always divided by the percentage change in the variable that *caused* the response.

104. (E) If you know that the price of eggplant has decreased by 4% and this prompted suppliers to reduce supply by 20%, then the price elasticity of supply is $(-20\%/-4\%)$ = 5. As a strategy for answering questions on price elasticity of supply, you can quickly eliminate any negative values as incorrect options. Barring the very unlikely possibility of a vertical supply curve, supply curves will slope upward and price elasticity of supply will always be a positive number.

105. (A) Anytime something doubles, it has experienced a 100% increase in size. Since the price elasticity of supply is equal to 3, the numerator of the formula must be three times the size as the price change in the denominator. Thus a 100% increase in price causes a 300% increase in quantity supplied. It is always helpful to quickly write the elasticity formula in the margin of your test book, include the information that you know, and solve for what you don't know. In this case, you are trying to find x in the equation $3 = x/100\%$.

106. (A) We believe that all measures of responsiveness are more elastic in the long run rather than the short run. Producers in this case, given more time, can find ways to increase production to take advantage of the higher price. If the price of the output has risen, the firms may be able to acquire more capital equipment, expand the production facility, or hire more labor to produce more output at the higher price.

107. (B) Price elasticity measures, whether supply or demand, change depending upon what we assume is the current price and quantity. When the price changes, we use the midpoint formula to compute price elasticity in between the two prices and quantities. The formula takes the percentage change between price and quantity, but uses the average price $\overline{P}$ and the average quantity $\overline{Q}_s$. The formula is as follows.

$$E_s = \left(\frac{\Delta Q_s}{\Delta P}\right)\left(\frac{\overline{P}}{\overline{Q}_s}\right) = \left(\frac{40}{4}\right)\left(\frac{12}{120}\right) = 1$$

108. (C) Much like the formula for price elasticity of supply, the price elasticity of demand measures the responsiveness of quantity demanded to a change in the price. A common mistake made by students is to invert the formula and put the percentage change in price in the numerator. Remember that the numerator always measures the percentage change in behavior, in this case the change in consumption. The denominator always measures the percentage change in the variable that instigated the change in behavior.

109. (C) If demand is considered inelastic, it means that for a given percentage change in price, the quantity demanded responds (in the opposite direction) with a lesser percentage change. Recall the following formula.

$$E_d = \left(\frac{\%\Delta Q_d}{\%\Delta P}\right)$$

An inelastic response would indicate that the numerator is less than the denominator and E_d is some value greater than zero, but less than one. If demand is elastic, the price elasticity is greater than one.

110. (E) To solve this, take a moment and write out the formula for price elasticity of demand. Insert the information that is given, and use a little bit of algebra to solve for what is being asked.

$$E_d = \left(\frac{\%\Delta Q_d}{\%\Delta P}\right) = .75 = \frac{\%\Delta Q_d}{+10\%}$$

Multiplying $(.75)(10\%)$ yields a solution of $\%\Delta Q_d = 7.5\%$, but remember that quantity demanded will always move in the opposite direction as the change in price. So make sure you eliminate any choices that include a price *increase* in this problem.

111. (B) A few factors typically affect whether demand for a product tends to be elastic or inelastic. Products have a more elastic demand if there are many substitutes for them, they account for a large share of a consumer's budget, and the consumer has lots of time to adjust behavior to a price change. Additionally, if a consumer considers the product a necessity, like food, then demand tends to be inelastic. The price can go up by a certain degree, but food consumption goes down by a lesser degree. But if a product is considered a luxury, like trips to a theme park, then if the price goes up, consumers can do without and quantity of luxury items goes down by a larger degree.

112. (D) When computing price elasticity using some formulas, the end result depends on whether we are starting at the lower price of $30 (and higher quantity of 70) or the higher price of $50 (and the lower quantity of 50). The midpoint formula eliminates this disparity by using the average price and average quantity between any two prices and quantities. The calculation isn't as difficult as it may seem.

$$E_d = \left(\frac{\Delta Q_d}{\Delta P}\right)\left(\frac{\overline{P}}{\overline{Q_d}}\right) = \left(\frac{20}{20}\right)\left(\frac{40}{60}\right) = .67$$

113. (A) Price elasticity of demand changes along a linear (straight line) demand curve. At prices below the midpoint of the curve, consumers are less responsive to small price changes and thus the price elasticity of demand is inelastic. At prices above the midpoint, consumers are more responsive to a small price change and thus the price elasticity of demand is elastic. The midpoint of this demand curve is at a price of $50 and quantity of 50 units. Because point z is clearly above the midpoint, we can assume an elastic response. Intuitively, at prices above the midpoint even small price increases represent fairly large absolute changes in dollar value, and this causes a larger impact on a consumer's budget. If the price was currently $10, a 10% increase would represent only a $1 increase in price. But if the price is currently $80, the same 10% increase in price would represent an $8 increase in price, and this would have a larger impact on the consumer's ability to purchase this item. Therefore, the consumer would be more sensitive at points like point z to an increase or decrease in the price.

114. (C) Total dollars consumers spent on a good is equal to the quantity of the good demanded multiplied by the price of the good ($P \times Q_d$). When the price changes, quantity demanded changes in the opposite direction; therefore, the change in total consumer spending depends upon price elasticity of demand. Point y is below the midpoint of this demand curve, so a small decrease in the price would result in an inelastic response in quantity demanded. Thus if the price were to fall by say 1%, quantity demanded would rise by less than 1%; total spending on this good would decline because the downward effect of price is larger than the upward effect of quantity.

115. (A) Total revenue received by a seller is equal to the price of the good multiplied by the units sold at that price. In other words, much like consumer spending on a good, total revenue $TR = (P \times Q_d)$. If Ruby knows there will be an elastic response to an increase in the price, she knows that the percentage increase in price will be offset by a larger decrease in quantity of her clothing demanded. This will cause total revenue dollars to decrease.

116. (E) A good is considered normal if consumption rises with income. The income elasticity of demand is the ratio of the percentage change in quantity demanded divided by the percentage change in income. If this ratio is positive, we know the good is a normal good. If it is negative, we know that it is an inferior good. A Giffen good is a particular type of inferior good that actually exhibits an upward-sloping demand curve.

117. (D) A good is considered inferior if consumption falls when income rises or rises when income falls. The income elasticity is calculated as follows.

$$E_I = \left(\frac{\%\Delta Q_d}{\%\Delta I} \right)$$

When income is rising in the numerator of this equation, and this results in a decrease in quantity of the good demanded in the denominator of the equation, E_I is going to be a negative number. This negative income elasticity identifies the inferior good. An income elasticity that is equal to zero does not identify a normal or an inferior good; it just tells us that consumption of that good is independent of income.

118. (C) Recall that the consumer behavior is always in the numerator of any elasticity formula. Very often students will invert the formula and incorrectly choose the inverse of the correct answer. Using the formula with the information that you know allows you to solve for what you don't know. Recall the income elasticity of demand equation.

$$E_I = \left(\frac{\%\Delta Q_d}{\%\Delta I} \right) = \frac{3\%}{5\%} = .60$$

119. (B) This question is very similar to the preceding one, but the small twist in this question is that it is describing margarine as an inferior good. Again we would recommend quickly jotting down the formula for the income elasticity of demand and solving for the correct answer.

$$E_I = \left(\frac{\%\Delta Q_d}{\%\Delta I} \right) = \frac{1\%}{-4\%} = -\frac{1}{4}$$

120. (C) This question gives you the income elasticity and an increase in income and requires you to rearrange the income elasticity formula to solve for the percentage change in quantity demanded. Because you are told that the income elasticity is a positive number, you can eliminate the one choice that describes a *decrease* in quantity demanded. This requires just a small amount of algebra and a little multiplication to reach the solution.

$$E_I = \left(\frac{\%\Delta Q_d}{\%\Delta I} \right) = \frac{\%\Delta Q_d}{6\%} = .40$$

To solve for $\%\Delta Q_d$, you must multiply $(.40) \times (6\%) = 2.4\%$.

121. (E) We must first know that an inferior good is a good for which a decrease in income actually causes consumers to consume *more*, rather than less, of that good. One way to think about problems such as this is to ask: "If income were to rise, would demand for this item decrease?" Food items like milk and granola may not be luxuries, but they are still likely to be normal goods. High-priced items like airplane tickets and televisions are certainly normal goods, but city bus tickets are most likely the inferior good. When people earn higher incomes, they tend to ride the bus less frequently and travel around town in their own cars.

122. (D) Luxury goods are described as having a very large consumption response to a given change in income. If the percentage change in quantity demanded exceeds the percentage change in income, the numerator of the income elasticity formula will be larger than the denominator; therefore, E_I will be greater than 1. Even if you have never heard of this distinction for luxury goods, having a good understanding of the income elasticity will allow you to deduce the correct choice from the description that is given in the question.

123. (D) Consumers alter their consumption of good X when the price of another good, good Y, changes. If the price of good Y rises, and we observe consumers buying more good X, those goods must be substitutes. If consumers buy less of good X, they must be complementary goods. The cross-price elasticity measures how responsive these substitute and complement relationships are. The formula is as follows.

$$E_{X,Y} = \left(\frac{\%\Delta Q_{dX}}{\%\Delta P_Y} \right)$$

Given the preceding intuition, substitute goods will exhibit a positive cross-price elasticity and complementary goods will exhibit a negative cross-price elasticity.

124. (C) Because we are looking for complementary goods, we are looking for a negative cross-price elasticity for goods A and B. If it helps with your intuition, think of goods A and B as some other complementary pair, like video games and game systems. If game systems became more expensive, fewer game systems would be purchased and fewer games would also be purchased. Therefore, the price of good B and the consumption of good A move in opposite directions; hence, the negative cross-price elasticity.

125. (A) Two brands of soft drinks are good examples of substitute goods, because when the price of one increases, the quantity of the other demanded increases. Use the following formula.

$$E_{\text{Diet Pepsi,Diet Coke}} = \left(\frac{\%\Delta Q_{d \text{ Diet Pepsi}}}{\%\Delta P_{\text{Diet Coke}}} \right) = \frac{4\%}{2\%} = 2$$

A common mistake is to invert the percentage changes. Remember that elasticity measures always have the behavioral change (a change in consumption) in the numerator.

126. (B) This question again tests your understanding of how cross-price elasticities distinguish between complementary goods and substitute goods. In this situation, the cross-price is positive 1.5, telling us that if the price of Cocoa Puffs increased 1%, the quantity of Frosted Flakes demanded would increase by 1.5%; they are substitutes. They may be normal or inferior goods—we don't know that from the information given. We would need to know income elasticities to make that distinction, so be sure not to jump to any conclusions—just use the provided information.

127. (B) Because you are given a negative cross-price elasticity, the goods must be complementary. Use the formula with the information given to fill in the blanks.

$$E_{bacon,eggs} = \left(\frac{\%\Delta Q_{d\ bacon}}{\%\Delta P_{eggs}} \right) = \frac{\%\Delta Q_{d\ bacon}}{3\%} = -.5$$

Solving for the percentage change in bacon consumption, we multiply $(3\%) \times (-.5)$, and we know that bacon consumption will fall by 1.5%.

128. (B) We are told that goods A and B are substitutes. If it helps, think of them as apples and bananas. If the price of bananas increases, people will switch to apples and the quantity of apples demanded increases. The cross-price elasticity will therefore be a positive number. Be careful to avoid choices like A because the value of zero stands out. A cross-price of zero simply means that the consumption of good A doesn't respond at all to a change in the price of good B; they're independent of each other.

129. (E) This question requires you to know not only the formula for cross-price elasticity but also how it tells us something. Because you are informed that the elasticity is "with respect to the price of catfish," the elasticity will be telling us about how salmon consumption responds to a change in the price of catfish. Ignore any choices that begin with the price of salmon changing. Again use the formula and the fact that we should be looking for a choice that begins with a change in the price of catfish.

$$E_{salmon,catfish} = \left(\frac{\%\Delta Q_{d\ salmon}}{\%\Delta P_{catfish}} \right) = \frac{\%\Delta Q_{d\ salmon}}{10\%} = .45$$

If the price of catfish were to increase by 10%, the formula would predict that salmon consumption increases by $(10\%) \times (.45)$, or 4.5%.

Chapter 5: Consumer and Producer Surplus

130. (A) A consumer's willingness to pay (WTP) is the maximum price he or she would pay for each unit of an item. If the consumer can pay a price that is below WTP, the consumer earns consumer surplus. Think about it this way: if you really wanted to see a newly released movie and you were willing to pay $20 to see it, you would see it as a monetary gain if you only had to pay $10 for a movie ticket—that is consumer surplus.

131. (D) A consumer will continue to buy a product until the price of the next muffin is below her willingness to pay. This means that Ellen will buy four muffins, but not the fifth. Consumer surplus is earned as each muffin is purchased and enjoyed and is calculated as the difference between what Ellen is willing to pay for that muffin and what she actually pays for that muffin. To determine total consumer surplus, we sum the consumer surplus at each muffin: $(10 - 3) + (8 - 3) + (6 - 3) + (4 - 3)$ equals $16. If you are trying to solve this graphically, remember that you should not solve this using a downward-sloping curve. Since Ellen cannot consume fractions of a muffin, this is a "stair step" demand that you may see in your textbook, rather than a continuous demand curve.

132. (B) This stair-step graph shows that Melanie's willingness to pay diminishes as more shoes are purchased. This occurs because her enjoyment of the next pair (her marginal benefit) diminishes. When willingness to pay equals $60, she stops buying shoes at that quantity for a total of five pairs of shoes. Consumer surplus is accumulated along the way up to the fifth pair: $(100 - 60) + (90 - 60) + (80 - 60) + (70 - 60) + (60 - 60)$ = $100. Note that in the graph, the consumer surplus for each pair of shoes is the area of a rectangle between the willingness to pay and the price of shoes. Even though she earns no consumer surplus on the fifth pair, she will still buy it. After all, if you're willing to pay $60 and the price is actually $60, you will buy that pair of shoes.

133. (D) The maximum price a consumer is willing to pay for the DVD player is another way of simply describing his willingness to pay. When the price is subtracted from this maximum price, we get the consumer surplus. Sometimes it helps to think of consumer surplus as a monetary "win" for the consumer. If this person was willing to pay $100 for the DVD player and only had to pay $80, he "wins" $20 because this is $20 he does not have to spend on the DVD player to bring it home. He can find an additional item that will bring him happiness and use the $20 to acquire it.

134. (E) The purchasing rule is the same for each consumer: buy cookies up to the point where the price (marginal cost) is equal to willingness to pay (marginal benefit). For Eli this occurs at five cookies; Max stops at four cookies. Another way to compute consumer surplus is to add up the willingness to pay values and then subtract how much money was spent on cookies. Consumer surplus for Eli is $(2 + 1.75 + 1.50 + 1.25 + 1) - (\$1 \times 5)$ = $2.50. Consumer surplus for Max is $(2.50 + 2 + 1.50 + 1) - (\$1 \times 4) = \$3$. Total consumer surplus is therefore $5.50.

135. (E) Producers earn producer surplus when they sell a unit of their good or service for a price that exceeds the marginal cost of producing that unit. If Terrell incurs $4 of marginal cost when he gives a customer a shave and a haircut, he would accept a minimum of $4 for this service. But if he can receive a price of $10, the difference $(\$10 - \$4)$ of $6 is his producer surplus for each customer. When he has seven customers, he earns a total of 6×7 = $42 in producer surplus.

136. (D) The marginal cost incurred for each unit is the minimum price the seller would accept to sell it. If the seller receives a higher price, the difference between that price and marginal cost is producer surplus. While choice A might have been tempting (subtract total cost from total revenue), this choice actually defines total profit earned from selling the product, which is not the same as producer surplus.

137. (A) Producer surplus is earned for each of the four tacos sold. We calculate the total producer surplus as $(4 - 1) + (4 - 2) + (4 - 3) + (4 - 4) = \$6$. The marginal cost of producing tacos rises, and because the price remains constant, producer surplus on each successive unit diminishes.

138. (B) This question is really just testing whether you know how to compute producer surplus. The marginal cost of producing a unit of output is the minimum price a seller would accept to sell that unit. If the seller can receive a price higher than that marginal cost, the seller earns producer surplus.

139. (B) Each producer will continue to sell kebabs so long as the price is greater than or equal to the marginal cost of producing a kebab. For Ali this is true up to three kebabs, and for Rahul it is true up to five kebabs. Producer surplus for Ali is $(1.50 - .50) + (1.50 - 1) + (1.50 - 1.50) = \$1.50$. Producer surplus for Rahul is $(1.50 - .50) + (1.50 - .75) + (1.50 - 1) + (1.50 - 1.25) + (1.50 - 1.50) = \$2.50$. Therefore, total producer surplus is \$4.

140. (C) The idea of consumer surplus is the difference between maximum willingness to pay (WTP) and the price of the unit purchased. The demand curve provides maximum WTP at every quantity. When a market is in equilibrium, price is at the intersection of supply and demand (here that would be point i, which is a quantity of g and a price of c). In a graph that shows a market, consumer surplus is the area under the demand curve (line ai) and above the price consumers pay (c) for all units consumed (g). When supply and demand are straight lines (linear), this amounts to the area of a triangle; in this case, the triangle is represented by aci.

141. (B) Producer surplus is the difference between the price and the marginal cost (MC) of the unit produced. The supply curve gives the MC at every quantity, and the price when a market is at equilibrium is at the intersection of supply and demand (point i). In a graph of a market, producer surplus is the area above the supply curve (line 0i) and under the price for all units sold (c). This is also the area of a triangle when supply and demand curves are linear.

142. (A) Price floors are legal minimum prices that are set above the equilibrium price because the government has concluded that the equilibrium price is "too low." Sellers cannot sell the good at a price below the controlled price. For a price floor to be effective, it must therefore be set above equilibrium. Such a price is sometimes called a "binding price floor." If it is set below equilibrium, it would be ineffective because market forces would drive the price upward to equilibrium, which is sometimes called a "nonbinding price floor."

143. (D) Price ceilings are legal maximum prices that are set below the equilibrium price because the government has concluded that the equilibrium price is "too high." Sellers cannot sell the good at a price above the controlled price. For a price ceiling to be effective, it must therefore be set below equilibrium. If it is set above equilibrium, it would be ineffective because market forces would drive the price downward to equilibrium. After all, a price ceiling doesn't forbid prices below the ceiling, only above.

144. (C) This question requires several steps to find the correct answer. First, you must know that a price ceiling lies below equilibrium, so an effective price ceiling in this market would be d. Second, you must know that quantity demanded at this price (which would be h) exceeds quantity supplied at the controlled price (f), and this defines a shortage of (h − f).

145. (A) This question requires you to understand several things about a price floor. First, you must know that a price floor lies above equilibrium, so in this market an effective price floor would be b. Second, you must know that quantity demanded at this price floor (in this case, e) is less than quantity supplied at the controlled price (in this case, r), and this defines a surplus. Finally, the size of the surplus is measured in units of output, and the difference between these defines a shortage (r − e).

146. (E) The sum of consumer gains (consumer surplus) and producer gains (producer surplus) is total surplus, or total welfare. At market equilibrium quantity, willingness to pay is equal to marginal cost. This maximizes total surplus and is considered efficient. Consider two cases. First, suppose the market produces 1 unit less than equilibrium. Here, willingness to pay (from demand) is still greater than marginal cost (from supply). In this case, there is a buyer and a seller who could make a profitable trade. If a buyer is willing to pay $6 and a seller has $4 marginal cost, they could each gain if they exchanged that unit at $5. If the market stopped here, it would not maximize total surplus. Second, suppose the market produced 1 unit more than equilibrium. Here, willingness to pay is below marginal cost. Imagine a producer has produced a unit at $8 marginal cost and his only potential customer has $4 willingness to pay. If they negotiated a $6 price, both lose surplus; total surplus isn't maximized. Thus any level of output besides the equilibrium level will not maximize total surplus; equilibrium output is the only efficient output.

147. (D) Deadweight loss refers to total surplus that could have been earned by producers, consumers, or both, but is not earned because of some external force. In some cases, it is the result of a government policy like a price control or an excise tax. In other areas of microeconomics, we see deadweight loss as the result of monopoly or externalities. We can also see such deadweight loss occur in trade when there are quotas or tariffs. In all of these instances, something is moving the market output away from the level that maximizes total surplus—deadweight loss exists.

148. (E) All of these statements accurately describe efficiency in competitive market equilibrium. When total surplus is maximized, there is no deadweight loss. And economists define this as an efficient outcome because all potential gains are realized; the market is producing neither too many units nor too few units of output. Any interference in such a market will necessarily cause total surplus to decrease.

149. (C) So long as Wilford's willingness to pay is greater than or equal to Rosemary's marginal costs, they should exchange servings of oatmeal. This is true for each of the first five servings. However, at the sixth serving, it costs Rosemary $4.50 to produce it, but Wilford is only willing to pay $3 to buy it. There is no way they will make this exchange, so they will stop at five servings as the efficient outcome.

150. (C) A minimum price of $6 is a price floor. Rosemary would love to sell all of her servings of oatmeal at this high price, but Wilford will buy only three servings, so only three will be exchanged. To find the deadweight loss, it might be easier to first see how many servings would be exchanged without the price floor. Without the price floor, five servings would be exchanged at price of $4. This means that consumer and producer surplus are lost on the fourth and fifth servings. For the fourth serving: Wilford loses $1 ($5 − $4) and Rosemary loses $.50 ($4 − $3.50), so the deadweight loss from this serving is $1.50. For the fifth serving: Wilford loses $0 ($4 − $4) and Rosemary loses $0 ($4 − $4). Because the price floor prevents the fourth and fifth servings from happening, the deadweight loss is $1.50.

151. (E) The maximum price of $3 is a price ceiling. At this lower price Rosemary will be able to supply only three servings, despite the fact that Wilford would like to buy six servings. To find the deadweight loss, it might be easier to first see how many servings would be exchanged without the price ceiling. Without the price ceiling, five servings would be exchanged at the price of $4. This means that consumer and producer surplus are lost on the fourth and fifth servings. For the fourth serving: Wilford loses $1 ($5 − $4) and Rosemary loses $.50 ($4 − $3.50), so the deadweight loss from this serving is $1.50. For the fifth serving: Wilford loses $0 ($4 − $4) and Rosemary loses $0 ($4 − $4). Because the price ceiling prevents the fourth and fifth servings from happening, the deadweight loss is $1.50.

152. (D) Total surplus is the sum of consumer surplus and producer surplus. When the market is in equilibrium, this area of total surplus is the greatest (i.e., it is maximized). Consumer surplus is a triangle that lies under the demand curve and above the price, or area P_1eP_4. Producer surplus is a triangle that lies under the price and above the supply curve, or area P_4e0. The combined area is thus P_1e0.

153. (D) To find deadweight loss from a price floor, it is usually helpful to find total surplus before the price floor. Before the price floor, the market is in equilibrium, total surplus is the sum of the consumer surplus triangle (P_1eP_4) and the producer surplus triangle (P_4e0), and Q_3 units are exchanged. When the price floor is instituted at P_2, only Q_1 units are exchanged, and a large area of the original total surplus triangle is not earned. The area of deadweight loss abe goes to neither the consumers nor the producers, so it is considered an inefficient result of the price floor.

154. (A) First locate consumer surplus before the price floor—when the price is P_4 and the quantity sold in the market is Q_3. The area under the demand and above the price is P_1eP_4. Once the price floor is enacted, the price increased to P_2, and only Q_1 units are bought and sold. So the new area of consumer surplus is much smaller because fewer units were bought and those were at a higher price. New consumer surplus is P_1aP_2, and when we subtract the new consumer surplus from the original consumer surplus area, we are left with P_2aeP_4.

155. **(A)** To find deadweight loss from a price ceiling, it will be helpful to find total surplus before the price ceiling. Before the price ceiling, the market is in equilibrium, total surplus is the sum of the consumer surplus triangle (P_1eP_4) and the producer surplus triangle (P_4e0), and Q_3 units are exchanged. When the price ceiling is instituted at P_5, only Q_2 units are exchanged, and a large area of the original total surplus triangle is lost. The area of deadweight loss cde goes to neither the consumers nor the producers.

156. **(C)** First locate producer surplus before the price ceiling. The area under the equilibrium price and above the supply curve at the quantity sold in the market Q_3 is P_4e0. Once the price ceiling is enacted, only Q_2 units are bought and sold, and the price decreased to P_5. So the new area of producer surplus is much smaller because fewer units were bought and those were at a lower price. Now producer surplus is P_5d0, and when we subtract the new amount of producer surplus from the original producer surplus area, we are left with P_4edP_5.

157. **(B)** Because the price floor artificially raises the price above equilibrium, it is going to hurt consumers. Consumers respond to the higher price by reducing the quantity of product demanded, and consumer surplus falls. Some of the lost consumer surplus goes to the producers because producers benefit from higher prices. But because the new level of output is below the competitive quantity, deadweight loss now exists.

158. **(E)** Because the price ceiling artificially lowers the price below equilibrium, it is going to hurt producers. Producers respond to the lower price by reducing the quantity of product supplied, and producer surplus falls. Some of the lost producer surplus goes to the consumers because consumers benefit from lower prices. But because the new level of output is below the competitive quantity, deadweight loss now exists.

159. **(B)** A price ceiling is set below the equilibrium price. Because the price falls, sellers reduce output below the equilibrium quantity, and deadweight loss begins to emerge in the market. If this reduction in output is large, the deadweight loss will be large. If we follow the logical reasoning, the lower the price ceiling, the larger the reduction in output below equilibrium and the larger the resulting deadweight loss.

160. **(D)** This is exactly what is happening in market equilibrium. The demand curve represents the consumer's maximum willingness to pay. The supply curve represents the producer's marginal cost, or the minimum price they would accept. Units are bought and sold so long as the price is somewhere in between willingness to pay and marginal cost. When this happens, total surplus continues to rise. When the diminishing willingness to pay intersects in the increasing marginal cost, no more beneficial transactions can be made, total surplus is maximized, and allocative efficiency is achieved.

161. (A) Economists like to think about how efficiently resources are allocated. If too much of a good is being produced, we think of the market having an "overallocation" of resources to that market. If too little of a good is being produced, there is an "underallocation" of resources to that market. But if the market is producing the perfect quantity, the quantity that maximizes total surplus, that market is experiencing allocative efficiency. This perfect quantity occurs when the competitive market comes to equilibrium and the demand curve intersects the supply curve.

162. (D) Price controls, whether floors or ceilings, reduce the number of transactions away from the equilibrium quantity. In both cases, not enough of the product is produced and the willingness to pay exceeds the marginal cost. If the market had been allowed to be in equilibrium, the price would have attracted the perfect amount of resources (labor, capital, land, and entrepreneurial ability) to produce the efficient quantity of output. The third statement is incorrect because other factors can create the same outcome. These other factors can include monopoly, externalities, excise taxes, and quotas.

Chapter 6: The Effects of Taxation

163. (C) An excise tax is a tax placed on each unit of production, for instance, $10 on each unit of a good that is sold. Another common type of tax is a proportional tax (sometimes called an ad valorem tax), such as a sales tax, which taxes the cost of each unit. For instance, for every $1 worth of goods sold, there is a tax of $0.08.

164. (B) The tax incidence is the distribution of a tax between the buyer and the seller of a good. Even though either the buyer or seller is taxed, both will share part of the burden of a tax (for this reason, your instructor also may have referred to this as the "tax burden").

165. (A) Lump sum taxes, such as a poll tax, are more efficient than per unit or ad valorem taxes. The reason that ad valorem or excise taxes are inefficient is that they alter the behavior of individuals. Lump sum taxes are taxes that are paid regardless of the units consumed or the value of the good. Because there is no incentive to alter behavior, there is no source of deadweight loss in a market. Unfortunately, this is a classic example of an efficiency-equity trade-off. Lump sum taxes are highly inequitable.

166. (D) A regressive tax is a tax that decreases as income increases, or a tax that places a greater burden on those with lower income. For instance, sales taxes are often regressive, because at lower incomes, people spend more of their income than save it and so would have to pay a higher proportion of their income on sales tax than someone who saves more. A positive statement is a statement such as "taxes rise." Statements about the fairness of the tax are normative.

167. (D) A marginal tax system is a tax system that pays higher and higher rates with additional units of income. This means that as income increases, one pays a higher and higher proportion of a tax, making it a progressive tax. Note that it is possible to have a regressive marginal tax system as well—Xela could have the tax rates decrease with each additional unit of income, rather than increase.

168. (C) As the amount of a tax increases, initially the amount of tax revenue will increase as well. However, this will eventually level out. Then as the amount of the tax increases, the total amount of tax revenue will actually decrease. Your instructor may have even graphed this relationship as an upside-down U-shaped curve called the Laffer curve. The price elasticity of demand explains this. Tax revenue is equal to the per-unit tax multiplied by how many units are bought and sold. If the price rises (due to a tax) by 1% and quantity demanded falls by more than 1%, tax revenues collected will fall. If quantity demanded falls by less than 1%, total tax revenue will rise.

169. (C) The incidence, or burden, of a tax will be greater on the side of the market that is more inelastic than the other. Note that elasticity is the ability to respond to a price change. To a buyer or a seller, a tax is an increase in the price. If an agent, the buyers or the sellers, cannot respond to an increase, they will end up bearing a higher burden than if they are able to respond by cutting back their quantity.

170. (B) The greater the price elasticity, the more elastic the curve. So a supply curve with a price elasticity of 3 is more elastic than a demand curve with an elasticity of 2. This allows us to conclude that suppliers are more able to respond to a tax than are the demanders, thus putting more of the tax burden on the buyers of this product.

171. (B) The tax incidence of the consumers is the dollar amount of the tax revenue that becomes the burden of the consumer. It is the equivalent of the area below the price that the consumer pays with the tax and above the price that the consumer pays without the tax, at the quantity that will actually be sold in the market with the tax. Without a tax the consumer would pay $12, and with the tax a consumer would pay $18. At $18, the consumer is willing to buy 10 units. So ($18 − $12) × 10 = $60. Note that this corresponds to the area of the rectangle represented by the letter *W*.

172. (A) Consumer surplus is the difference between the amount that consumers are willing to pay and the amount that they actually pay, at the quantity that they actually buy. Before the tax is imposed on this market, consumers pay a price of $12 and buy 19 units, and their consumer surplus is represented by the areas V + W + U. However, after the tax consumers pay $18 and buy 10 units, so consumer surplus is now only the area V. So what happened to W and U? W is part of the tax revenue that goes to the government. However, when the consumers reduced their consumption from 19 to 10 units, there are 9 units that never get bought (or sold), and part of the consumer surplus that used to exist, U, simply disappears.

173. (C) In Figure 6.1, the consumer's tax incidence is $60. The producer's tax incidence is the area represented by Z, the difference between the price that the producer would get with no tax and the price that they get with the tax, at the quantity that they actually sell. In this case, this is ($12 − $8) × 10 = $40. Since the tax burden of the consumer is higher than the tax burden of the producer, we know that the demand curve is more inelastic than the supply curve.

174. (D) We can tell that the supplier is being taxed in this situation because the supply curve has shifted up by the amount of the tax. After the tax, consumers pay $18 and the producers receive a price of $8 after they pay the tax. Therefore, a $10 wedge has been driven between the price that producers get and the price that consumers pay, which is the amount of the tax.

175. (E) Total surplus = consumer surplus + producer surplus + tax revenue. Here, consumer surplus after the tax is represented by the area S. Tax revenue is represented by the area V + W. Producer surplus is represented by the area Z. Students are sometimes confused as to why tax revenue is counted as surplus, since we tend to think of surplus as some benefit that is gained by the existence of a market. Tax revenue is counted as surplus because it is assumed that the benefit of the tax goes somewhere, whether to build roads or even to be enjoyed by a less-than-benevolent dictator.

176. (E) Tax revenue is the total value of the taxes collected. Each of the 10 units that are sold in this market are taxed $10, so tax revenue = $10 \times 10 = 100$. This is equivalent to the areas represented by the rectangles W (the consumer's tax incidence) and Z (the producer's tax incidence). Students are sometimes tempted to calculate the tax revenue using the quantity that would be sold in the market without a tax (19 units in this case). This is not correct. Once the tax is imposed, the amount that is sold will decrease.

177. (E) Before a tax is imposed in this market, f units are sold at a price of c. At this equilibrium, producer surplus is represented by the areas $\varphi + \delta + \tau$. After the tax is imposed, only e units are sold, and the seller only gets a price of d, so the producer surplus with the tax is represented by the area of triangle τ, and the area represented by the rectangle φ becomes the producer's tax incidence. The area of the triangle represented by δ is deadweight loss that used to be part of producer surplus.

178. (B) With a tax on the market, producer surplus is represented by the area τ. If the tax on this market is lifted, the price that sellers receive will increase to c and the quantity that they sell will increase to f. As a result, the producer surplus will increase to $\varphi + \delta + \tau$ if the tax is lifted.

179. (A) Elasticity relates to the incidence of a tax. Whichever side of the market is more inelastic will bear a higher tax burden. If the elasticities are equal, then each side of the market will bear the same incidence of the tax. Here the tax incidence of suppliers is represented by the area of the rectangle φ, and the tax incidence of demanders is represented by the area of the rectangle β. So the area of the rectangle φ will be equal to the area of the rectangle β only if the elasticities of the two curves are equal.

180. (C) Total surplus without a tax in this market would be represented by the area $\alpha + \beta + \rho + \varphi + \delta + \tau$. After a tax is imposed in this market, the total surplus would be $\alpha + \beta + \delta + \tau$, where α is the consumer surplus, $\beta + \varphi$ is the tax revenue, and τ is the producer surplus. The areas represented by ρ and δ are the deadweight loss, or inefficiency, meaning that this is surplus that used to exist but now basically disappears. Note that there is not really any interpretation of the areas σ or μ; they are merely distractors.

181. (A) The efficiency loss that occurs when an efficiently operating market is taxed is due to the change in incentives to consume. When consumers have to pay a higher price as the result of a tax, they cut back on their consumption. A lump sum is a tax that is imposed regardless of the quantity or value of a market—you are taxed the same whether you consume zero units or a million units of a good. So even though a tax is imposed, there is no incentive to change consumption and therefore no efficiency loss. Note that this is also a very inequitable form of taxation, because even if you consume nothing from this market, you would still be taxed.

182. (C) *Deadweight loss* is the term that economists give to the efficiency loss that occurs in a perfectly functioning market when you impose a tax or any other kind of interference with market prices, such as price ceilings or price floors. There is a notable difference between the price controls and taxes, however, in that no shortage or surplus exists.

183. (A) The supply curve in this market has shifted up by the amount of the tax. We can tell the amount of the tax in one of two ways. First, the new intersection of the supply curve with the price axis will be the amount of the tax. Second, we can figure out the amount of the tax by looking at the wedge that is placed between what the buyer must pay with the tax—in this case $55—and the price that the seller receives—in this case $35. So $55 − $35 = $20.

184. (E) In this market 40 units are sold after the $20 tax is imposed. The consumer tax incidence is ($55 − $47) × 20 = $160. The producer tax incidence is ($47 − $35) × 40 = $480. The producer pays the higher tax incidence in this market, so we can infer that the supply curve is more inelastic than the demand curve.

185. (B) Anytime a market is taxed, the burden of that tax is shared, with the higher burden of that tax falling on the side of the market with the most inelastic curve. The side of the market with the most elastic curve bears the least burden. In case of a market with a perfectly elastic curve, the side of a market with a perfectly elastic curve would pay no burden at all. So if buyers had a perfectly elastic demand curve, the entire burden of any tax would fall solely on the producer of the market as long as the producer did not also have a perfectly elastic supply curve.

Chapter 7: Consumer Choice

186. (D) Economists describe the happiness (or satisfaction) we receive from consumption as "utility." If consuming (or doing) something makes you happier than you were prior to consuming it, your total utility has increased. For example, a person who is very thirsty will experience higher total utility once the person has had a cold glass of water. When we experience things that make us less happy, they are said to have brought us "disutility," and consumers seek to avoid such experiences.

187. (C) Marginal utility is the change in total utility when another unit of a good or service is consumed. Economists sometimes describe a unit of utility as a "util." For example, if Jacob sees his total utility rise from 0 utils to 20 utils after the first cup of tea, we know that his marginal utility has been positive 20. Similarly, if Jacob sees his total utility from consuming two cups of tea rise from 20 utils to 30 utils, we know his marginal utility of the second cup was 10 utils. Anytime marginal utility is positive, it tells us that a person is seeing his total utility rise with successive units of a good. However, if Jacob's fifth cup of tea gives him a headache and makes him unproductive, that fifth cup is lowering his total utility. Thus the marginal utility of the fifth cup is negative. For instance, he had a total utility of 40 utils from 4 cups of tea and 37 utils from 5 cups of tea. If Jacob knows this happens with the fifth cup, he will never choose to consume it and he will stop at four cups.

188. (E) A utility-maximizing consumer would continue to eat hot dogs so long as total utility continues to climb. Total utility rises for the first six hot dogs, but the seventh causes total utility to fall. If the consumer knows that this will happen with the seventh hot dog, he or she will never consume it, even if it is free.

189. (A) Marginal utility is the change in total utility caused by a change in consumption. The formula for marginal utility is $MU_X = \Delta TU / \Delta X$. When consumption rises by 1 unit at a time, as it does in the table, we simply subtract the total utility from having four hot dogs (38 utils) from the total utility from having five hot dogs (40 utils). The difference of 2 utils is the marginal utility of the fifth hot dog.

190. (A) Lucy is a consumer with a budget constraint and would seek to maximize her utility within the limits of this budget. A combination of lipstick and magazines that amounts to more than $48 of spending would provide more utility, but she cannot afford such combinations (choices B and D). A combination that amounts to less than $48 of spending would be affordable, but would not provide as much total utility as she could potentially enjoy (choices C and E). We must find a combination of lipstick and magazines that uses exactly all of her $48 of income. One lipstick and nine magazines do add up to $48 = 1 × $12 + 9 × $4 = $12 + $36.

191. (D) When a consumer like Lucy is spending all of her income to buy more of one good (lipstick), she must reallocate her spending and decrease consumption of the other good (magazines). Buying a lipstick requires $12, and since magazines are $4 each, she must reduce her magazine consumption by three magazines.

192. (B) Given that Mr. Chang is buying only two goods, we can use the information provided to answer this question. The y-intercept on the graph tells us that if he spends all of his income on burritos, he can buy 45 burritos. Since a burrito costs $6 each, his income must be $6 × 45 = $270. The x-intercept on the graph tells us that if he spends all of his income on toothpaste, he can buy 90 of them. Now that we know how much income he has, we can determine the price of toothpaste as $270/90 = $3 each.

193. (C) A budget constraint is similar to a production possibility frontier. Combinations that lie beyond the budget constraint are unaffordable, though they would certainly provide Mr. Chang with more utility. A combination that lies inside the budget constraint is affordable but inferior to combinations that lie along the constraint, because not all income is being used (much like a point that lies inside of a production possibilities frontier is inferior because not all resources are being used). Note that one affordable choice, point F, could maximize Mr. Chang's utility, but because it represents the *x*-intercept, it could only be a utility-maximizing point if he received absolutely no happiness from burritos.

194. (D) If the price of toothpaste falls, the budget constraint will rotate outward along the toothpaste axis. A previously unaffordable point like point E could now become affordable along the new budget constraint and could become the new utility-maximizing combination of toothpaste and burritos. Note that this also reinforces our utility-maximizing rule that the optimal consumption bundle will be a combination of goods where $MU_x/P_x = MU_y/P_y$. If the price of good X falls, then this equation is no longer equal, and the consumption of X should increase.

195. (A) If the price of burritos rises, the budget constraint will rotate inward along the burrito axis. A point that previously fell inside the budget constraint, like point B, could now become a point along the new budget constraint and become the new utility-maximizing combination of toothpaste and burritos.

196. (A) Consumers maximize their utility between two goods when they find the point where the marginal utility per dollar is equal for both goods (mathematically, for two goods X and Y, this would be expressed as $Mu_x/P_x = MU_y/P_y$). Maddy's marginal utility of milk is 40 utils, but when divided by the price of $4, he gets 10 utils per dollar. His marginal utility of fish is much higher at 100 utils, but the price is also higher at $15 each. Fish provides him with only 6.67 utils per dollar (100/$15). Since milk gives Maddy more happiness per dollar, he can increase his total utility by spending more of his income on milk and spending less of his income on fish. This also makes sense on an intuitive level: if you are getting more "bang for your buck" by consuming milk, it makes sense to consume more milk.

197. (E) This condition is also called the utility-maximizing rule. When the marginal utility per dollar is equal for both goods, there is no way to reallocate your spending to increase your total utility. To see this, suppose that each good has a price of $1, and the marginal utility of good X is 10 utils and the marginal utility of good Y is 4 utils ($MU_x > MU_y$). You can spend $1 more on good X, spend $1 less on good Y, and increase your overall happiness by 6 utils. So long as you're getting more bang for your buck from good X, you will continue to make this substitution until $MU_x = MU_y$. Of course, the same process would occur in reverse if you were at a point where $MU_x < MU_y$; you would buy more good Y and less good X.

198. (B) The principle of diminishing marginal utility helps explain why demand curves are downward sloping. Suppose a consumer can eat free tacos. As she eats more and more tacos, the marginal utility of the next taco is smaller and smaller. This means that she enjoys the third taco less than she enjoyed the second taco. If she must now pay for the third taco, her willingness to pay for that taco will be lower than her willingness to pay for the second taco. She will only pay for the third taco if the price falls to meet her lower willingness to pay. Thus her diminishing marginal utility for tacos implies an inverse relationship between price and quantity of tacos demanded—a downward-sloping demand.

199. (E) All of these statements accurately describe the relationship between utility and demand. A diminishing marginal utility curve means the additional happiness for the next unit of good X is lower than it was for the previous unit. Because of this, the consumer's willingness to pay for the next unit also falls. A consumer responds to a lower price of good X by consuming more of good X because a lower price gives that consumer higher marginal utility per dollar. Utility for this good now comes at a bargain, so more of that good is purchased. The substitution effect from a lower price means that good X is now a bargain relative to other goods, and the consumer can increase utility by purchasing more of X and less of the alternative.

200. (A) Since Julie is already maximizing utility, she is already at the point where $MU_A/P_A = MU_B/P_B$. When the price of good B rises, it creates a situation where the marginal utility of good B divided by the higher price is less than the marginal utility of good A divided by its price. This prompts Julie to make a substitution: more of good A and less of good B. She will continue to substitute until she is back in equilibrium and the ratios of marginal utility per dollar are again equal.

201. (C) If Manny considers pizza to be a normal good, both the substitution effect and income effect will prompt him to buy more pizza when the price falls. Because pizza is now a less pricey food option, the substitution effect will cause him to decrease consumption of a pizza substitute and increase pizza consumption. Manny's income hasn't increased, but the lower price of pizza gives him more purchasing power in his budget. This feeling of more income prompts him to buy more of all normal goods, thus reinforcing the substitution effect.

202. (B) When a good is inferior, the substitution effect and income effect work against each other. The higher price of good Z creates a substitution effect wherein fewer units of good Z are demanded. However, a higher price of good Z causes a consumer to lose purchasing power. This feeling of lost income would cause an increase in consumption of inferior goods. If the income effect of an inferior good (more units of Z) is stronger than the substitution effect (fewer units of Z), it is possible for a demand curve to be upward sloping.

203. (E) Because tacos are normal goods, the substitution and income effects work in the same direction. A higher price of tacos will cause a consumer to look for substitutes that are now a relative bargain; quantity of tacos demanded falls. A higher price causes a loss of purchasing power and a feeling of lost income. Because tacos are a normal good, this also prompts a decrease in quantity demanded.

204. (D) We know that both Gilligan and Ginger have experienced a lower price of coconuts, and both have the same substitution effect. Only two possibilities explain why Ginger has increased her coconut consumption more than Gilligan did. It is possible that both consider coconuts to be normal goods, but Ginger's income effect is larger than Gilligan's. This is not one of the choices given in the question. If Ginger considers coconuts to be normal, a lower price will reinforce the substitution effect and increase consumption. If Gilligan considers them to be inferior, this would partially counter his substitution effect and explain the disparity.

205. (C) A vertical demand curve means that if the price of crackers changes up or down, Max will not alter his consumption of crackers. It is possible that he has absolutely no substitution or income effects, but this is not one of the choices given in the question. The other possibility is that he does have a substitution effect, but it is exactly offset by an income effect for an inferior good.

Chapter 8: Production and Costs

206. (B) The short run is a period of time too brief to adjust the hiring of all of the production inputs. If an input can be quickly increased or decreased to produce more or less output, it is described as a variable input. Thus variable inputs can be adjusted in the short run. Anything that can be changed in the short run is by definition also able to be changed in the long run. So variable inputs can be changed in the short run or the long run. However, if an input cannot be quickly increased or decreased, it is a fixed input. These inputs are therefore fixed in the short run, but variable in the long run. In the long run, all inputs can be adjusted to produce more or less output.

207. (C) If the ice cream shop wanted to operate longer hours to serve more customers, the shop would need to increase the hiring of variable inputs like hourly part-time (or noncontract) labor, supplies, electricity, and key ingredients. However, the monthly rent will remain constant no matter if the shop is busy, quiet, or even closed. Buildings, whether owned or rented, are considered part of the firm's capital input, and the cost of employing capital is almost always considered a fixed short-run cost.

208. (B) Because there are fixed inputs in the short run, there are fixed costs in the short run, which are constant at all levels of output. However, the firm must employ more variable inputs to produce more units of output, and if output is zero, total variable costs are also zero. In other words, total fixed cost is not a function of output (it's the same), and total variable cost is a function of output. Total cost is the sum of total variable cost and total fixed cost. So when output is zero, total cost is equal to total fixed cost. In the short run, economic profit could be positive, negative, or zero.

209. (B) When one more unit of a variable input (like labor) is employed, the additional unit of labor causes a change in total output (or total product of labor). This change in total output is the marginal impact, or marginal product, of the additional unit of labor. Marginal product is equal to $MPL = (\Delta TPL)/(\Delta L)$. If output increased with more labor, the marginal product is positive; if output decreased, the marginal product is negative.

210. (A) When more labor is added to a fixed amount of capital, eventually the labor either runs out of equipment or space to work with, so marginal product of labor begins to fall. A closer look at the formula MPL = $(\Delta TPL)/(\Delta L)$ tells us something interesting about marginal product. The total product curve is plotted in a graph with TPL on the y-axis and L on the x-axis; so our marginal product equation could be written as MPL = $(\Delta y)/(\Delta x)$, or the slope of the total product curve. So long as the marginal product is positive, it tells us that total product is rising. But if total product is rising and getting flatter, the slope is getting smaller. This shows that marginal product must be falling. If the marginal product ever becomes negative, the total product must be falling.

211. (C) When the ninth worker is hired, total output rises from 80 to 81 units; thus the marginal product of that worker is 1 unit of output. Average product of labor, or output per worker, is simply the total output divided by the quantity of labor that was employed to produce that output. So when total output at nine workers is 81 total units, on average each worker is producing 9 units per worker (81 units/9 workers). We calculate the average product of labor as APL = TPL/L.

212. (B) The marginal product is the additional contribution of the next worker. The average product is the current average output per worker hired. The relationship between the two can be seen with exam scores in a class. Suppose your current average exam score is 80%, but your next exam (the marginal exam) is a 90%. Your average just went up! Had your marginal exam been a 70%, the average would have been pulled down. This allows us to generalize back to production: if the marginal product exceeds the current average, the average will come up. If the marginal product is below the current average, the average will come down. Of course, if the marginal product is equal to the average product, average product will neither rise nor fall.

213. (D) The key to knowing that Curve Y is total variable cost is that the curve begins at $0 when output is zero. Because variable inputs are not hired when nothing is being produced, no variable costs are associated with hiring them. Curve Z is horizontal, telling us that this cost curve doesn't rise or fall with output; this curve represents total fixed cost. Another way to tell that Y, rather than X, is the short-run cost curve is that Curve Y is always less than Curve X: variable costs are always less than total costs, which are represented by Curve X.

214. (B) In the short run, there are both fixed and variable costs. The total cost (TC) of producing any level of short-run output is the sum of total variable cost (TVC) and total fixed cost (TFC). In the graph, Curve X represents the sum of the TFC (a constant cost represented by the horizontal Curve X) and the rising TVC (Curve Y). Notice that the total cost curve, at output of zero, begins on the vertical cost axis. This happens because at zero units of output, there still exists total fixed cost.

215. (E) The short run is too short a time span to change the fixed inputs (usually capital such as factories, equipment, or buildings), so there are total fixed costs in the short run. When the cost of employing variable inputs (total variable cost) is added to the cost of the fixed capital inputs, the firm has accounted for all of the production costs. In equation form, the total cost of producing Q units is the sum of fixed costs that don't vary based on the Q units produced, and variable costs, which do depend on the Q units produced, or TC(Q) = TFC + TVC(Q). Choice C might appear to be correct, but the sum of average variable cost and average fixed cost is average total cost, or the total production cost per unit of output produced.

216. (E) Marginal cost is the additional cost of producing the next unit of output or the change in the total cost that is required to produce one more unit. Equivalently it is cal-culated as MC = ΔTC/ΔQ = Δ TVC/ΔQ. If the quantity of output is changing 1 unit at a time, we can simply see what happens to total cost when the firm moves from 4 units to 5 units of output. The change in total cost going from 4 units to 5 units, or ΔTC, is $33 − $27 = $6. Therefore, $6/1 = $6.

217. (A) Average fixed costs are equal to AFC(Q) = TFC/Q. It might appear that we can-not figure out average fixed cost from Table 8.1 because fixed costs are not given. However, Table 8.1 indicates that total cost is always $10 higher than total variable cost. This $10 difference is the level of total fixed cost (TFC = TC(Q) − TVC(Q)). Another way to find the fixed cost is to note that when Q = 0, variable costs are equal to zero; so from the total cost curve TC(0) = TFC + TVC(0) = TFC. To find the fixed cost of production, look at what production costs are when there is no output. Average fixed cost, or fixed cost per unit, is total fixed cost divided by units of output, or AFC(Q) = $10/2 = $5 per unit. Although TFC does not change with output, AFC declines with output, because as output increases, the same number (10) is divided by a larger and larger number. Note that while total fixed costs are not a function of Q (the value of total fixed costs does not change depending on Q), average fixed costs (AFC(Q)) are a function of Q.

218. (C) To get a mental picture of what the marginal cost curve looks like, subtract total cost (or total variable cost) from one level of output to the next. The marginal cost of pro-ducing the first unit is $5 because total cost rises from $10 to $15. The marginal cost of producing the second unit is lower and equal to $3, because total cost rises from $15 to $18. But beyond the second unit of output, marginal cost begins to rise. The marginal cost of the third unit is $4, the marginal cost of the fourth unit is $5, and so on. This is a pretty typical pattern where the marginal cost curve initially falls but quickly becomes an increasing func-tion as more output is produced (similar to a "check mark").

219. (A) Because average variable cost, or variable cost per unit, is total variable cost divided by units of output, we calculate AVC(Q) = $30/6 = $5 per unit. Average variable cost typically falls with more output, eventually reaches a minimum level, and then rises as output continues to increase. Graphically it is drawn as a U-shaped curve.

220. (D) When economists use the word *marginal*, it helps to think "additional" or "incremental change." So when we compute marginal cost, we are calculating the additional cost of producing an additional unit of output. If output is rising by 1 unit at a time, we get the marginal cost by subtracting the total cost before the unit was produced from the total cost after it was produced. Sometimes output rises by more than 1 unit. Suppose that output rises by 5 units and total cost rises by $100. The marginal cost of 1 additional unit is found by calculating MC = (ΔTC/ΔQ) = ($100/5) = $20.

221. (D) In the short run, the sum of total variable cost and total fixed cost is total cost (TC(Q) = TVC(Q) + TFC). If we divide both sides of this equation by output (Q), we can see a similar relationship in the per-unit costs: TC(Q)/Q = TVC(Q)/Q + TFC/Q. Thus the average total cost is equal to the sum of the average variable cost and the average fixed cost: ATC(Q) = AVC(Q) + AFC(Q).

222. (B) The key to understanding the shape of the average fixed cost curve is to know how average fixed cost is computed and how to visualize that computation. We divide the total fixed cost, which does not change in the short run, by output. As output rises, we are dividing the same number by more and more units of output; AFC(Q) gets smaller and smaller. For example, suppose TFC = $300. For the first unit, AFC(1) = $300/1 = $300; for the second unit AFC(2) = $300/2 = $150; for the third unit AFC(3) = $300/3 = $100, and so on.

223. (E) The best way to see the inverse relationship between marginal cost (MC) and marginal product of labor (MPL) is to make a couple of quick simplifications and use a little algebra. Suppose the firm's only variable input is labor (L), and labor is paid a constant market wage of $W. This implies that total variable cost TVC = W × L. The formula for marginal cost recall is as follows.

$$MC = \frac{\Delta TC}{\Delta Q} = \frac{\Delta TVC}{\Delta Q} = \frac{\Delta(W \times L)}{\Delta Q}$$

Since the wage doesn't change, we can show the following.

$$MC = \frac{\Delta TVC}{\Delta Q} = \frac{W\Delta L}{\Delta Q}$$

The marginal product of labor is the change in output caused by a change in the quantity of labor hired. Finally, we recognize that our marginal cost equation is really just the market wage multiplied by the inverse of this marginal product of labor equation. We know that MPL declines as more labor is hired to a fixed quantity of capital. So as MPL declines, MC must rise. This tells us that each unit of labor is marginally less productive, so the cost of producing more output must rise because it now takes more labor to produce the additional output.

224. (C) If we assume that hiring zero units of labor corresponds to zero units of output, then an upward shift of the total product of labor will create a steeper total product of labor curve (it still begins at the graphical origin). Marginal product of labor (MPL) is the slope of total product of labor, which implies that the marginal product curve shifts upward. Better production technology implies workers are using better capital tools; this allows each additional worker to produce more additional output. Because MPL is the inverse of marginal cost (MC) of production, an upward shift in MPL must correspond to a downward shift in MC.

225. (A) Just as the marginal product of labor is inversely related to marginal cost, average product of labor (APL) is inversely related to average variable cost (AVC(Q)). A technological catastrophe that causes total product of labor to shift downward will cause average product of all workers to decline, because average product is calculated by dividing TPL/L. If the APL is shifting downward, the AVC(Q) must be shifting upward.

226. (D) Suppose the firm's only variable input is labor (L), and labor is paid a constant market wage of $W. This implies that total variable cost TVC(Q) = W × L (where a specific unit of labor will produce a given amount of Q). The formula for average variable cost is as follows.

$$AVC = \frac{TVC}{Q} = \frac{(W \times L)}{Q}$$

The average product of labor (APL) is the total output per unit of labor hired. Finally, we recognize that our average variable cost equation is really just the market wage multiplied by the inverse of this average product of labor equation. So long as there are diminishing marginal returns to hiring labor, the average product of labor first rises and then falls. Because APL is a hill-shaped curve and is inversely related to AVC, then AVC must be a U-shaped curve that first falls and then rises.

227. (E) While cost functions and cost curves can be confusing and complicated to calculate, total revenue is very straightforward. The total revenue (TR) collected from selling a product is equal to how many units are sold (Q) multiplied by the price (P) at which they were sold; thus TR = P × Q.

228. (A) Think of total revenue as the money collected by Fred when he sells the hot dogs to his customers. He sells 100 hot dogs, and he receives $3 for each of the hot dogs sold, so he collects $300 from his customers. While the marginal cost information will be necessary to compute other important things, like perhaps profit, it is irrelevant to determining total revenue.

229. (C) Marginal revenue is the change in total revenue from the next unit sold. Suppose the firm can sell a Zurg for $10 and that price stays the same no matter how many they sell. If one Zurg is sold, total revenue rises from zero to $10. If a second Zurg is sold, total revenue rises from $10 to $20. We can see that total revenue rises by $10, the price, every time another unit is sold. In this case, price and marginal revenue are the same.

230. (B) We see in the table a demand schedule: the quantity of a product demanded at different prices. If the firm can sell 12 units at a price of $5, total revenue received from those sales will amount to $60 ($5 × 12 units). It is important to go slowly through these types of questions and read them carefully.

231. (C) This is a difficult question because it asks for the marginal revenue when the price changes, rather than explicitly asking about a change in quantity. Of course, we see from the table that when the price rises from $3 to $4, quantity declines from 16 to 14 units, a 2-unit decrease. Marginal revenue is the change in total revenue divided by the change in quantity sold, calculated as follows.

$$MR = \frac{\Delta TR}{\Delta Q} = \frac{(\$56 - \$48)}{2} = \$4$$

232. (D) Profit is often hastily described as the difference between total revenue (TR) and total cost (TC). However, an economist and an accountant see total cost differently; an accountant will usually recognize only the direct out-of-pocket expenses of hiring inputs. If we subtract only the explicit costs from total revenue, we get accounting profit (πA). Explicit costs would include wages paid to employees, the cost of machinery, and any form of utilities. An economist readily acknowledges these explicit costs in the computation of accounting profit, but also includes any opportunities forgone by the owner of the firm. When these implicit costs are also subtracted from accounting profit, we are left with economic profit (πE).

233. (D) One of the most important implicit costs that an entrepreneur should consider is a forgone salary. An accurate reckoning of economic profit should begin with subtracting explicit production costs from total revenue (TR), but any implicit costs such as Linda's current salary should also be subtracted. To break even, economic profit must at least equal zero: $\pi E = TR -$ explicit costs $- \$19,000 = 0$. If we solve for total revenue: TR = explicit costs + $19,000.

234. (A) Whether we are describing accounting or economic profit, profit maximization is the same: find the output where the difference between total revenue and total cost is the greatest. Total revenue is a function of output, and total cost (at least the variable component) is also a function of output, so profit fluctuates depending upon the level of output chosen.

235. (D) The cornerstone of production theory, or theory of the firm, is that owners of firms act to maximize profit. While revenue maximization might be a tempting choice, revenue is only one part of the profit computation. When output is produced and sold, monetary revenues flow into the firm. But to hire inputs to do that production, monetary costs flow out of the firm. While it is true that not every firm is profitable and some firms go out of business due to overwhelming losses, the goal of each firm is to be as profitable as possible.

236. (E) When a unit of output is sold, two things happen: marginal revenue dollars are earned and marginal cost dollars are incurred. If the marginal revenue dollars are greater than the marginal cost dollars, profit rises. In fact, the difference between marginal revenue and marginal cost on the next unit is called marginal profit. But marginal cost rises as more output is produced, so the gap between marginal revenue and marginal cost begins to narrow and marginal profit falls. At some point the marginal revenue is equal to the marginal cost; the next unit will create a situation where marginal cost exceeds marginal revenue, and marginal profit on that unit would be negative. So to maximize total profit, the firm would stop at the output where the dollars of marginal revenue earned are exactly offset by the dollars of marginal cost incurred.

237. (B) Since we are told that the price will be a constant $70, this informs us that marginal revenue of any unit sold is also $70. To find profit maximization, we look for the point where marginal cost is equal to $70. The difference between total cost at 5 units ($420) and 4 units ($350) is exactly $70, so the fifth unit will be sold, but not the sixth (marginal cost of $80).

238. (C) This question tells us that total revenue rises by $90 each time a unit is sold. In other words, marginal revenue is $90. We use the table to find where total cost (or total variable cost) rises by $90, and this is the output where profit will be maximized. Total cost at the seventh unit is exactly $90 higher than it is for the sixth unit ($590 − $500), so the firm should produce 7 units.

239. (A) We must first find the output where marginal revenue equals marginal cost and $80. This occurs at the sixth unit of output, because total cost rises from $420 to $500. Profit is now found by computing total revenue (P × Q) and subtracting from that total cost found in the table at 6 units of output. Profit is therefore equal to $80 × 6 − $500 = −$20.

240. (A) Since we are told that the firm has maximized profit at 8 units, it must be the case that marginal revenue equals marginal cost at this level of output. The table informs us that marginal cost is $100 because total cost rises from $590 to $690 at the eighth unit.

241. (C) A key distinction between the long run and the short run has to do with the ability of the firm to be more flexible in their long-run hiring of inputs than they can be in the short run. In the long run, there is enough time to change all inputs, including capital, so all costs become variable in the long run. In the short run, at least one cost is fixed.

242. (E) In the long run, the firm can adjust all inputs to either grow the overall size of the firm (often referred to as "scale") or reduce it. If the firm sees that long-run expansion causes per-unit costs to fall, a downward-sloping LRATC curve, it is said to be experiencing economies of scale. Economies of scale can result from a larger firm being able to spread the high costs of large machinery or buildings over many units of output. A factory might be expensive to build, but if it can produce millions and millions of units of output, the per-unit costs decline.

243. (B) Sometimes a firm can expand so much that it becomes less efficient, not more efficient, to grow the scale. If the firm sees that long-run expansion causes per-unit costs to rise, an upward-sloping LRATC curve, it is said to be experiencing diseconomies of scale. Diseconomies of scale can result from a larger firm that finds it more difficult to monitor quality control or finds it more difficult to quickly adapt to market changes or new rivals. If the firm is becoming less efficient or less able to adapt, inefficiencies result and per-unit costs rise.

Chapter 9: Perfect Competition

244. (D) One of the key assumptions of perfect competition is that there are many producers in the market, each of which has a relatively small share of the market. At the heart of the most competitive of the four main market structures is the assumption that no large firm dominates, or heavily influences, the marketplace. In other words, each of these small firms produces an insignificant fraction of the overall market output.

245. (A) Every firm in perfect competition produces a product that is identical to the products of the other firms. This standardized (sometimes called *homogeneous*) product reinforces that no firm has the ability to set the price. Because each product is identical, if one firm tries to raise the price of its product, they will not sell any of it, since a buyer could get an identical product at a lower price.

246. (B) Firms in perfect competition must take the market price as given. They are each so small and sell a homogeneous product, so no one firm can affect the market price through their actions. They each sell such a tiny fraction of the overall market that if one firm wanted to create a shortage by withholding their output from the market or a surplus by flooding the market with their product, it would have no impact on the market price. Additionally, because the firms are all selling identical products and cannot get a price higher than the market price, they have no incentive to advertise. If they were to advertise, they wouldn't garner any additional production (or a higher price) and would just be lowering their profit by incurring an additional expense.

247. (C) Because no firm can actually set the price, firms must accept the market price as a given. This behavior is known as "price-taking" and sets perfectly competitive firms apart from the firms in other market structures. Firms will get this price regardless of the quantity that they produce. Since each firm makes up a small share of the market production, changing the quantity that they produce will have a negligible impact on the market.

248. (E) Two characteristics of the model of perfect competition create outcomes unique to this market structure. When firms are so small that they cannot affect the market price, and when those firms are assumed to produce a homogenous product, we have the most competitive of all market structures. In other market structures, firms have the ability to affect the market price.

249. (B) Remember that demand curves are the relationship between the price of a firm's product and the quantity of that product demanded. A downward-sloping demand curve implies that firms have a choice of many different prices. While the market for wheat still has a downward-sloping demand curve, when a firm is perfectly competitive, they have no ability to affect the price. So the demand for that firm's product is not downward sloping—it is horizontal or perfectly elastic.

250. (A) The market demand for a product is downward sloping. Like the demand for any product, if the price were to fall in the market, all else equal, the quantity of geezums demanded will fall. However, for any given price, the demand for the product of each of the many small price-taking firms is horizontal, as they have no control over the price of their own products.

251. (C) Each bean grower produces a bean that is identical to the beans of every other grower. For price-taking bean growers, the demand for each firm's product is horizontal and equal to the price. If the price of beans in the market were to rise, this would cause a vertical shift upward of this horizontal demand curve.

252. (B) When studying the model of perfect competition, we must remember that the law of demand for the product still holds in the market. Consumers in the market for a perfectly competitive product (e.g., wheat) will still reduce their quantity demanded when the price rises. When looking for the market demand for a product, look for a downward-sloping curve.

253. (D) The law of demand in the market for a perfectly competitive product is downward sloping. However, when we focus our attention to the demand for a particular firm's product, the demand for this firm's product is horizontal. It isn't horizontal because consumers don't respond to lower prices; it's horizontal because these firms have no choice over the price that can be offered. The price comes from the market, it is fixed, and the firm produces as much as possible at that price.

254. (B) Because the perfectly competitive firms are price takers, the price is equal to marginal revenue. Every additional unit sold increases total revenue by exactly the market price. Firms maximize profit by finding the output where marginal revenue of a quantity equals marginal cost of that quantity. Thus it is always true that $P = MR = MC$.

255. (C) As the price (and marginal revenue) rises and falls with changes in the market, the firm is adjusting output such that the price equals marginal cost. When the price rises, the firm increases output along the marginal cost curve. If the price were to fall, the firm would decrease output along the marginal cost curve. Hence the marginal cost curve serves as the supply curve. However, if the price were to fall below average variable cost, the firm would produce zero units of output.

256. (E) If the price of a variable input decreases, it will obviously not cause the average fixed cost curve to change at all. The average variable cost (TVC/Q) will clearly decrease because total variable cost has decreased. Average total cost is the sum of average variable cost and average fixed cost, so it will also decrease. Marginal cost is the change in total cost divided by a change in output. Now each unit of output can be produced at lower cost, so the additional cost of another unit of output has also fallen.

257. (C) When the price of a fixed input rises, the total fixed costs (TFC) increase. Clearly the average fixed cost curve (TFC/Q) must also increase when total fixed cost increases. Since the variable costs are unaffected, the average variable cost curve will not change. Average total cost will increase because it is the sum of average variable and average fixed costs. Because this change has not affected the variable cost of production, marginal cost is also unaffected.

258. (A) To maximize profit, the firm sets output at the point where price (and since it is perfectly competitive, price = marginal revenue) equals marginal cost. If the price increases, the initial level of output is no longer where P = MR = MC. In fact, it is now the case that P = MR > MC. Since the sale of the next unit of output brings in more dollars of revenue than it costs to produce, output increases.

259. (D) Economic profit, the difference between total revenue and total cost, can be seen in graphs such as this one by comparing the current price to average total cost, at the profit-maximizing level of output. To see this, let's look at how profit is calculated. Profit (we use the symbol $\prod$) is a function of output (Q) and is equal to $\prod(Q) = TR(Q) - TC(Q)$. Dividing both total revenue and total cost by the output where price equals marginal cost gives us $\prod(Q) = Q \times (P - ATC(Q))$. If price is greater than average total cost, as it is at P_1, profits are positive.

260. (B) Recall that the economic profits earned by the firm are equal to the difference between total revenue and total cost. This relationship can be rephrased as $\prod(Q) = Q \times (P - ATC(Q))$. The difference between price and average total cost gives us profit per unit. When we multiply this by Q, the number of units produced, we are back to total profit. The only way for profit to be zero, or the break-even level, is if price equals average total cost. Looking at the graph, we see that at the price of P_2, the firm is breaking even.

261. (E) When total cost is subtracted from total revenue, the result is equal to profit. If total revenue is greater than total cost, economic profit is positive, and if total revenue is less than total cost, profit is negative (losses). Both total revenue and total cost are functions of output, and since the perfectly competitive firm is a price taker, we can see positive and negative profits by looking at the relationship between per-unit revenue and per-unit cost. Revenue per unit is price, and cost per unit is average total cost. Since P_4 lies below average total cost, we know that per-unit profit is negative and thus total profit is negative.

262. (B) When a firm produces any level of output in the short run, total revenues are earned and total variable costs are incurred. If the total revenue falls below the total variable cost, the firm should not produce anything in the short run. This decision to shut down is the same if revenue per unit, or price, is compared to average variable cost. If the price is below average variable cost, the best decision is to shut down.

263. (A) If a firm decides to shut down in the short run, it has determined that price is below average variable cost. In this situation, any output at all will only cause greater and greater losses because the price is not even covering the variable cost of production. But in the short run, producing zero units of output does not eliminate the total fixed costs that still exist: $\Pi = TR - TVC - TFC = 0 - 0 - TFC = -TFC$.

264. (C) Profit per unit is equal to revenue per unit (price) minus cost per unit (average total cost). Because only the variable costs are affected when output is produced, a firm must really determine whether the price is going to be high enough to pay for the average variable costs that are incurred. After all, the average fixed costs are paid whether the firm produces zero units or a million units. If the price falls below the minimum of the average variable cost curve, the profit-maximizing decision is to shut down and produce zero units.

265. (D) The profit-maximizing decision is really just marginal analysis. The additional benefit of producing the next unit of output is marginal revenue, and because perfectly competitive firms are price takers, marginal revenue is also equal to the price. The additional cost of producing the next unit of output is marginal cost. Every last penny of profit is earned when price, marginal revenue, and marginal cost are all equal. However, if the price is not above the average variable cost, any level of production will lower profit.

266. (E) Once we are told that the firm is maximizing profit, we know that one thing is true: price is equal to marginal cost. But just because a firm is maximizing profit, we don't know if those profits are negative, zero, or positive until we know where price lies in relation to average total cost. Because we are also told that economic profits are positive, it must be the case that price is above average total cost.

267. (B) We need to use the information in the table to find the marginal cost of each unit of output to figure out the quantity that the firm will choose. The firm will maximize profit at the unit of output where marginal cost is $7, the same as the market price. At the fifth unit total cost is $33, and at the sixth unit total cost is $40, so the marginal cost of the sixth unit is $7. Profit is $42 of total revenue from this quantity ($7 × 6) minus $40 of total cost of this quantity, which yields an economic profit of $2.

268. (C) The long-run adjustment to short-run economic profits begins with the entry of new firms into the market. As more firms enter the market, the market supply curve shifts outward and the market price begins to fall. As the price begins to fall, each firm reduces output because now MR < MC, and this lowers firm profits. This adjustment continues until entry stops because economic profits have been eliminated.

269. (D) Positive profits in the short run attract entry of firms into the perfectly competitive market. With more firms producing, market supply shifts to the right, and equilibrium output in the market increases. However, the rightward shift of market supply causes price to fall, and positive economic profits decline to the break-even level.

270. (E) If there are short-run negative profits (or losses), some firms will exit the market. With fewer firms in the market, the market supply curve shifts to the left, which will increase the market price. As the market price rises, each remaining firm increases output because MR > MC and will do so until the price reaches average total cost and profits are zero.

271. (A) The firm in perfect competition maximizes profit when marginal revenue equals marginal cost. Because this firm is a price taker, price is also equal to marginal revenue and marginal cost. Economic profit can be positive or negative in the short run, but will always end up being zero in the long run. For profits to be equal to zero, it must be the case that price is equal to average total cost. Thus we can say in the long run that P = MR = MC = ATC.

272. (B) One of the key assumptions of the model of perfect competition is that there are no barriers to entry or exit. This means that in the long run, firms will enter the market if profits are positive and firms will leave the market if profits are negative. This process of entry and exit forces short-run profits to be zero in the long run. When profits are zero, there is no incentive for firms to enter or exit. This is known as long-run equilibrium.

273. (C) Allocative efficiency is an outcome of perfect competition that shows each firm in the market producing just the right amount: not too few and not too many. If the firm produces at a point where price is greater than marginal cost, the firm is not producing enough to maximize profit. If the firm produces at a point where marginal cost is greater than price, the firm is producing too much.

274. (E) Another way of describing allocative efficiency is to describe it as the outcome where the sum of consumer surplus and producer surplus is maximized. Firms achieve allocative efficiency by producing the profit-maximizing output where price is equal to marginal cost. When each firm produces at the point where price equals marginal cost, the entire market is allocatively efficient.

275. (C) When firms are producing the output where marginal revenue is equal to marginal cost, they are maximizing profit. Because perfectly competitive firms accept the market price and cannot change it, price is also equal to marginal cost and this creates allocative efficiency. In the long run, perfectly competitive firms end up producing at the minimum of the average total cost curve and this defines productive efficiency.

276. (D) Regardless of whether short-run profits are positive, zero, or negative, the perfectly competitive firm will have maximized them at the point where price and marginal revenue equal marginal cost. Because price equals marginal cost, allocative efficiency is always achieved in the short run and in the long run. In the long run, we know that short-run profits will be eliminated through entry and exit of firms. When long-run profits are equal to zero, the firm is producing at the minimum of average total cost; thus productive efficiency exists only in the long run.

277. (A) When price is equal to marginal cost, the firm is allocatively efficient. The word *allocative* refers to the resources that are allocated to the production of the good. Because the firm is producing neither too many nor too few units, it must be hiring the perfect quantities of labor and capital to produce those units. When those units are also being produced at the lowest per-unit costs, the firm is also productively efficient. Price is equal to the minimum of average total cost in the long run, and therefore, the firm achieves allocative and productive efficiency in the long run because P = MC = minimum ATC.

278. (B) Perfectly competitive firms can earn positive or negative economic profits in the short run. If there were barriers to entry or exit, those profits or losses may last into the long run because it is the entry and exit of firms that drives down the price of a good. In the case of positive profits, the entry of new firms drives a high price down to break-even levels. When there are negative profits, the exit of some existing firms brings the price up to break-even levels.

279. (C) In perfect competition each firm produces a product that is identical to the other firms' products. All products are perfect substitutes for each other, and there are no differentiating characteristics. Because there is a complete absence of product differentiation, perfectly competitive firms would not have an incentive to engage in any advertising.

280. (A) The assumption that firms can freely enter and exit the perfectly competitive market ensures that long-run economic profits will be zero. Whenever firms are able to enter and exit a market, price will adjust until the price is on the average total cost curve. For perfectly competitive firms, this occurs at the bottom of the average total cost curve (when average total costs are as low as possible). The fact that firms are price takers means that the price is equal to marginal revenue. In the long run, firms will earn zero economic profit because P = MR = MC = ATC.

281. (D) Because perfectly competitive firms are price takers, each unit that they sell increases total revenue by exactly the price; thus marginal revenue equals price. As profit maximizers, firms set price and marginal revenue equal to marginal cost. Allocative efficiency occurs when price is equal to marginal cost, so allocative efficiency is really the result of price-taking behavior.

282. (E) A firm that spends money on advertising does so to persuade consumers to either purchase more of their product (instead of another firm's product) or pay a higher price for their product than for other firms' products. The firm does this by asserting that its products are different and better than the products of its rivals. In perfect competition, all products are perfect substitutes for all the other products and there are no differentiating characteristics. Without product differentiation, advertising would be a very ineffective, additional expense for the firm to incur.

Chapter 10: Monopoly

283. (B) As long-run average total cost falls with more output, the firm is said to have economies of scale. This is a common barrier to entry for firms with monopoly power. The lower per-unit costs provide a big advantage for the monopolist. If a smaller firm without the same economies of scale were to attempt entry into the market, they would be forced to charge a higher price for the same product. This higher price would give the monopolist the means by which the firm could price out the new entrant and maintain the monopoly.

284. (A) A patent is issued by the government to an inventor to protect, sell, and hopefully, profit from his or her ideas. In the realm of barriers to entry, it gives the inventor (the firm) the sole right to produce a patent-protected product or to use a patent-protected production technology. For a period of several years, no other firm can replicate these new goods or technologies, and this gives the holder of the patent a barrier to entry.

285. (C) When a firm can control the critical raw material necessary to produce a product, the firm likely has an effective barrier preventing entry into that market. Imagine if one firm owned most of the world's copper or magnesium deposits. In that case, any firm that needed to use copper or magnesium for a final product would be blocked from producing that product.

286. (D) Economies of scale, or declining long-run average total costs (LRATC), can give monopolies a barrier to entry because they allow the monopolist to charge a lower price than any potential entrant. A firm's profit is positive if the firm can sell the product at a price that exceeds LRATC. Because the monopolist has lower LRATC than new entrants, it is much more difficult for the new firms to be profitable; thus a barrier is created.

287. (D) Barriers to entry can be created through regulation. In this case, the city of Montrose has created a monopoly by restricting other competitors from entering the market. This gives the public utility monopoly pricing power. It is not true, however, that the utility company can charge whatever price they want. Like any other monopolist, the price a monopoly can charge is still limited by consumers' willingness and ability to pay.

288. (A) Monopoly, by its strictest definition, is an industry with only one seller. The reason that there exists only one seller is because there is at least one barrier to entry. These barriers prevent other firms from entering the market and competing against the monopolist. The other choices describe other market characteristics like those seen in perfect competition and oligopoly.

289. (C) Because a monopolist is the only firm selling the good or service in the market, the firm is the market. Quantity demanded will still fall if the price rises. The fact is that the monopolist has the ability to set the price at any point on the demand curve. So long as there is the ability to set the price (rather than accept the market price), the monopolist operates in a very different way than a perfectly competitive firm.

290. (C) A monopolist is, strictly speaking, the only firm in the market producing a good with no close substitutes. If there is a very large firm with 99% of the market and one small competitor with 1% of the market, the market is technically not a pure monopoly. The demand for the monopoly product is not perfectly elastic, as this would imply no control of the price.

291. (B) A monopolist can set the price of its good, and the amount that the monopolist will be able to sell at that price will depend on consumers' demand for that good. This means that every time the monopolist wants to increase the number of units that it sells, it must lower the price of the good.

292. (E) The monopolist is the only seller in the market because there exists at least one barrier to entry. As a result of the barriers, the firm ends up being the only producer of this good that has no close substitutes. Because there are no close substitutes, the firm is able to set the price of the product at the level that maximizes the firm's profits.

293. (B) Unlike a perfectly competitive firm's marginal revenue curve (which is equal to the price and is the same as the demand curve for the firm's product), the monopolist's marginal revenue curve lies below the demand for the product. In perfect competition, the price-taking firms sell the next unit of output and receive as marginal revenue exactly the market price for that unit. Under the monopoly conditions, if the monopolist wants to sell 1 more unit of output, the firm must lower the price of all units. Thus the marginal revenue of the next unit of output is not the price, but something less than the price.

294. (C) A monopolist may be able to set the price, but the firm cannot avoid the law of demand: to sell additional units of output, the firm must lower the price of the product. However, the firm cannot lower just the price of the additional units of output, the firm must lower the price on all units of output. This means that revenue from the additional units (marginal revenue) is not equal to the price; it must be a dollar value less than the price.

295. (A) When the firm is selling 3 units at $5 each, the firm is earning total revenue of $15 (3 × $5 = $15). To sell 1 more unit, the firm lowers the price of all units to $4 each and sells 4 units of output. Total revenue is now $16 (4 × $4 = $16). Therefore, the marginal revenue of the fourth unit is $1 ($16 − $15 = $1), which is less than the price at which the fourth unit was sold.

296. (E) Profit is maximized at the level of output where marginal revenue is equal to the marginal cost, which occurs at Q_1 in Figure 10.1. The price required to sell the output of Q_1 is read from the demand curve, or P_1. A common mistake is to choose P_4 at the intersection of MR = MC. It is important to remember that price always comes from a demand curve. The intuition behind this is clear: if the firm produces Q_1 units, then the MR of the fourth unit is P_4 and the MC of the fourth unit is P_4. The firm could charge P_4, but doing so would not maximize their profit—in fact, they would only be covering their marginal cost. The demand curve, however, tells us that the most that people are willing to pay for Q_1 units is P_1. So the firm would make the most profit by charging the highest price that they could sell Q_1 units for.

297. (D) Profit is the difference between total revenue and total cost. The profit-maximizing choice of quantity is Q_1. Profit is calculated by multiplying per-unit profit, or the difference between price and average total cost, by the number of units produced. In the graph, this is also the area of a rectangle that is Q_1 units wide and $(P_1 - P_3)$ dollars high. Note that you can see this if you rearrange the profit function: Profit = TR(Q) − TC(Q) = P × Q − TC(Q). If we multiply TC(Q) by Q/Q (in other words, multiply it by 1), we get Profit = P × Q − TC(Q) Q/Q. Note that TC(Q)/Q is the same as ATC(Q), so this becomes Profit = P × Q − ATC(Q) × Q = Q × (P − ATC(Q)).

298. (D) The firm must find the level of output where marginal revenue equals the marginal cost of $4. Total revenue is price multiplied by quantity, and marginal revenue is the change in total revenue when 1 more unit is sold. The total revenue at 4 units of output is $36 (4 × $9), and the total revenue at 5 units is $40 (5 × $8). The marginal revenue of the fifth unit is $4 ($40 − $36). Profit is total revenue minus total cost. There are no fixed costs, and since the marginal cost of producing each unit is $4, and 5 units are produced, the total cost of producing those 5 units is $20 (5 × $4). Profit is therefore $40 − $20 = $20.

299. (B) The monopoly firm, because it is able to set the price, reduces the level of output below the perfectly competitive output, and in so doing, it is able to raise the price. There are barriers to entry in the monopoly market, so economic profits are able to last into the long run. Finally, because the monopoly price is greater than marginal cost, allocative efficiency is not achieved and deadweight loss exists.

300. (E) Allocative efficiency, an outcome of perfect competition in which there is no deadweight loss, does not exist in the monopoly market. The allocatively efficient level of output occurs when price is equal to marginal cost, but the monopolist reduces output to the level where marginal revenue, not price, is equal to marginal cost. This reduction in output means that some transactions that could be made are not made, and this creates the deadweight loss to society.

301. (A) The reason that area def is the monopoly deadweight loss is that those transactions from g units to h units of output should be made in a competitive market. Point d on the demand curve represents a buyer who is willing to pay a price that exceeds the firm's marginal cost (at point e) of producing that good. In this case, the buyer and the seller should be able to make a mutually beneficial transaction (negotiate a price) that is somewhere between point d and point e. The buyer would get consumer surplus, and the producer would get producer surplus from the transaction. But the monopoly firm will not produce the units between g and h, so all of those transactions go unmade and the surplus goes to nobody.

302. (C) If the market is initially competitive, the price would be at point c and h units of output would be produced. Because price equals average total cost at point h, the firm would not earn any economic profit or consumer surplus. The entire area under the demand curve and above the marginal cost curve would be consumer surplus: the triangle acf. If a monopoly exists, output is reduced to g units and the price is increased to point b. Consumer surplus declines to a much smaller triangle: the area of abd. The difference between the large triangle acf and the new smaller triangle abd is what the consumer lost.

303. (D) Monopoly profit is the level of output multiplied by the difference between price and average total cost. In the graph, it can be seen as the area of a rectangle that is g units wide and (b − c) dollars high. The area of profit is therefore bcde, and if the market became perfectly competitive, this would be part of consumer surplus.

304. (B) Price discrimination can take many different forms, but the outcome is the same: two different consumers pay different prices for the same product. Sometimes this is obvious, like when a senior citizen receives a discounted sandwich at a restaurant. Other times it is more subtle, like when a person buys a case of sodas and pays a lower price per soda than a person who buys from the vending machine.

305. (C) Airlines have mastered the art of price discrimination. Customers are separated by how far in advance they have reserved their seat. The airline knows that a last-minute buyer is probably very desperate to fly to that destination and is therefore willing to pay a much higher price than a person who buys a month in advance. The one who buys months in advance is likely much more sensitive to a price and has the time to shop around for a better deal.

306. (A) An extreme form of price discrimination is one in which a customer pays a price equal to his or her maximum willingness to pay price. In this form of price discrimination, sometimes called perfect or first-degree price discrimination, if Sally would pay $10 for that book, that is the price she is charged. If James would pay only $5 for that book, that is the price he is charged at the same time Sally is charged $10 for the identical book. In this pricing scheme, all consumer surplus is taken by the firm. The difficulty, of course, is the firm's challenge in actually determining what each consumer is willing to pay.

307. (B) Only firms that have the ability to set different prices for their products have the possibility of engaging in price discrimination. It is also important that the firm prevents resale between customer groups. Suppose a child could buy a ticket to the movie for $4, but the adult must pay $8. An enterprising 10-year-old could buy many child tickets and resell them to adults in the parking lot for $6. If this happens, the price discrimination will not be effective. The firm will always try to determine which group of customers is least sensitive to a higher price and charge that group the higher price.

308. (A) If the firm has two or more groups of customers, each with different levels of price sensitivity, the firm will seek to exploit those differences in price elasticity of demand by charging the least sensitive group the highest of prices. After all, for that particular group, any percentage increase in price will be met with a smaller percentage decrease in quantity demanded, and total revenues from this group will rise. If a group is relatively elastic in their demand for movie tickets, any percentage decrease in price will cause a larger percentage increase in quantity demanded, and total revenues from that group will rise.

309. (D) A special kind of monopoly is a natural monopoly. These are extremely large producers, like public utilities, that can produce additional units of output at very low marginal and average total costs. Because of the large capital investment (a power plant) and infrastructure (the power grid), it is more cost-effective to have one large utility to supply power to an entire geographic region than it would be for several smaller firms to do the same, each at a smaller scale.

310. (E) The key to a natural monopoly is that the firm is so large that it is more efficient for this monopolist to supply the entire market than it would be for several smaller firms to divide the market. Efficiency in this case is measured by how cheaply the product can be produced. A huge firm with a vast range of economies of scale has, by definition, a long-run average total cost curve that diminishes with output.

311. (C) The primary reason that a monopolist can enjoy profits in the long run is because there are no firms competing for those profits. In perfect competition, short-run profitability is eliminated by long-run entry of new firms. As firms enter, the price is driven down and profits are driven to zero. The barriers to entry in a monopoly market protect those profits from competition—no firms entering means that the firm's profits will not decrease.

312. (A) Because the firm produces a product with no close substitutes, the demand for the firm's product is the same as the market demand for the product. This creates a situation such that the firm, rather than accepting a price set in the market, is able to set the price at the level that maximizes profit. For this reason, monopolies are sometimes called price makers to distinguish them from perfectly competitive price takers.

313. (B) The monopoly firm has a downward-sloping demand curve for its product; in fact, the demand for its product is also the market demand for the product. If the firm's price of each unit sold was equal to marginal revenue from that sold unit, the monopolist would produce the same quantity as would a perfectly competitive industry. But the marginal revenue for a monopolist is less than the price, so the point where marginal revenue intersects marginal cost occurs at a level of output that is below the competitive market output.

314. (C) Anytime a price is greater than average total cost, the firm is earning positive economic profit. This occurs for the monopolist, both in the short run and the long run, because there are barriers to entry. If new firms could enter the market, the price would fall until the profits were equal to zero.

315. (D) A firm in perfect competition has no control over the price, so every unit they sell earns marginal revenue equal to exactly the price. But if a monopoly firm has the ability to set the price, a lower price will increase quantity demanded, but the marginal revenue earned is less than the price. This happens because the monopolist must lower the price for all units, not just the next unit. Because the marginal revenue is less than the price, when the firm sets marginal revenue equal to marginal cost, the price will ultimately exceed marginal cost.

316. (C) Economic profit is the difference between the price of each unit sold, minus the average total cost of each unit produced, multiplied by the level of output. If the price is equal to the average total cost of each unit, the firm will just break even. To find this in the graph, find the intersection of average total cost and demand, because the demand curve gives the price for any quantity of output sold.

317. (D) The socially efficient (or allocatively efficient) level of output is produced at the output where price is equal to marginal cost. This is also the level of output that, because of its efficiency, produces zero deadweight loss. To find this point of efficiency, find the intersection of demand and marginal cost.

318. (A) An unregulated monopolist would produce where profits are maximized, and output (Q_1) is where marginal revenue equals marginal cost. The price (P_1) associated with this output is at the demand curve above Q_1. Regulating this firm would require output (Q_2) to be where price (P_3) is equal to average total cost. Thus the regulation would increase output by ($Q_2 - Q_1$) units and lower the price by ($P_1 - P_3$).

319. (E) A regulated monopolist that is required to break even would produce at output (Q_2) to be where price (P_3) is equal to average total cost. A new regulation requiring the firm to produce with no deadweight loss would require a price P_4 equal to marginal cost at output level Q_2. This particular regulation would increase output by ($Q_3 - Q_2$) units and decrease the price by ($P_3 - P_4$) dollars.

320. (D) The socially efficient level of output corresponds to the output where price is equal to marginal cost. A complete deregulation of the market would allow the firm to move to the profit-maximizing output and price combination. This type of deregulation decreases output by $(Q_3 - Q_1)$ units and increases the price by $(P_1 - P_4)$ dollars.

Chapter 11: Oligopoly

321. (B) Oligopoly industries are characterized by a few large producers who make up the majority share of production in an industry. For example, suppose an industry has 1,000 firms. Even though this is a large number of firms, the industry would be considered an oligopoly if two of those firms produced 90% of the goods in the market. Oligopoly industries are also characterized by barriers to entry. This is fairly intuitive: if these industries were easy to enter or easy to compete with on the basis of quantity, we would not see them dominated by a few large producers for very long. Finally, oligopoly markets can have either differentiated or standardized products, so seeing only one or the other doesn't really give us a clue about the market structure of the industry.

322. (D) In some sense, oligopolies are the vaguest type of industry in terms of their defining characteristics, having some things in common with monopolies and monopolistic competition. Barriers to entry such as patents and copyrights can exist in either monopolies or oligopolies. Since oligopolies and monopolistically competitive firms both can have differentiated products, there is incentive to advertise and further differentiate their goods (to get a higher price). The one true defining characteristic of oligopolies is mutual interdependence of price and quantity.

323. (A) Perfectly competitive industries have homogeneous (meaning standardized or identical) products, no barriers to entry, and many firms, each of which have little to no market power. Oligopoly firms are characterized by having either homogeneous or heterogeneous (meaning differentiated) products, so the two types of industries can have the feature of homogenous products in common. The degree of market power in an industry is sometimes measured in concentration ratios, which determine the degree to which a few industries control the production in the market. Note that an oligopoly would be characterized by a fairly high concentration ratio; a perfectly competitive industry on the other hand would have a concentration ratio at or near zero.

324. (C) Oligopolies can be described as being somewhere in between perfectly competitive markets and monopolies. A perfectly competitive market will always have the lowest price and highest quantity. A monopoly will have the highest price and lowest quantity. Therefore, it is not surprising that oligopoly industries tend to produce more than a monopoly, but also charge a higher price than a perfectly competitive industry would.

325. (B) An oligopoly industry is somewhere between a monopoly and perfect competition. A single-firm industry would be a monopoly, so there would need to be at least two firms in an industry for it to be considered an oligopoly. Such an industry with two firms is sometimes called a duopoly and is frequently used to illustrate many of the findings that we see in oligopoly industries in the simplest way.

326. (C) While there is no strict definition of the number of firms (in this case, babysitters would be the firms) in an industry, whenever there are only a few firms, it is very likely that the industry will behave as an oligopoly. A college campus with a single bookstore and a town with a single utility provider both describe monopolies. With its many suppliers and buyers, the market for tutoring would be perfectly competitive. The market for labor in which there are many sellers but only one buyer is a variation on monopoly called a monopsony.

327. (A) Oligopolies are sometimes determined not by the number of firms in an industry, but by how much of the market share a small number of firms have in a market. That is, even if there are many firms in a market, if a few firms dominate that market, then the industry will act as an oligopoly. One of the ways to measure the degree to which a few firms dominate an industry is to use a concentration ratio, which is simply the sum of the shares of a certain number of the largest firms. In this example, a four-firm concentration ratio would simply be the sum of the shares of the market held by each of the four largest firms, in this case, 35% + 25% + 11% + 6% = 77%, which means these four firms control 77% of the market for coffee in this town. The higher the degree of concentration, the more likely an industry is to behave as an oligopoly.

328. (C) An industry with a concentration ratio over 50% is likely to be an oligopoly. In general, concentration ratios between 50% and 80% are considered to be medium or moderately concentrated and are likely to behave as an oligopoly. Concentration over 80% is considered highly concentrated. Note that a concentration ratio of 100% is actually a single firm controlling the entire market, which would be a monopoly. An oligopsony is a special case of an oligopoly in which there are only a few sellers and only a few buyers.

329. (C) A cartel is a group of firms that agree to set either price or quantity in a market in order to generate an industrywide profit that is identical to what a monopoly would earn. By cooperating and choosing a price, firms can get a higher profit than they would if they were competing against each other.

330. (E) Oligopoly firms would like to be able to form cartels and earn monopoly profits. Unfortunately, several factors make it unlikely for firms to be able to successfully collude. First, collusion (such as price fixing) is illegal in the United States through a variety of anti-trust legislation, such as the Sherman Antitrust Act. Second, even if collusion were legal, once firms have agreed on a fixed price or quantity, they have incentives to "cheat" because doing so would be in their best interest. Firms that can secretly cheat on such agreements hope to increase profits even more than they would had they followed the agreement.

331. (B) The potential for long-run profits exist only for two kinds of industries: monopolies and oligopolies. For both, it is the existence of barriers to entry that create the potential for long-run profits. In the other types of industries, long-run profits become zero because anytime firms in an industry experience profits, more firms will enter and drive the profits down for the existing firms.

332. (D) Price leadership, where one firm first sets its price and other firms follow that firm's lead, is a form of tacit price collusion. In such a case, firms are essentially agreeing to not compete on the basis of price. While explicit pricing agreements are illegal in the United States, price leadership is not uncommon.

333. (B) There is an inherent tension in oligopolies between a firm's self-interest and the potential benefit of cooperating. If firms are able to cooperate, they could act as a monopoly and earn higher profits. However, once an agreement is made between firms, an oligopolist is frequently better off by breaking that agreement, which leads to the agreement ultimately breaking down. This is one of the reasons that even if there are no regulations against collusion, cartels have the tendency to break down.

334. (E) This question illustrates the interdependence of price in an oligopoly using the simplest kind of oligopoly, a duopoly (i.e., an oligopoly comprising two firms). The market price of Gloomps will depend on the number of Gloomps that are being sold in the market. If one firm produces 5 and the other firm produces 3, the market quantity, Q, is 8. Plugging Q = 8 into the market demand curve yields $8 = 20 - 2P$. Solving for P yields P = $6.

335. (C) This is an example of what is called a Cournot (or Cournot-Nash) duopoly, in which there are two firms that can produce a good at zero cost. If firms can collude, they then simply need to choose the market quantity that will give them the most revenue (firms are profit maximizers, but Profit = TR − TC, and since TC = 0, this means Profit = TR). To find profit, multiply the quantity that the cartel chooses by the price that the cartel will get for that quantity. If the cartel produces Q = 20, then $20 = 20 - 2P$ yields a price of zero, and the firm gets zero profits. If the duopoly produces 5 units, Q = 5 and $5 = 20 - 2P$ yields a price of $7.50, and a total revenue of $37.50. If you work through all of the possible combinations of P and Q in this market, a market quantity of 10, which yields a price of $5, yields the highest profit. (Hint: Construct a table with three columns: Q, P, and profit. Calculate the value of P and profit for each quantity, starting with 0, then 1, then 2, until you get to Q = 20. Then look for the line where profit is the highest.)

336. (B) This is an example of what is called a Bertrand duopoly. It is similar to a Cournot duopoly, but here firms choose a price that they want to get in the market and then produce the amount that gets them that price. At a price of $12 the industry profit is $48, which is the highest profit that the industry can get, and the two firms will produce a total of 4 units of the good.

337. (D) If the two firms are able to agree upon a price and quantity, they will set these at Q = 4 and P = $12 because this combination gives the industry the highest profits (industry profit = $48). If they split this equally between the two, each firm produces 2 units, which they each sell at a price of $12, which yields each firm a profit of $24. If one firm decides to increase their production by 1 unit, while the other firm remains at the agreed-upon quantity, the cheating firm will produce 3 units, the market quantity will be Q = 5, and each producer will get a price of $9. The cheating firm will get a profit of 3 × $9 = $27, and the firm that kept the agreement will make a profit of $18. This is why cartels tend to fall apart: unless the firms can enforce this agreement, they each have incentive to cheat.

338. (E) Tacit collusion can occur when regulation makes it illegal to make explicit agreements to set price or output. When firms engage in pricing strategies such as price wars, this may end up being very damaging to all of the firms involved. Instead, they may engage in actions such as price leadership to keep a price war from occurring.

339. (A) Game theory is a method of analyzing situations where strategic behavior occurs. In an oligopoly, a firm's profit will depend not just on its actions, but also on the actions of all of the other firms in a market. Therefore, oligopoly markets are ideally suited for analysis using game theory, as unlike the other types of industries, firms must behave strategically.

340. (B) The term *dominant strategy* refers to a strategy that a player should always play because it is always the best response to any strategy that the other player may do. If a strategy dominates other strategies, it means that the player will always get a better payoff playing the dominant strategy than he would get by playing any other strategies, regardless of what the other player or players do. A "best response," on the other hand, is a strategy that is the best choice to make, given a particular action taken by the other player or players.

341. (D) A Nash equilibrium is an outcome in which a player is playing his or her best response to another player's best response. It is a noncooperative outcome in the sense that this is the outcome we would expect to see if there is no cooperation between players. Each player takes an action that is in his or her best interest, given that all of the other players are also doing what is in their best interest as well, and do not take into account the effect of their actions on each other.

342. (E) Table 11.3 shows a payoff matrix for a two-firm taco industry. The Fajita Wagon's best choices will depend on what the other firm does, and for this reason they are called "best responses." If the Taco Bus chooses a low-price strategy, the Fajita Wagon will be better off if they also choose a low price. So the Fajita Wagon's best response to Taco Bus playing the low-price strategy is to play the low-price strategy. If the Taco Bus chooses a high price, the Fajita Wagon is best off if they play the low-price strategy, so the Fajita Wagon's best response to the other firm choosing a high price is to choose a low price.

343. (E) A Nash equilibrium occurs when all players are playing best responses to other players also playing best responses. Note that a Nash equilibrium is expressed as a combination of strategies and not the payoffs to those strategies. In this case, if Taco Bus plays the low-price strategy, Fajita Wagon's best response to that is to play the low-price strategy, and the best response for the Taco Bus to play if Fajita Wagon is choosing "low price" is also to play "low price."

344. (A) The reason that a Nash equilibrium is an equilibrium is that firms are doing the best they can in terms of maximizing their profit, given that other firms are also doing the best they can. Additionally, it is an equilibrium in the sense that once firms are playing these strategies, they have no incentive to alter their strategy. For instance, if Firm 1 were to suddenly change their strategy to Y, their profit would go down; so Firm 1 has no incentive to alter their strategy. Likewise, if Firm 2 changed their strategy to A, their profit would go down, so it would not make any sense for Firm 2 to change their strategy.

345. (C) A noncooperative equilibrium is another way of saying a Nash equilibrium. To find the noncooperative equilibrium, we find the equilibrium that we would expect to see if firms were unable to coordinate their actions. The Nash equilibrium in this situation is when Firm 1 plays the strategy X and Firm 2 plays the strategy B. Payoffs to a particular combination of strategies are read from the table as payoff to the player on the left, payoff to the player on the top.

346. (A) The set of strategies {A, Y} are unlikely to be played, because at least one player can make herself better off by altering her strategies if that is played. If the set of strategies {A, Y} is played, then Firm 1 has a payoff of $13 and Firm 2 has a payoff of $20. However, if Firm 1 knows that Firm 2 is going to play the strategy A, they could increase their payoff from $13 to $15 by changing their strategy to X.

347. (B) A dominant strategy is a strategy that one player always plays regardless what the other player does, because that one strategy is always the best response to anything the other player does. Whether Firm 2 plays A or B, Firm 1's best response is always to play the strategy X. Therefore, Firm 1 has a dominant strategy of X (and a dominated strategy of Y, since they would never play Y). Firm 2, on the other hand, does not have a dominant strategy. If Firm 1 plays the strategy X, Firm 2 is best off if they play the strategy B. However, if Firm 1 plays the strategy Y, Firm 2 is better off if they play the strategy A.

348. (D) Scott's dominant strategy is to confess. Note that this is a dominant strategy because it is the best strategy to choose for any of Ian's possible choices. It would not be correct that a dominant strategy is a dominant strategy only in certain situations. That would, by definition, make it not a dominant strategy because a dominant strategy is a strategy that is always the best strategy to play.

349. (C) This is a classic game known as the prisoner's dilemma. In this situation, the Nash equilibrium is (confess, confess) because it is a noncooperative outcome. The players would actually be better off if they could somehow cooperate and choose the strategies (don't confess, don't confess) because in that situation they each spend only two years in prison. Unfortunately, if they do play that set of strategies, both players immediately have an incentive to change their strategies, since if one player doesn't confess, the other player is better off by confessing. As a result, they both end up with a less than optimal outcome.

350. (E) The optimal set of strategies is the strategies that make players the best off possible without regard to strategy. In this situation, the optimal outcome is that each player spends only two years in prison. Note that this would be difficult to achieve, however, if both players are acting in their own interest.

351. (A) The outcome that would be predicted in this market is a Nash equilibrium outcome, because both firms act in their own self-interest, knowing that the other firm is also doing the same. If you set up a table that shows the strategies as well as the payoffs to the strategies each player can make, given what the other player chooses, you will find that both firms will advertise, and any attempt to change from that set of strategies will make the firm that alters its strategy worse off.

352. (C) Antitrust policies are designed to foster competitive markets and to deter the behaviors and anticompetitive outcomes of monopoly power. It is important to understand that antitrust laws do not forbid the growth of firms into very large and very profitable enterprises. They are in place to prevent business practices that can serve to manipulate markets, unfairly exploit consumers, or oppress competitors and suppliers.

353. (E) The Sherman Antitrust Act was really the landmark piece of legislation to attempt to curb some of the corporate abuses seen in the nineteenth century. At the time, prevailing opinion was that large firms were fixing prices and raising them to artificially high levels that could only be maintained through collusive cartel-like behavior. While more than 100 years old, the Sherman Act is still one of the foundations of antitrust laws today.

354. (D) If firms wish to form an illegal cartel to reduce output, raise prices, and earn monopoly profits, they must first come to an agreement on how best to accomplish this outcome. It is much easier to come to a collusive price-fixing agreement if the number of firms is small, they are of similar size, and they have similar cost structures. The more diverse the firms in the cartel, the more difficult it will be to form an agreement that suits all firms. If the agreement favors some firms over others, it is more likely to come undone.

Chapter 12: Monopolistic Competition

355. (C) Like other industries, the profit-maximizing choice of quantity for a firm in a monopolistically competitive industry is where the marginal revenue of that quantity is equal to the marginal cost of that quantity (MR = MC). However, a firm in a monopolistically competitive industry will have some control over the price it can charge as it faces a downward-sloping demand curve. Therefore, they will then go up to the demand curve to find the price that consumers are willing and able to pay for that quantity.

356. (B) Monopolistically competitive industries are similar to perfectly competitive industries in several ways, including having a large number of firms and no barriers to entry. The key way in which they differ, however, is that firms in monopolistically competitive industries sell products that are slightly different from each other, and as a result each firm has some control over price.

357. (E) Monopolistically competitive firms in essence have a monopoly over their own good, but they are competitive in the sense that there are a large number of other firms selling similar products. For instance, in the market for potato chips, one firm may have a distinctive kind of potato chip and be the only ones selling that distinctive chip, but there are many other firms also selling their own style of potato chips. At first glance, C may appear to be correct because monopolistically competitive firms do in fact choose the quantity where MR = MC. However, since firms in all four of the industries do this, it does not make them distinctively monopoly-like in nature.

358. (E) Monopolistically competitive industries are characterized by (i) a large number of firms with a small share of the market (similar to perfect competition), (ii) each producing a slightly differentiated product (like a monopoly, since they have a "monopoly" over their own distinct good), and (iii) having low barriers to entry (similar to perfect competition).

359. (B) The monopolistically competitive firm has the same profit-maximizing rule as in other types of industries: the profit-maximizing choice of quantity will be the point at which the marginal cost curve intersects the marginal revenue curve. This intersection occurs at the quantity of Q_1. However, the firm then chooses to set a price on the demand curve by finding the price (in the graph, it is P_a) on the demand curve that corresponds to that quantity.

360. (D) The output Q_1 represents the profit-maximizing choice of quantity for this firm. To find the marginal cost of Q_1 units, we find the point on the marginal cost curve associated with this quantity, which is P_d (also the point where MR = MC). Note, however, that the price that this firm will charge for Q_1 units is P_a, so in this situation $P_a > P_d$, which means that the price exceeds the marginal cost for this quantity.

361. (B) The area is a rectangle represented by the difference between the price of the good (P_a), the cost per unit of producing the good that can be found on the ATC curve (P_c), and the quantity that is sold in the market (Q_1). Students frequently (and mistakenly) use the point on the marginal cost curve to calculate the cost. However, the marginal cost tells you only what it cost to make the last unit of production (in other words, what it cost to produce the Q_1th unit) but not what the typical cost per unit is.

362. (D) In the long run, monopolistically competitive firms earn zero economic profit, so the price will be at a point just tangent to the average total cost (ATC) curve. Since this firm is currently earning positive profits in the short run (at price P_a), the price must eventually fall below this short-run price. Price P_d is below the ATC curve and would never be a long-run price. Note that this also implies that even in the long run, the price that the firm charges will be higher than marginal cost.

363. (C) In a monopolistically competitive industry, if firms are earning economic profits, as the firm in Figure 12.1 is, then other firms will enter the industry as well. This effectively reduces the size of the market for this firm, so the demand curve for their product (along with the marginal revenue curve) will decrease. This will continue until the firm is earning zero economic profits.

364. (B) The firm shown in Figure 12.1 is making positive economic profits because the price that the good is being sold at is greater than the average total cost of the quantity being sold. It could not be a monopolistically competitive firm in the long run. The monopoly graph is identical in the long run and in the short run, so neither A nor D is correct. Since the graph has a downward-sloping demand for the firm's good, it cannot be a perfectly competitive firm in the short run or the long run.

365. (C) Of these types of firms, only the monopolistically competitive industry has incentive to advertise. While not a choice, whether or not a monopoly has an incentive to advertise is debatable. On the one hand, the monopolist is the only firm in its industry, so it doesn't need to persuade customers to buy their good versus another firm's good. On the other hand, advertising would shift the monopoly demand curve to the right, increasing profits without sparking entry of new firms. A perfectly competitive industry doesn't have any incentive to advertise either: it can already sell whatever quantity it desires at the market price and cannot control price, so the only effect advertising would have is to increase their costs.

366. (A) The profit-maximizing rule says that a firm will always choose the quantity where MC = MR. In the long run, however, the monopolistically competitive firm will face a smaller and smaller market (due to entry of new firms) for their good until the demand curve is just tangent to the ATC. This means that when they find the Q where MC = MR and then go up to the demand curve to set the price, they will be setting the price where P = ATC.

367. (D) People enjoy variety, and even if this is not an explicit goal of buyers or sellers in a monopolistically competitive industry, it is a side effect of each producer selling a slightly differentiated good. For instance, consider the market for potato chips. In a perfectly competitive industry, there is only one style and one flavor of potato chips. Similarly, in a monopoly, there is also only one style or flavor. However, suppose someone wants to enter the potato chip market and it is monopolistically competitive. For a firm to take business away from the existing firms, they will need to introduce something new and different, and since consumers like variety, they get a positive benefit of another firm entering by virtue of another choice.

368. (B) Unfortunately, when another firm enters a monopolistically competitive market, all the firms already in the market suffer. Consider, for instance, the market for apartments in a university town where there is a fixed pool of potential tenants of 10,000 students. If there are 200 apartment complexes, then the students are split among these 200 firms. However, if the 201st firm opens, the pool of 10,000 students will be divided by 201 firms. Because another firm has entered, all existing firms are made worse off even if they haven't changed.

369. (C) A monopolistically competitive firm engages in advertising to differentiate their products, which may slow down the entry of new firms in the market. However, advertising does not erect barriers to entry, so the industry will eventually return to break-even profits. The firm is able to slow down or reverse the loss of market share to new firms, but ultimately it cannot stop other firms from entering.

370. (D) If P > MC, the firm must have some control over the price of their product. This occurs with monopolies and monopolistically competitive industries. For a perfectly competitive firm, it is true that P = MC = MR, and the firm can sell whatever quantity it wants and cannot reduce output to raise revenue. A monopoly has P > MC, but they have a small incentive to advertise because it is impossible for firms to enter the market and take away market share. The only firm with a strong incentive to advertise would therefore be the one who had control over their price (P > MC) and had the potential to lose market share to competitors (no barriers to entry).

371. (B) In the long run, as firms enter a monopolistically competitive industry with short-run profits, the demand curve that each firm faces shifts to the left. It will continue to shift to the left as more firms enter until the demand curve is just tangent to the average total cost curve. If the industry is experiencing short-run losses, firms will exit. The demand curve for each existing firm shifts to the right until demand is tangent to average total cost. In either case, in the long run the monopolistically competitive firm is producing at the point where MR = MC, and the price that they charge for the good is P = ATC; the firm is not making any profit.

372. (E) This graph represents a monopolistically competitive firm in the long run. We can determine this because the demand curve is just tangent with the average total cost curve at the point where MR = MC. At the quantity where MR = MC, the marginal cost of that quantity is u, the cost per unit (ATC) of that quantity is s, and the price that is charged for that quantity is also s. Since (P − ATC) = ($s − s$) = 0, the profit for each of the units produced is zero.

373. (D) Firms in monopolistically competitive industries produce a quantity where P > MC because they have some control over price. This price is also equal to average total cost (P = ATC) because the demand for the firm's good will adjust until the firm is earning zero profits in the long run. The quantity that the firm chooses will be smaller than the quantity that minimizes the cost per unit of production. Because the firm charges P > MC, there is deadweight loss; however, because the firm has less control over price than a monopolist does, the firm would have less deadweight loss than a monopolist.

374. (A) Excess capacity is the additional quantity that could be produced if a firm is not using all of its resources in a cost-effective way, achieving productive efficiency. If the firm increased its production from v to z units, it would be producing a productively efficient quantity because this is where average total cost is minimized. In this graph, the productively efficient quantity is z, and the quantity that the firm will choose to produce will be v. Therefore, the difference between these, z − v, is the excess capacity.

375. (E) Deadweight loss occurs when a firm does not produce a quantity where the demand curve intersects the marginal cost curve. The marginal cost and demand curves intersect each other at quantity w, but since MR = MC at v units, this is the amount that the firm produces. Deadweight loss also occurs when the firm charges a price where P > MC. Here, the firm will charge a price of s for v units, but the marginal cost of v units is only u. This deadweight loss is the area of a triangle with a height of (s − u) and a width of (w − v) units.

376. (A) Allocative efficiency refers to a situation in which there is no deadweight loss. This only occurs when a firm charges a price equal to the marginal cost of production (P = MC). Productive efficiency occurs when a firm produces the quantity that minimizes the cost per unit of production (i.e., at the lowest point on the ATC curve). A monopolistically competitive industry is neither productively efficient nor allocatively efficient in the long run or the short run.

377. (C) The definition of excess capacity is producing an output less than the output that would minimize average total cost. What this means is that the firm is underutilizing its plant or equipment and is producing a less than optimal output. If a firm has excess capacity, it would lower its cost per unit if it increased its capacity.

378. (C) The absence of barriers to entry is what drives a monopolistically competitive firm's long-run profits to zero. Suppose that firms are earning positive profits in the short run. When a new firm enters the market, even if the new product offered by the new firm is slightly different from the incumbent firm, the new firm will "steal" some of the market share from the incumbent firm. This will cause the demand for the incumbent firm's product to decrease until P = ATC.

379. (A) When a firm sells a product that is slightly different from other goods, they have some control over their price. While a perfectly competitive firm will charge a price equal to marginal cost (P = MC = MR), the monopolistically competitive firm will choose the quantity where MR = MC, but because people are willing and able to pay a price above the MR for that quantity, the price charged will be higher than that of a perfectly competitive firm.

380. (B) Because each firm produces a product that is similar, but differentiated from, the products sold by the other firms, each firm has a product with characteristics that can be advertised to consumers. We might think of several restaurants in town that each has a slightly different menu. They each sell appetizers, entrées, salads, and desserts, but they offer the dining customer a different menu and experience. These differences can be advertised to steal customers from rival restaurants and increase short-run profits for each firm.

381. (B) Because a monopolistically competitive firm has some control over the price it charges for its good as its good is slightly different from all other goods, the firm charges a P > MC. Whenever a firm charges a price greater than MC, it drives a wedge between the price that people are willing to pay for a good and the amount that it actually cost to produce that last good.

382. (C) Perfectly competitive industries produce the largest quantity because they have no control over price. It might be tempting to say that perfectly competitive industries produce the most because they have no barriers to entry. Note, however, that monopolistically competitive industries produce less than perfectly competitive industries, yet they also have no barriers to entry.

383. (D) Holding other factors constant, as the number of firms increases, the market becomes more competitive. If an oligopoly of 4 firms grows to include 40 firms or even 400 firms, the market outcome starts to become closer to that of a perfectly competitive industry. As more firms enter, the market power (i.e., the ability to individually control the price) of a firm goes down. The simplest comparison is that of monopoly to perfect competition. In monopoly, there is only one producer with absolute control over the price. In perfect competition, there are many firms, each with no control over the price. Naturally there are other factors, like product differentiation and barriers to entry, but all else equal, we can generally say that as the number of firms increases, the industry will become more and more competitive.

384. (D) The source of long-run profits is barriers to entry. Both monopolies and oligopolies have barriers to entry, which means that these industries have the potential for long-run profits. Because monopolistically competitive markets and perfectly competitive markets have no barriers to entry, in each of these types of industries, firms will enter and push down price until each firm is making no economic profit.

385. (E) Allocative efficiency means that there is no deadweight loss. This occurs only if firms charge a price that is equal to marginal cost. This occurs only in two situations. First, if a firm has no control over price, P = MR for all units sold, so when profit is maximized, P = MR = MC. The other situation is if a firm, usually a monopoly, is able to perfectly price discriminate. For this firm, price will equal marginal revenue for each unit sold and the firm will sell to the point where P = MR = MC. In this situation, however, there is no consumer surplus.

386. (D) The market for published books is monopolistically competitive, since there are a large number of sellers, the authors, selling slightly differentiated products. Because there are no barriers to entry (anyone can write and sell a book), this will push long-run profits to zero. If the books were identical to each other, then this would be a perfectly competitive market, and the price in a perfectly competitive market is lower than the price in a monopolistically competitive market.

387. (B) The two extremes of competition, monopoly and perfect competition, are actually the rarest of the four industries. If you consider the features of the goods and services that are offered around you, it is apparent that you rarely, if ever, see markets that exhibit these features. Oligopolies and monopolistically competitive industries are far more common in the real world.

Chapter 13: Factor Markets

388. (C) Supply and demand analysis in factor markets is done in the very same way as it is done in output markets. The only difference is that the product and factor markets are connected because the output of one (peppers) is a function of the other (pepper pickers). An increase in demand for the product causes an increase in the labor required to produce the product. The increase in demand causes equilibrium wages to rise and employment to rise in the labor market.

389. (B) The weak demand for large appliances causes the equilibrium price of appliances to fall. Because the demand for the workers that assemble the appliances is a function of both the marginal productivity and the price of the output (value of the marginal product), a falling price of appliances causes the demand for assembly workers to also decrease. As the demand for workers falls, it causes both wages and employment to fall.

390. (A) When we talk about production functions, we say that output is a function of the quantity of labor employed. While this is true, it is also true that the quantity of labor employed is a function of how much output is being sold and the price at which the output is selling. Thus the demand for factors of production is said to be derived from the demand for the product being produced by the factor.

391. (E) Since we are told that wages and employment in the market for autoworkers have both increased, it is likely due to an increase in the demand for autoworkers. The rising demand for labor can occur if the price of a substitute factor rises, the price of a complementary factor falls, the marginal productivity of the labor rises, or the price of the product rises. A rising demand for cars would increase the quantity of cars bought and the price of cars, thus boosting the demand for the autoworkers.

392. (D) The labor market for carpenters will be very sensitive to the demand for construction projects. A recession decreases the demand for many products, but because new homes are so expensive, the demand for new homes will fall by a great amount. A decreased demand for new homes will also cause the price of the homes to fall in the housing market. All other choices describe situations that would cause the demand for housing or other construction projects to increase.

393. (B) As mobile phones become more popular, the demand for phones increases, increasing the equilibrium price of mobile phones. The rising price and rising output of the phones both cause the demand for the assembly workers to increase. The stronger demand for the workers would also cause the wage of those workers and their total employment to rise.

394. (C) Each worker, through his or her production, contributes dollar value to the firm. This dollar value is the marginal product of that worker multiplied by the price at which the additional output is sold. Given the price of the good (P), this value of the marginal product for any worker is $VMP_L = P \times MP_L$. Because the price of the output is $2 and the marginal product of the fifth worker is 12 units, the $VMP_L = \$2 \times 12 = \$24$.

395. (A) A worker's value of the marginal product to the firm is the price of the product multiplied by that worker's marginal product. Because the $VMP_L = P \times MP_L$, we can use what we know to solve for the thing that we don't know. We know from Table 13.1 that the marginal product of the seventh worker is 6 units of output, and we are told that the value of the marginal product is $15 for that worker. We can then use the equation to solve for price: $P = VMP_L/MP_L = \$15/6 = \$2.50$.

396. (E) A firm hires labor up to the point where the additional dollars earned from the unit of labor are equal to the additional cost of employing that unit of labor. The additional cost of a unit of labor is the competitive wage of $45. The additional dollars earned are found by computing the value of the marginal product for each worker: $VMP_L = P \times MP_L$. We are told that the competitive price of output is $3, so we multiply each marginal product in Table 13.1 by $3 and see that the value of the marginal product is $45 at the fourth unit of labor. The fifth unit of labor won't be employed, because VMP_L of $36 falls below the wage of $45. In other words, the fifth unit of labor is only worth $36, so if a firm has to pay $45 for that unit of labor, it won't be willing to hire that unit.

397. (D) The demand for labor can be thought of as the maximum price a firm would pay to employ a particular quantity of labor. To derive this maximum price, we must figure out how much benefit the firm receives from each unit of labor employed. This benefit is the value of the marginal product, and this is the price of the product being sold multiplied by the marginal product of labor: $VMP_L = P \times MP_L$. Because the marginal product of labor diminishes with more labor employed, the firm's demand for labor is downward sloping.

398. (B) The labor demand curve is the value of the marginal product (VMP_L), and this curve slopes downward due to the diminishing marginal product of labor. If the wage were to fall in the labor market, Jerry would increase employment along the fixed VMP_L curve. However, if the price of crunks increases in the product market, the VMP_L increases for any quantity of labor. This creates an upward (or rightward) shift of the curve. Since the competitive market wage is constant, Jerry will find that he can increase his profits by hiring more workers.

399. (A) There are many combinations of labor and capital that can produce a given level of output, but only one combination produces that output at the lowest possible cost. Suppose that the ratio of MP_L/w (marginal product of labor per dollar spent on labor) is greater than the MP_K/r (marginal product of capital per dollar spent on capital). In other words: $MP_L/w > MP_K/r$. This inequality tells us that the firm can spend one dollar hiring labor and that labor will provide more production than a dollar spent on capital; the firm should hire more labor and less capital. As more labor is hired, the MP_L falls, and as less capital is hired, the MP_K rises. On the other hand, what if $MP_L/w < MP_K/r$? This inequality tells us that the firm can spend one dollar hiring capital and that capital will provide more production than a dollar spent on labor; the firm should hire more capital and less labor. In each of these cases, the firm can reshuffle the hiring of labor and capital to produce the same level of output at lower and lower cost. The only time such cost savings are impossible is when $MP_L/w = MP_K/r$.

400. (C) If Sarah were using the least-cost combination of labor and capital to produce a certain level of output, she will have found the combination such that $MP_L/w = MP_K/r$. To check, we use the information given. The marginal product of labor per dollar is (5 units)/$20 = .25 units per dollar. The marginal product of capital per dollar is (2 units)/$20 = .10 units per dollar. This comparison tells us that Sarah should reallocate her money by employing more labor and less capital. This will allow her to produce the same level of output but at lower total cost.

401. (D) Although Ricky has already found his least-cost combination of labor and capital, a changing price of capital can disrupt this equilibrium and cause him to recalibrate his optimal hiring. Initially, it is true that $MP_L/w = MP_K/r$. Once the price of capital falls, it is now the case that $MP_L/w < MP_K/r$, and capital is now providing more output per dollar. As Ricky starts to increase his hiring of capital, he reduces his hiring of labor, and thus the ratio of capital to labor (K/L) begins to increase.

402. (E) Each individual makes his own labor supply decision at each market wage. The total market supply of labor is the sum of each individual decision. Therefore, at a wage of $20, the total labor hours supplied is 120 hours (20 + 60 + 40). The total labor hours supplied at a wage of $30 is 130 hours (40 + 50 + 40).

403. (B) Each worker, at any given wage, has to choose how many hours of work to supply to the labor market and how many hours of leisure to consume. If the worker chooses to consume an hour of leisure, there is an opportunity cost equal to the wage that could have been earned by working. When the wage rises, it creates conflicting effects on this decision. On the one hand, each hour of leisure is now more costly and this prompts a substitution effect where the worker increases hours of labor and decreases hours of leisure. On the other hand, earnings are now higher at any hours of work supplied, which creates an income effect, assuming that leisure is a normal good, that prompts more consumption of leisure and fewer hours of labor supplied. If a higher wage causes the worker to supply more hours of labor, it must be the case that the substitution effect outweighs the income effect and the labor supply curve is upward sloping. However, if the income effect outweighs the substitution effect, the labor supply curve will bend backward and be downward sloping. Ted is the only worker who exhibits fewer hours of labor supplied at a higher wage.

404. (C) The first two statements are incorrect. Jeffrey's labor supply curve is upward sloping because he continues to increase his hours of labor supplied as the wage rises; his labor supply curve does not have a downward-sloping range. Between the wages of $10 and $20, Ted increases his hours of work. The higher wage creates a substitution effect that would cause him to increase work and decrease leisure, but the higher wage also causes an income effect that would cause him to increase leisure and decrease work. Since we know that he has actually increased work, his substitution effect must be stronger than his income effect between those two wages. John's labor supply curve is vertical, or perfectly inelastic, because he continues to supply 40 hours of work at all wages.

405. (B) Relative to current equilibrium, point a is on the demand curve and left of point c. This location indicates that the supply of labor must have decreased along the demand curve. If the government were to create something that made it more difficult for individuals to offer labor in this market, the supply curve would shift to the left. This type of rule exists in some occupations that require licensing, a certification, or the passing of an exam before a person can work.

406. (D) Relative to current equilibrium, point b is on the supply curve and right of point c. This location indicates that the demand for labor must have increased along the supply curve. If the price of a substitute factor has increased, firms will increase their demand for the labor as a way to produce the same output at lower production costs.

407. (A) Relative to current equilibrium, point d is on the demand curve and right of point c. This location indicates that the supply of labor must have increased along the demand curve. If more workers qualify for this occupation, the supply curve will shift outward. This can happen because of demographic trends, immigration, or growing popularity of a particular field of study in high school and college.

408. (C) Relative to current equilibrium, point e is on the supply curve and left of point c. This location indicates that the demand for labor must have decreased along the supply curve. If the demand for the good being produced by the labor is getting weaker, both the equilibrium price and quantity are falling in that product market. These two changes in the output market contribute to a decreased demand for this labor in the factor market.

409. (E) An effective minimum wage is a price floor in the labor market (your text may also refer to it as a *binding minimum wage*). The minimum wage is set at a wage that exceeds the equilibrium wage and creates a gap between the quantity of labor supplied and the quantity of labor demanded. The higher wage causes more workers to supply hours to the market but reduces the quantity of hours demanded by employers. This surplus in the labor market won't be resolved by market forces, because the law prevents the wage from falling back to equilibrium.

410. (D) When only one producer exists in an output market, we call it a monopoly. When only one buyer (or employer) exists in a factor market, we call it a monopsony. A monopsonist employer is hard to imagine in a large urban setting where there are plenty of firms competing for available workers, but it can emerge in a small town or isolated community. For example, if there is only one hospital in a rural community, there is only one place for a person with a nursing degree to find employment, unless he or she wants to relocate to another town.

411. (A) The total factor cost (TFC) is the quantity of the factor employed (labor in this case) multiplied by the wage each unit of labor is paid. In other words, total factor cost is the total payment made to labor, or payroll. Marginal factor cost (MFC) is the change in total factor cost divided by the change in the quantity of labor employed: MFC = (ΔTFC/ΔL). In this problem, labor is being employed 1 unit at a time. The total factor cost of employing six workers is TFC = 9×6 = $54, and the total factor cost of employing seven workers is TFC = 10×7 = $70, so the marginal factor cost of the seventh worker is $70 − $54 = $16.

412. (B) A monopsonist employer must find the quantity of labor where the value of the marginal product is equal to the marginal factor cost. The value of the marginal product of labor is given in Table 13.3, and it represents the labor demand curve. The marginal factor cost (MFC) is the change in total factor cost (TFC) at each level of employment. At 3 units of labor, TFC = $18, and at 4 units of labor, TFC = $28, so the MFC for the fourth worker is $10. The value of the marginal product at the fourth worker is also $10, so the firm will employ four workers. However, the wage is not $10, it is the $7 wage necessary to entice four workers to supply their labor. It is important to note that a wage-setting monopsonist is a firm that ends up paying their workers a wage that is below the value of the marginal product.

413. (A) Melanie, like any employer, must find the quantity of labor where the marginal cost is equal to the marginal benefit of employment. Because the labor market is competitive, the marginal cost of employment is the wage. The marginal benefit of employment is the value of the marginal product. If the output market was competitive, the VMP_L = $P \times MP_L$. Because Melanie is a monopolist, she doesn't receive exactly the price for each unit of output sold, she receives marginal revenue that is less than the price. Melanie's VMP_L (or more correctly called the marginal revenue product MRP_L) therefore lies below, or to the left of, a perfectly competitive firm's VMP_L. This situation produces an outcome where the intersection of Melanie's labor demand curve with the wage will happen at a quantity of labor that is to the left of a perfectly competitive firm's intersection.

414. (C) A factor market for capital operates in much the same way as the factor market for labor. If labor is a substitute factor for many employers, and the price of labor falls, firms will increase employment of labor and decrease the demand for capital. In the capital market, equilibrium price (or the rate) and quantity both fall.

415. (A) A government subsidy for capital investment effectively lowers the cost of purchasing capital equipment for the firm. This subsidy would shift the supply curve in the capital market to the right (an increase in supply), thus putting downward pressure on the capital rate. In equilibrium the quantity of capital employed will increase.

416. (E) Capital is a substitute factor for labor. This means that employers can use capital and labor interchangeably. But capital and land are complementary factors, so this means that if more of one input is being used, more of the other input will also be used. Since capital is now less expensive, the demand for the substitute, labor, will decrease. Since more capital is being used (and also because it is less expensive), we will see firms increase their demand for land.

417. (C) A decrease in the supply of capital in the capital market will cause the capital rate to increase, and less capital would be employed by firms. Because the other factors, land and labor, are complementary with the capital, this will cause the demand for land and the demand for labor to both decrease.

Chapter 14: Externalities

418. (C) We expect a good to provide benefit to those who actually consume it, but sometimes one person's consumption of a good provides benefit to another person who is not directly consuming that good. When a third party (i.e., someone who is neither a buyer nor seller in an exchange) receives this external benefit from the consumption or production of a good, it is called a positive externality.

419. (B) Ted is receiving the private benefit from the sale of his honey, but in the process of producing the honey, his bees are benefiting Jane's orange grove. Jane is the recipient of this external benefit, and therefore we would say that a positive externality exists in the production of honey.

420. (A) When buyers and sellers exchange a good or a service in a market, both parties expect to gain from the transaction. The buyer receives private benefit, and the seller receives revenue. However, there are times when this private exchange generates benefit to third parties not actually involved in the exchange. This external benefit is referred to as a positive externality.

421. (D) Public education is a positive externality because the benefits from education go beyond the private benefits received by the students receiving the education. A more educated community is typically more prosperous and has higher property values, more tax revenue for government services, less crime, and fewer social problems. The other choices in the question are situations usually associated with pollution and risks to our health.

422. (E) A flu shot reduces the chance that Steve gets the flu, but this is the private benefit enjoyed by the recipient of the shot. The reason the flu shot is a positive externality is that other people, like his teachers and classmates, also receive a benefit (a lower chance of getting the flu) from Steve's vaccination.

423. (A) The production of paper creates costs, in the form of inputs that must be employed, for the Houseweyer firm, but these are the private costs of producing paper. If the neighborhood downwind of the paper plant is experiencing an unpleasant smell and lower property values, then there are external costs of producing paper. These external costs are the essence of a negative externality. In other words, the firm is not considering the full costs of its production when making decisions.

424. (C) A transaction in a market creates both cost and benefit for buyers and sellers. The seller must incur the private cost in hiring inputs to produce the good or service, but sometimes third parties outside of the market suffer costs. When this happens, it is said that the market is generating a negative externality. A good example of external costs is the adverse health effect of pollution.

425. (D) When the production or consumption of a good or service creates an external cost on a third party, it is called a negative externality. These costs can often come in the form of pollution (air, water, noise, etc.) that is a by-product of market activities. Deadweight loss is the result of a negative externality, not the factor that generates the externality; the external costs to third parties cause the deadweight loss.

426. (C) When Jesse purchased the stereo, he incurred private cost and the stereo store received a private benefit. Jesse enjoys a private benefit from the use of his stereo, but JJ does not. Because of the loud music, the rattling of the windows, and the difficulty sleeping, JJ is experiencing a negative externality from the stereo.

427. (E) A corporation's factory employs factors of production (inputs) and incurs private costs in that employment. However, if the production process also creates harmful pollution, then the factors of production are not the only costs of producing that good. The harm from the pollution imposes external costs on society, and this is a negative externality in the market.

428. (B) Whenever there is a positive externality, at each level of output society benefits more than the individual(s) buying the product. In other words, the marginal social benefit (MSB) of a good is higher than the marginal private benefit (MPB) of the good at each quantity. Graphically, this appears as a marginal social benefit curve that is above the demand curve (which represents private social benefit).

429. (A) The graph shows a marginal social cost (MSC) curve that lies above the marginal private cost (MPC) curve. The MPC curve represents the costs incurred by producers of gizmos in their employment of inputs. The vertical distance between MSC and MPC is the external cost upon society from the production of gizmos; a negative externality exists.

430. (B) The market for gizmos will not recognize the marginal social cost, only the marginal private cost of producing gizmos. Therefore, the market comes to equilibrium at the intersection of the MPC and MSB = MPB curves; Q_2 units are produced at a price of P_2. Due to the presence of the external costs, the socially efficient quantity of gizmos would occur at the intersection of the MSC and the MSB = MPB curves; Q_1 units should be produced at a higher price of P_1.

431. (C) The market for gizmos is generating a negative externality because the marginal social cost exceeds the marginal private cost of producing them. The market will fail to recognize the external cost (the vertical distance between MSC and MPC), so the market will produce too many gizmos at Q_2 at a low price of P_2. If those external costs were internalized, the efficient quantity of gizmos would be lower at Q_1 and the price would reflect those external costs at the higher P_1. At this quantity and price, MPB = MSB = MSC, but MSC > MPC.

432. (D) This is the very definition of a positive externality. Whenever a positive externality exists, as it does in the market for education, there are external benefits to the broader society on top of the private benefits to consumers of education. On an incremental basis, this tells us that the marginal social benefit (MSB) curve lies above the marginal private benefit (MPB) curve.

433. (D) The market price of a goozum is $12, so this tells us that the marginal private benefit to consumers of goozums is $12. But if the private consumption of a goozum creates $1 of extra benefit to someone else, it must be the case that the marginal social benefit is $13. For any quantity of goozums, the marginal social benefit is the market price (or marginal private benefit) plus the external benefit to third parties.

434. (B) The graph shows that the MSB curve lies above the MPB curve. This vertical distance is the external benefit society receives from the market for smoke grinders. The market will not recognize these external benefits, so it will produce a quantity Q_2 (where MPB = MSC = MPC) that is lower than the efficient quantity of Q_3 (where MSB = MSC = MPC). The market price P_2 will be lower than the efficient price of P_3. Deadweight loss exists because the market is producing below the socially efficient level.

435. (A) Deadweight loss exists because the socially efficient quantity of smoke grinders is not being produced in this market. The efficient quantity exists only if there is some way for the market to recognize that there are external benefits to society (MSB > MPB) from consuming and producing smoke grinders. If this is not the case, not enough smoke grinders will be produced.

436. (C) The smoke grinder market is producing a quantity of Q_2 at a price of P_3, but because of the positive externality, this quantity is inefficiently low and the price is too low. If the external benefits were internalized, the efficient quantity would be Q_3 smoke grinders at a price of P_2. The triangle between the efficient and inefficient quantities, and bounded by the MSB and MPB curves, gives us the deadweight loss. This triangle is $(Q_3 - Q_2)$ units wide and $(P_1 - P_3)$ dollars high.

437. (E) When pollution, a common source of negative externality, exists in a market, the external costs of that pollution will not be captured by the market. This creates a gap between the marginal private costs and the higher marginal social costs of production. Because the market ignores the marginal social costs, too much of this good will be produced, thus generating deadweight loss.

438. (D) The table tells us that there are marginal social costs in the market for plastics; a negative externality exists. The market equilibrium will not recognize those $4 of marginal social costs, so the equilibrium will occur where the MSB = MPB = MPC, and this occurs at a price of $10 and quantity of 6 units.

439. (A) The socially efficient quantity of plastics would be produced if the marginal social cost of producing plastics were equal to the marginal social and private benefit. The marginal social cost is the sum of the marginal private cost column and the external cost column of data. The MSC = MSB = MPB occurs at a quantity of 4 and a price of $12.

440. (B) Because the market for plastics will recognize only the marginal private costs, the Pigouvian (or per-unit) tax on plastics must be added to the MPC data so that the market will move to the efficient quantity. The optimal tax must therefore be equal to the external cost of producing plastics, and in the table that cost is equal to $4 per unit.

441. (C) The premise of the Coase theorem is that direct negotiations between parties can remedy the impact of a negative externality if the right to pollute, or the right to be safe from pollution, is clearly established. In this case, Danielle is the victim of a negative externality. The Coase theorem suggests that the sewage treatment facility could continue to occasionally pollute the river but would compensate Danielle for the damage to her profits. While a tax would lessen the pollution, this would not be a solution suggested by the Coase theorem.

442. (D) When the government dictates strict limits on pollution, the policies are deemed command-and-control. The government gives the command to producers like Killdeer, and then Killdeer must act to control their sludge emissions. These policies can be effective, but economists find them to usually be an inefficient way to reduce pollution. Per-unit taxes and tradable pollution permits can often achieve the same goal of reducing pollution at lower cost to society.

443. (E) The Coase theorem offered an alternative to direct intervention by the government in solving the market failures of externalities. The idea is very simple. If the number of people affected by the externality is small, the parties should be able to meet to discuss a solution. Theoretically, this solution would be efficient and less costly than involving government regulators or litigation.

444. (A) When a positive externality exists in a market, the market is not producing enough of the good or service, because the marginal social benefit of flu shots exceeds the marginal private benefit. If buyers of flu shots were given a subsidy equal to the external benefit, more people would pay for a flu shot and the market would get closer to the efficient quantity.

445. (C) When there is a free-rider effect, it means that some people are enjoying the benefit of a good or service without paying for it. In other words, the good or service is non-excludable. In this situation, private firms will find it impossible to profitably supply the good or service; not enough will be supplied by the market. Since the good or service is underproduced by the market, the government or nonprofit charities must step in to provide it.

446. (A) A negative production externality describes a situation where there are spillover costs to society that go above and beyond the direct private costs of producing a good. The market supply curve reflects only the marginal private cost (MPC) of hiring inputs, but the spillover costs should be added to those marginal private costs to compute marginal social costs (MSC); therefore, MSC > MPC.

447. (B) Positive externalities in market X mean that there are spillover benefits to society that are added to the private benefits. The private benefits are enjoyed by consumers making purchases in market X. However, if there are spillover benefits, others outside the market (third parties) are also enjoying something about the good in market X.

Chapter 15: Public and Private Goods

448. (A) A compact car is a private good because it has two important characteristics: it is rival and it is excludable. Private goods are rival because once a consumer has purchased that particular car, nobody else can buy that same car. Private goods are also excludable because the seller can prevent a person from owning a car if that person is unwilling or unable to pay the going price.

449. (E) Public goods, like space exploration and other forms of scientific research, are those things that are both nonrival and nonexcludable. Something is nonrival if one person's consuming of 1 unit of the good does not prevent the next person from consuming that unit. There are really no consumable units for space research. A public good is nonexcludable if there is no way to prevent someone from the benefits of the good even if he or she is not paying for it. The knowledge gained from research or exploration is knowledge that all persons benefit from.

450. (B) The excludability characteristic of private goods is what allows for them to be exchanged in a market. Sellers can exclude a potential buyer from buying a good if that person is not willing or able to pay the price. If the good is distributed in a market, it ends up being sold to those who are willing and able to pay the market price.

451. (E) A gallon of gasoline is a private good for two reasons: it is excludable and rival. The excludability characteristic is very important. If the owner of a gas station must give a gallon of gasoline to every person who wants one, even if they were not going to pay the price for it, the seller would not be in business very long.

452. (A) Dottie's bakery is happy to sell a customer an apple pie but will only do so if that person has $10 to spend on the pie. This property of excludability makes Dottie's apple pies an example of a private good. If the pies were nonexcludable, she could not profitably sell them, because she would be giving her pies to all persons, even those who did not have $10 to spend on a pie.

453. (D) The private good characteristic of rivalry means that consumers are rivals when it comes to buying scarce goods like the apple pies. Once Jason buys the last pie, that pie cannot be purchased by Jennifer or anyone else. The fact that pies are scarce and therefore rival means that there is a price that Dottie can charge in the market for pies and hope to earn a profit from the sale.

454. (C) This is the very nature of excludability, and it tells a lot about how private goods are distributed to consumers. Private goods are distributed in markets to those who can afford the market price that is determined by the intersection of market supply and market demand. If an individual's income or willingness is insufficient to pay the going price, they will not receive a unit of this good.

455. (B) The characteristic of rivalry is also important in defining private goods and understanding how they are effectively exchanged in markets. The characteristic of rivalry means that a particular unit of a good cannot be bought and consumed by two different consumers. If one person buys a gallon of milk, the next person cannot also buy that same gallon of milk.

456. (D) When it comes to purchasing units of a scarce private good, consumers are certainly rivals. This is never truer than during the holiday shopping rush to buy the very last units of a particularly popular toy or gadget. Only so many units of the item are on the shelf, and once a particular unit has been purchased, it cannot be purchased by another person.

457. (E) The nature of rivalry in markets for private goods is that once Stan has purchased and consumed that last soda, it cannot be consumed by Sharon or anyone else. Sodas, like all goods and services, are scarce and thus limited in availability. Choice A alludes to the excludability of private goods. Sharon wants a soda but cannot come up with the money to pay for it, so she is, at least temporarily, excluded from that market.

458. (D) The leather coat and sunglasses are both private goods because both are rival and excludable and will be effectively exchanged in a market. For both goods, they are rival because once a particular coat or sunglasses are purchased, they cannot also be purchased by another person. They are both excludable because only those who can pay the market price will be able to buy the goods.

459. (C) A meatball sub sandwich is both rival and excludable, making it a private good. The good is excludable because the sandwich shop can refuse the sale of a sandwich to a person who doesn't want to pay the going price. The sandwich also has the rivalry characteristic because once a person has consumed that sub, it cannot be consumed by another person.

460. (A) Streetlights are considered public goods because they are both nonrival and nonexcludable and are therefore unlikely to be exchanged in a market. The streetlights are nonrival, because if a person enjoys the light, that person does not prevent someone else from enjoying the light. In this way, the light is not scarce. It would also be impossible to make a person pay for the use of the light when that person could just continue walking down a darkened street without paying. Because there is really no price that could exclude anyone, a market will fail to emerge for it.

461. (A) When one person sees and reacts to the stoplight, it does not go away for the next person who sees it. In other words, the benefit of the stoplight is not going to be exhausted if many people pass through that intersection. It would also be highly impractical for an entrepreneur to sell individuals a peek at the stoplight and prevent people from viewing the light if they were unwilling to pay. The light must be provided to all and is therefore nonexcludable.

462. (B) These three goods and services are classic examples of public goods because they are nonrival and nonexcludable. City parks, protective services (like fire and police departments), and scientific research cannot be provided by markets, because consumers will enjoy the benefits without paying (nonexcludable) and there are no real units to be consumed (nonrival). These goods and services benefit everyone and therefore must be provided by the government.

463. (B) The sculpture, like any piece of public art, is nonrival. Just because Susan views the artwork does not mean she has reduced the inventory of art by 1 unit. The city could try to charge $2 to view the art, but people could always view the sculpture by viewing it from a distance or by not going to the park at all.

464. (B) Common resources, like the wild mushrooms in a public forest, are rival. If Melanie and Max harvest a wild mushroom, Eric and Eli cannot also harvest that same mushroom. Because the forest is public, anyone can walk into the forest and begin to search for the mushrooms. This should lead to a rush to harvest the scarce mushrooms.

465. (C) Schools of fish in the ocean are nonexcludable because virtually anyone can access the ocean and try to catch the fish. However, once the fish is caught by one person, it is rival because it cannot be caught by another person. This combination of rival and nonexcludable characteristics means that the fish will be overharvested. After all, if I don't catch that fish, someone else will.

466. (D) Timber on public land is a classic example of a common resource. The trees in the public forest are nonexcludable because anyone can come to harvest a tree. However, the tree is also rival because once it is cut down by one person, it cannot be felled by another person.

467. (E) Lobsters, like all fish and shellfish in the ocean, are common resources. They are rival because if Sven catches a lobster in his trap, his buddy Ollie can't also catch that lobster. They are also nonexcludable because the ocean is open to anyone who wants to drop a lobster trap and try to harvest lobster.

468. (B) The tragedy of the commons refers to the likely outcome of having an absence of property rights for a common resource that is both rival and nonexcludable. If a common resource, like wild mushrooms in a public forest, is not owned by anyone, it will be overharvested. After all, nobody is there to prevent a person from harvesting mushrooms, and the scarcity of the mushrooms causes everyone to harvest as many as possible, as quickly as possible.

469. (C) If a good like the fireworks show is nonexcludable, it will create a situation where people will choose to view the show without paying for it. If the fireworks are ignited for the pleasure of one, they are going to be visible for the pleasure of all. As a result, nobody will pay for the show, they will be free riders, and the city must provide it.

470. (A) Any student who has worked on a group project like this has experience with the free-riding behavior of people like George. If the student knows he will receive the same grade as the hardest-working member of the group, that free-riding student will put forth less than maximum effort.

471. (E) Suppose that a person can attend the public art museum and enjoy all of the exhibits without contributing any cash to the voluntary collection box. Economists would describe this free-riding behavior as entirely rational and would expect that not much cash will be collected from the museum visitors. Because of this, museums must conduct fundraising drives and receive government financial support.

472. (C) Because a person cannot get the pay-per-view movie unless he or she pays the price of $10, the movie is excludable. However, in this situation a person's consumption of the movie does nothing to prevent thousands of other people from consuming the very same movie at the very same time. This makes the movie nonrival in consumption.

473. (D) Satellite television programming is excludable because the satellite TV company will not connect a person to their network unless that person pays the price they are charging. However, once a person has paid the price and hooked up to the programming, that person can consume those television shows without reducing the quantity available to other viewers.

474. (A) The state forest pass is excludable because I cannot receive access to the hiking trails if I am unwilling or unable to pay the fee. However, once I have paid the fee, I can hike in the forest as much as I like without consuming "units" of the hiking experience away from other pass holders. When goods are excludable but nonrival, they are sometimes referred to as "artificially scarce" goods or "club" goods.

475. (D) A common resource, like an oyster in Chesapeake Bay, is both rival and nonexcludable. It is nonexcludable because the bay is open for anyone with sufficient equipment to harvest oysters and consume or sell them. The oysters are rival in that once a person harvests that oyster, it cannot be harvested by another person.

476. (C) The tragedy of the commons emerges when there is a common resource that is rival and nonexcludable. Natural resources like ducks are rival because once a duck has been bagged by one hunter, it cannot be bagged by another. However, ducks are nonexcludable because anyone can go out and harvest ducks. If the harvest of ducks, fish, deer, and other wildlife is not regulated with licensing and limits, these species are likely to be greatly depleted.

477. (E) Markets are effective in exchanging private goods, so we must look for the choice that identifies a good that is both rival and excludable. An apartment is rival because a tenant cannot rent the apartment from the landlord unless he or she is paying the rent. The apartment is also excludable because once it is rented to one person, it cannot also be rented to the next person. The other choices represent public goods either at the local, national, or international level.

Chapter 16: Income Inequality and Poverty, and Taxes

478. (C) The poverty line describes a level of income that is set by a government (or other agency such as the World Bank). Anyone earning an income less that that level of income is considered to be living "in poverty." The amount of income that qualifies as being the poverty line varies by country. A poverty line is a "threshold" measure in the sense that anyone earning beneath the poverty line is in poverty, but even $1 more in income makes someone not in poverty.

479. (B) The poverty line in the United States is based on the amount of money that is required to obtain an adequate diet. This is because the Department of Agriculture determined that a family of three spent approximately ⅓ of their income on food. This amount is adjusted annually to account for inflation.

480. (E) Differences in income, and thus differences in income inequality, can depend on any factor that causes incomes to differ. Differences in innate ability may lead to differences in marginal productivity and thus differences in income. There are life-cycle effects of income as well, where the very old and very young earn less than people somewhere in between. Finally, more education can lead to higher productivity.

481. (B) According to the idea of diminishing marginal returns, wealth and income also have diminishing marginal returns. This means the benefit of $1 of additional income is much greater the lower the income level. If there is a great deal of income inequality with the majority of income earned by a small number of people, the total benefit of wealth to society is likely to be low.

482. (B) Line A represents the line of equality. That is, any point on Line A represents the proportion of the population such that each income group earns exactly that level of income. For instance, along Line A, the 20th percentile income group earns exactly 20% of income, and the 80th percentile group earns exactly 80% of income. The line of equality is at a 45-degree angle from each axis.

483. (C) Line B represents the Lorenz curve. This curve represents the cumulative distribution of wealth in a country. Each point along the Lorenz curve represents the cumulative amount of income that a particular percentile of wealth earns. For instance, if the population axis is broken down by quintiles (i.e., by fifths of the population, so 20% of the population, 40%, 60%, 80%, and 100%) and the point at 50% of the population is 10%, this is saying that 50% of the population cumulatively earns just 10% of the income.

484. (A) The farther a Lorenz curve is from the line of perfect equality, the more unequally distributed the income is in the nation. In other words, the farther away the actual distribution of income is from what would be perfectly equal, the greater the amount of income inequality. The distance between these two curves is exactly what the Gini coefficient measures.

485. (E) The idea behind the Gini coefficient is that it calculates the total area (Y) between the line of perfect equality and the Lorenz curve. The bigger this area, the further away this society is from having equitable income distribution. Taken as a ratio, the Gini coefficient is the area Y divided by the sum of areas Y and Z. The Gini is useful, because the greater this coefficient, the greater the degree of income inequality.

486. (E) The Gini coefficient measures the area between the two curves as a ratio of the total area underneath the line of equality. The Gini coefficient represents the degree of income inequality that exists. In other words, the Gini coefficient measures how far away the Lorenz curve is from the line of equality. The larger the Gini coefficient, the more unequal the income distribution, and the smaller the Gini coefficient, the closer the economy is to having perfect income equality.

487. (C) The Lorenz curve reflects a cumulative distribution, so each point on the Lorenz curve represents the cumulative amount of income earned by that group. For instance, suppose the total amount of income in this country is $400,000 and the population is 100 people. The 20th percentile represents the 20 people earning the least. Earning 10% of the total income means that the total earnings of these 20 people are $40,000.

488. (A) The Gini coefficient measures the degree of income inequality only, not the extent of poverty. In fact, it is entirely possible for a country to have a very low Gini coefficient and a very high degree of poverty (e.g., if everyone in a country had income that was equally distributed, but all lived beneath the poverty line). Since the Gini coefficient measures the distance between the Lorenz curve and the line of equality, a Gini coefficient of zero effectively says that they are the same curve.

489. (C) The marginal tax rate is the amount that each additional dollar of income is taxed. Since Jenny pays $100 in tax on $1,000 in income, she pays a $100/$1,000 = 10% marginal tax rate. Since Samford pays $400 in tax on $1,000 in income, $400/$1,000 = 40% marginal tax rate. While it may be tempting to say that this is a proportional tax, because each pays a proportion of their income in tax, a proportional tax is when each person pays the same proportion of tax, regardless of income. For example, if there was a 10% proportional tax on income, Jenny would pay a total of $1,100 in tax and Samford would pay a total of $4,100 in tax.

490. (B) Jenny and Samford are under a progressive tax system, meaning as income increases, the average tax rate increases. For instance, suppose that each pay the same tax rate of 20% on their initial level of income. This means that if Jenny earns an additional $1,000 of income, she will pay 20% × $10,000 + 10% × 100 = $2,100 in tax, or an average tax rate of 2,100/11,000 = 19.1%. If Samford earns an additional $1,000 in income, he will pay 20% × 40,000 + 40% × 1,000 = $8,000 + $400 = $8,400, which gives him an average tax rate of about 20.5%. Since he pays a higher average tax rate at a higher income, this is considered a progressive system.

491. (C) If Charles spends $2,000 of his income on food and 3% of this is taxed, Charles would pay $60 in tax, giving him an average tax rate of 0.3%. If Prodigy spends 8% of his income on food, he spends $2,400 on food and pays $72 in tax, giving him an average tax rate of 0.24%. Since Prodigy pays a lower average tax rate even though his income is higher, this would be an example of a regressive tax.

492. (E) If the labor supply curve is elastic, this means that peoples' work effort would be very responsive to changes in income. If redistributive income policies lead to less additional income for more effort and people are responsive to this, then wealthier people may respond to redistributive wealth policies by reducing work effort. This is one of the reasons that some policy makers oppose redistributive wealth policies.

493. (C) If the labor supply curve is elastic and if net income after tax increases, then individuals will provide more work effort to earn more. If there is a regressive tax, the more you earn, the lower your effective tax rate, thus giving incentives to work harder and minimizing inefficiency from taxation. Unfortunately, the trade-off for this efficiency is equity—this would result in the least amount of wealth redistribution from higher-income people to lower-income people.

494. (B) A progressive income tax is a redistributive wealth policy. This is because those at higher incomes pay a greater share of the tax as a proportion of their earnings, while lower-income individuals, who are more likely to use public services, pay a lower share of tax as a share of their own earnings. Therefore, if a policy maker was more concerned about equity than efficiency, he or she would choose a redistributive wealth policy such as a progressive income tax.

495. (A) The average tax rate measures the true share of an individual's income that he or she pays in taxes and is in fact the effective rate of taxation. For instance, if a person earns $10,000 per year and pays a 10% tax rate on the first $5,000 in income, and a 20% tax rate on the next $5,000 in income, that individual pays a total of ($5,000 × .10) + ($5,000 × .20) = $1,500 in taxes. We can then divide $1,500/$10,000 = 15%, and see that this person has an overall, or average, tax rate of 15%.

496. (D) The idea behind the equity-efficiency trade-off is that these two goals are mutually exclusive: to obtain a higher degree of equity through redistributive policies, you alter individual incentives, which may lead to inefficiencies (which we capture with the concept of deadweight loss). Therefore, policy makers with one of these objectives in mind would need to be willing to sacrifice the other objective to achieve that goal.

497. (E) The higher income that each individual earns, the greater the effective tax rate that each person pays. This is the definition of a progressive tax. Note that one person pays no tax and receives a tax refund, even though that person hasn't paid any taxes. This negative income tax is effectively a subsidy.

498. (C) The Lorenz curves shown in Figure 16.2(i) and 16.2(ii) only inform us of the income distribution of each country. We can tell by the area between the Lorenz curve and line of equality for each country that Morgonia has a higher degree of income inequality than Eccelson. However, this does not give any indication of the source of the inequality or even the poverty level in each country.

499. (E) The United States has a Gini coefficient that has ranged from about .45 to .47 over the period 2000–2011. Other countries with a similar degree of income inequality are the People's Republic of China, Pakistan, and Argentina. The United States has a relatively greater degree of income inequality compared to other developed nations such as Canada and the United Kingdom.

500. (B) The highest degree of income inequality, and thus the highest Gini coefficient, is found in far southern Africa. South Africa, Botswana, Lesotho, and Namibia all have Gini coefficients greater than .6. The smallest amount of income inequality, and thus the smallest Gini coefficients, is found in Northern European countries such as Sweden and Norway.